LABOUR IN SCOTLAND

LABOUR
IN SCOTLAND
A PICTORIAL HISTORY
FROM THE EIGHTEENTH CENTURY TO THE PRESENT

IAN MACDOUGALL

MAINSTREAM
PUBLISHING·EDINBURGH

First published in 1985 by
MAINSTREAM PUBLISHING COMPANY (EDINBURGH) LTD.
7 Albany Street
Edinburgh EH1 3UG

ISBN 0 906391 64 4 (cloth)
ISBN 0 906391 65 2 (limp)

Typeset by Studioscope in conjunction with Mainstream Publishing.
Printed and bound by Clark Constable (1982) Ltd., Edinburgh.

Table of Contents

Sponsors 7

Foreword 9

Introduction 11

Acknowledgements 13

Some Relevant Events 17

Eighteenth Century Beginnings 21

The Nineteenth Century:
    First Half 41
    Second Half 87

The Twentieth Century:
    1900-14 153
    1914-18 179
    Between The Wars, 1919-39 197
    Second World War, 1939-45 243
    Since 1945 251

Some Further Reading 271

Sponsors

The following individuals and organisations have given this book their financial and moral support. It is doubtful whether publication could have taken place without their generosity.

Scottish Arts Council
Aberdeen Trades Council
Amalgamated Union of Engineering Workers (Engineering Section), Region No 1.
Amalgamated Union of Engineering Workers, Technical, Administrative and Supervisory Section, National Executive Committee.
Ancient Order of Foresters Friendly Society
Association of Cinematograph Television and Allied Technicians

British Labour Group in the European Parliament
Gordon Brown, M.P.

The Civil and Public Health Services Association
Confederation of Health Service Employees, Scottish Region
Co-operative Union Ltd.
Co-operative Union Ltd., Education Department
Co-operative Wholesale Society Ltd.

Educational Institute of Scotland
Edinburgh Trades Council
Electrical Electronic Telecommunication and Plumbing Union, Scottish Political Committee.
Equity, Scottish Committee

Falkirk Trades Council

General, Municipal, Boilermakers and Allied Trades Union, G.M.W. Section, Scottish Region.

The Merchant Navy and Airline Officers' Association
Hugh McCartney, M.P.

National Union of the Footwear, Leather and Allied Trades
National Union of Mineworkers (Scottish Area)
National Graphical Association
National and Local Government Officers' Association, Aberdeen City Branch
National and Local Government Officers' Association, Edinburgh District Branch
National Union of Public Employees
National Union of Public Employees, Scottish Division
National Union of Railwaymen

Scottish Labour Group of Members of Parliament
Scottish Secondary Teachers' Association
Scottish Trades Union Congress
Society of Graphical and Allied Trades, Edinburgh and Forth District Branch
Society of Graphical and Allied Trades, Glasgow and West of Scotland Branch
Socialist Group of the European Parliament

Transport and General Workers' Union, Ayr District Committee
Transport and General Workers' Union, Dumfries District Committee
Transport and General Workers' Union, Edinburgh District Committee
Transport and General Workers' Union, Grampian and Northern Isles District Committee
Transport and General Workers' Union, Scottish Regional Councils

Union of Construction, Allied Trades and Technicians, Scottish Regional Council

Foreword

THE HISTORY OF the trade union and labour movement in Scotland is long and varied. Above all it demonstrates the power and ability of ordinary men and women to influence beneficially their lot in a basically unequal and unjust society.

It always amazes me to hear people who should know better say that it was a Whig Government and Lord Shaftesbury who introduced the first labour protection legislation and that it was a Tory Government that finally repealed the Combination Acts. Don't they know of the struggles waged by workers to win the vote, their struggle to form unions and to seek some redress for the terrible conditions under which they worked and lived? Some paid dearly for their endeavours: some with their lives, and others sent to Botany Bay. Many ended their days in the workhouse because they were denied the possibility of employment. They were the heroes, they were the people who made history and I suggest that this is still the case. One of the mainsprings for the generation of the better society will be the trade union and labour movement.

This book is another substantial contribution by Ian MacDougall, who has already done much to preserve and catalogue labour records. He has already published a 500-page catalogue of records of the labour movement, where they are housed and where they can be seen. Unfortunately, despite his untiring efforts much valuable material has been lost or destroyed: this illustrated book is an effort to bring at least significant parts of Scottish labour movement history to a wider audience. The more we know of it, the better will we be able to cope with our everyday problems.

Mrs Thatcher has been telling us that many of the problems of our society would disappear if we could return to sound Victorian values. I can well understand her logic, because in Victorian Britain it was said that everybody knew their place in society: but not everybody was pleased with their place, and certainly working people had little to enthuse over. Perhaps she had in mind that we could find work for our school leavers by training them as chimney sweeps.

The study of labour history is well established in our universities, in our central institutions and in further education. In our schools there is a welcome new emphasis placed on it, but we cannot allow the study of labour history to become the realm solely of the specialist. I hope this book, therefore, will be read in the main by working men and women and that it will whet their appetite for more. There are already available many books dealing with aspects of the history of our movement. Ian MacDougall is not only an enthusiast, he is well qualified to write this book because he has a unique knowledge of the subject it deals with and he is of course a professional historian.

I commend it to you, reader. I am sure you will find it both interesting and instructive.

James Milne,
General Secretary,
Scottish Trades Union Congress.

Introduction

THE ROOTS OF organised labour in Scotland lie in the eighteenth century. Then it was that the distinctive organisations of working people — trade unions, co-operative societies, friendly or benefit societies — began to emerge, to be joined early in the nineteenth century by distinctively working class political organisations.

Industrial disputes and trade unionism predated the Industrial Revolution, whose coming in Scotland in the later eighteenth century, accompanied by the additional pressures or stimulations of the French Revolution and the French Revolutionary and Napoleonic Wars, raised to a new plane economic, social and political issues.

By the early decades of the nineteenth century a working class had emerged in Scotland. With many vicissitudes working class organisation — industrial, political, and co-operative — thereafter became more, or much more, widespread and also more continuous or at least less ephemeral.

This volume attempts to illustrate by means of photographs, banners, and a few extracts from newspapers and other documents, some of the history of labour in Scotland since the eighteenth century. It makes no claim to provide a comprehensive or systematic narrative or analysis of that history.

To some extent the volume has arisen out of the ongoing work by the Scottish Labour History Society to find, catalogue, and encourage permanent preservation of all surviving records and relics of labour in Scotland and to help make them accessible to everyone with a *bona fide* interest. Any royalties from the sale of the book will go to the Society to help it further that work.

Labour history in Scotland, as in other countries, has attracted in the past quarter of a century or so much more attention than before. But there remain many aspects that invite research, discussion, publication. To these activities it is hoped this volume will contribute its mite. It is also hoped that it will help arouse wider and keener interest among working people in Scotland, and elsewhere, in their own history — in the sorts of issues, organisations, events, publications, rank-and-file activists and leaders, and not least 'ordinary' workers some of whom or which are mentioned in the following pages. One further hope the volume carries is that it will help publicise and attract support for the proposal by the Scottish Labour History Society that a Scottish Labour History Centre or Museum be established where photographs, documents, banners, etc., could be exhibited and tape-recordings played.

A large number of friends and colleagues, trade union, Co-operative and political party rank-and-file members and officials, councillors, M.P.s, librarians, archivists, museum curators, newspaper staffs, photographers, and others have provided information, given access to relevant material, loaned items for copying, or helped in other ways in the preparation of this volume. To all of them my warmest thanks are offered. I am particularly grateful to those trade unions, M.P.s, and other sponsors whose financial support, along with a generous grant in aid of publication from the Scottish Arts Council, has enabled the volume to appear sooner than might otherwise have been possible.

Bill Campbell and Peter Mackenzie of Mainstream Publishing have been patient guides and invaluable supporters. My greatest debt as always is to my wife Sandra for her encouragement, help and patience.

Finally, any inaccuracies or infelicities (and, alas, there are sure to be some) in this volume are to be blamed on me alone.

Ian MacDougall
January 1985

Acknowledgements

For permission to reproduce photographs, documents and other items in this book acknowledgement is made to:
(N.B. Numbers refer to illustrations, not pages)

Scottish Record Office: 4, 15, 59 (*The Liberator*), 63, 65, 67, 75, 77, 183

Public Record Office and the Controller of H.M. Stationery Office: 11, 16, 17, 19, 22, 23, 24, 27, 28, 29, 31, 34, 35, 42, 43, 44, 51

National Library of Scotland: 3, 5, 6, 7, 14, 25, 47, 48, 55, 60, 64, 68, 70, 99, 107, 111, 119, 122, 125, 127 (Glasier), 130, 132, 135, 139, 143, 145, 155, 160, 163, 166, 177, 196, 210, 211, 215, 217, 231, 232, 233, 238, 254, 257, 276, 279, 290

Mitchell Library, Glasgow: 9, 10, 30, 32, 59 (*Herald to the Trades Advocate*), 70, 88, 131, 154, 162

Huntly House Museum, Edinburgh: 1, 36, 38, 45, 53, 54, 69, 81, 82, 84, 85, 90, 91, 92, 93, 94, 95, 147, 185, 186, 187, 295

Hamilton District Libraries and Museum: 2, 98, 189

The Museum, Rothesay, and Mr Russell Darling, Council of Buteshire Natural History Society: 8

Roxburgh District Council: 12, 115, 116

National Coal Board: 13

Scottish National Portrait Gallery: 18 (Muir and Palmer)

Highland Regional Museums Service: 118

National Museum of Antiquities of Scotland: 20, 105, 109, 140, 144, 149, 150, 153, 156, 178, 179, 192, 197, 220, 223, 225, 240, 245, 251, 258, 259, 267, 270, 275, 278, 280, 281, 297, 298, 303, 304

Anne Baxter, Golspie: 26

Stirling Smith Art Gallery and Museum: 33

British Library of Political and Economic Science: 37

Airdrie Library: 39

Glasgow Museums (People's Palace): 40, 46, 62, 80, 171, 175, 184

Paisley Central Library: 41

Co-operative Wholesale Society: 49, 100, 101, 212, 288, 294

Royal Commission on the Ancient and Historical Monuments of Scotland: 50
Private Collection: 52
Strathkelvin District Museums: 56
Edinburgh City Libraries: 57, 134, 253
North Angus Co-operative Society Ltd: 58
Biggar Museum Trust: 66
Dumfries and Galloway Regional Council, Ewart Library: 71, 172
Perth and Kinross District Libraries: 72
Kyle and Carrick District Library and Museums Service: 73
Borders Regional Library: 74
City Art Centre, Edinburgh: 76
Dundee District Library: 79, 86, 120
Art Gallery and Museums, Aberdeen: 83, 104, 137, 146
Co-operative Union Ltd (Scottish Section): 87, 102
City of Dundee District Council Archive and Record Centre: 97, 242
Royal Scottish Museum: 103
Mr John Tweedie, Currie: 105, 150
R. Clapperton, Photographer, Selkirk: 108, 142, 151, 244, 246
Cumbernauld and Kilsyth District Council: 112, 113
Strathclyde Regional Archives: 114, 157, 164, 226, 265
Edinburgh Central Constituency Labour Party: 123
International Institute of Social History, Amsterdam: 126
Communist Party Picture Library and Archive, London: 127 (Mahon), 193, 235, 248, 271,
     272, 273, 274, 286
Aberdeen Central Library: 117, 129
National Museum of Ireland: 133
Transport & General Workers' Union: 136, 148
Falkirk Museums: 138
National Union of Seamen: 141
City of Dundee Museums and Art Galleries: 152, 180
The late J.M. Morrison, Clydebank: 283
Glasgow Herald Picture Library: 158, 161 (Adamson), 168, 201, 202, 203, 216, 218, 219, 228,
     229, 230, 237, 239, 250, 261, 263, 264, 266, 285, 293, 299, 300, 301, 305, 307, 309, 310
Glencoe and North Lorn Folk Museum: 159
Trades Union Congress Library: 161 (Wilkie), 181
Arbroath Herald: 165

Some Relevant Events

1661 Re-enactment of Act of 1617 by Scots Parliament authorising magistrates to regulate wages and conditions of labour.

1748 Strike by Edinburgh journeymen tailors over wages.

1750 Ploughmen in Stirlingshire formed a combination.

1760 Aberdeen journeymen woolcombers accused of forming an unlawful combination.

1769 Foundation of first co-operative store in Britain by weavers at Fenwick, Ayrshire.

1778 Edinburgh building and furnishing workers form a workers' co-operative.

1783 American War of Independence ended. Industrial Revolution and Highland Clearances under way.

1787 Glasgow weavers' strike: six shot by troops.

1789 French Revolution began.

1792 Friends of the People societies formed in Scotland.

1793 Britain entered French Revolutionary Wars. Sedition trials of the 'Martyrs of 1793'. First general Act passed concerning friendly societies.

1797 Riots against Militia Act.

1798 George Mealmaker, United Scotsmen, sentenced to fourteen years' transportation for sedition.

1799 Anti-Combination Laws passed—not implemented in Scotland. Robert Owen bought the cotton mills at New Lanark. Scots colliers emancipated from serfdom.

1804 Edinburgh compositors' interlocutor from Court of Session.

c.1806 Glasgow Cottonspinners' Union formed.

1812-13 Strike by handloom weavers and imprisonment of their leaders: combinations became unlawful in Scotland under Common Law.

1813-14 End of state regulation of wages and apprenticeship.

1815 End of Napoleonic Wars. Revival of Radical agitation.

1820 Radical War.

1824 Repeal of Combination Laws and end of illegality of unions under Scots Common Law. Formation of Ayrshire Colliers' union.

1825-28 Owenite Utopian community at Orbiston.

1830-32 Great Reform Bill agitation.

1830s Trade union 'boom'.

1834 Tolpuddle Martyrs sentenced to transportation. West of Scotland calico printers' strikes.

1837-38 Glasgow Cottonspinners' Union strike and trial and sentence of leaders.

1838-48 Chartist movement.

1848 The Year of Revolutions in Europe.

1851 Formation of Amalgamated Society of Engineers, first "New Model" union.

c.1853 Edinburgh Trades Council formed.

1858 Glasgow Trades Council formed.

1859-61 Unification of Italy.

1861 *Address to the Working Men of the United Kingdom* issued by Glasgow Trades Council. Edinburgh stonemasons became first building trade workers in Britain to win nine hours' day.

1861-65 American Civil War.

1863 Polish Revolt. Glasgow Trades Council initiated national campaign to reform Master and Servant Laws.

1864 First International Working Men's Association founded.

1866-67 Second Reform Bill agitation; many urban workers won right to vote.

1866-75 Struggle over Labour Laws.

1868 Foundation of Trades Union Congress and of Scottish Co-operative Wholesale Society.

1870 Fife miners became first in Europe to win eight hours' day.

1871 Engineers on north-east coast of England won nine hours' day. Criminal Law Amendment Act passed: picketing made very difficult.

1874 Alexander McDonald and Thomas Burt, miners' leaders, elected Liberal-Labour M.P.s in England.

1874-87 Industrial depression.

1877 Blantyre Colliery disaster.

1880s Socialist Revival: formation of Social Democratic Federation, Fabian Society, Socialist League.

1882-88 Crofters' War in Highlands.

1884 Third Reform Bill: right to vote won by many rural workers, including miners.

1887-89 The 'New Unionism' emerged: London Dock Strike.

1888 Scottish Labour Party formed by Keir Hardie.

1890 Scottish railwaymen's strike.

1892 Scottish United Trades Councils' Labour Party formed.

1893 Independent Labour Party formed.

1894 Scottish miners' strike.

1895 Trades Councils excluded from Trades Union Congress.

1897 National lock-out of engineers. Foundation of Scottish Trades Union Congress.

1900 Foundation of Labour Party and of Scottish Workers' Parliamentary Elections Committee.

1901 Taff Vale decision.

1903 Socialist Labour Party formed.

1905 Revolution in Russia.

1906 First Labour M.P.s elected in Scotland. Foundation of Glasgow Catholic Socialist Society and of weekly labour paper *Forward*. Industrial Workers of the World founded in America.

1909 Osborne Judgement.

1910-14 The 'Great Unrest' of labour.

1911 National strikes by seamen, dockers, and railwaymen. Strike at Singers, Clydebank.

1912 National strike by miners. *Miners' Next Step* published. Scottish Farm Servants' Union formed.

1913 Dublin Tramways strike; Irish Citizen Army formed.

1914-18 Great War.

1915 Clyde engineers' strike. Dilution of labour began. Shop Stewards' Movement emerged. Death of Keir Hardie. Rent Strike in Glasgow.

1916 Conscription imposed. Deportation of Clyde shop stewards. John Maclean sentenced to penal servitude for sedition. Easter Rising in Ireland.

1917 Two Revolutions in Russia, February/March and (Bolshevik) October/November. Workers' and Soldiers' Council in Glasgow.

1918 John Maclean sentenced to further term of penal servitude. Franchise conceded to women over thirty. Labour won seven seats in general election in Scotland. 'The Troubles' began in Ireland.

1919 Forty Hours' Strike: George Square Riot. Sankey Commission on coal industry. National railwaymen's strike. Communist International founded.

1920 Inter-War Depression and mass unemployment began. Communist Party of Great Britain founded. Rent Strike in Scotland.

1921 National lock-out of miners. Collapse of Triple Industrial Alliance. National Unemployed Workers' Movement founded. Red International of Labour Unions founded in Moscow.

1922 Breakthrough for Labour Party in general election. First national Hunger March. Mussolini and Fascists gained power in Italy.

1923 Ruhr occupied by French and Belgian armies. Abortive *putsch* by Hitler in Germany. Split in Fife miners' union. Death of John Maclean.

1924 First Labour Government. Minority Movement founded. A.J. Cook elected General Secretary of Miners' Federation of Great Britain. Death of Lenin.

1925 'Red Friday': crisis over coal industry postponed.

1926 General Strike and miners' lock-out.

1927 Trades Disputes Act. Stalin dominant in Soviet Union.

1929 Wall Street Crash. Second Labour Government formed. United Mineworkers of Scotland formed.

1930 Death of John Wheatley.

1931 End of Second Labour Government and formation by Ramsay MacDonald of 'National' Government: Labour heavily defeated in general election.

1932 I.L.P. disaffiliated from Labour Party. Mass unemployment at its worst in Britain. Mosley formed British Union of Fascists.

1933 Hitler and Nazis won power in Germany.

1935 Abyssinia invaded by Fascist Italy.

1936 Spanish Civil War began: International Brigade.

1938 Munich Crisis.

1939 Nazi-Soviet Non-Aggression Pact.

1939-45 Second World War.

1940 Dunkirk. Blitz began. Death of Robert Smillie.

1941 Nazis invaded Soviet Union. Clydebank Blitz. Tom Johnston appointed Secretary of State for Scotland in Churchill Coalition Government.

1942 Engineering Union decided to admit women members.

1944 Allied D-Day landings in Normandy: Second Front begun. Miners' Federation of Great Britain reconstituted as National Union of Mineworkers.

1945 Atomic bombs dropped on Japan. End of Second World War. Labour won landslide victory in general election.

1946 Death of James Maxton.

1947 Nationalisation of coal industry.

1948 Nationalisation of railways and several other industries. 'Wage freeze' introduced by Labour Government.

1949 North Atlantic Treaty Organisation founded.

1950 Labour majority drastically reduced in general election. William Gallacher, Communist M.P., defeated in West Fife.

1951 Knockshinnoch Castle Colliery disaster. Labour lost office in general election.

1953 Death of Stalin.

1955 Labour again lost general election.

1956 Suez War. Hungarian uprising. Communist Party of Great Britain lost many members. 'New Left' formed.

1957 Increasing closures of coal pits began.

1958 Formation of Campaign for Nuclear Disarmament.

1959 Labour lost third successive general election.

1960 Unilateral nuclear disarmament briefly adopted by Labour Party.

1963 Beeching Report: railway closures.

1964 Labour won general election.

1965 Highlands and Islands Development Board founded.

1966 Seamen's strike. Labour again won general election.

1967 Exploration for oil began off coast of Scotland. Labour Party lost Hamilton by-election to S.N.P.

1970 Labour defeated in general election.

1971 Upper Clyde Shipbuilders crisis and 'work-in'. Industrial Relations Act passed.

1972 Miners' national strike. Britain entered Common Market.

1973 Scottish Co-operative Wholesale Society merged into Co-operative Wholesale Society. Fascist military coup in Chile.

1974 Miners' national strike. Labour won general elections of February and October. New local government structure in Scotland.

1975 *Scottish Daily News* workers' co-operative formed. Scottish Development Agency founded.

1976 Scottish Labour Party founded.

1977 Bullock Report on industrial democracy. Scottish Trades Union Congress affiliations reached one million.

1978-79 'Winter of Discontent' among trade unionists.

1979 Referendum on devolution for Scotland. Labour defeated at general election.

1980 Unemployment in Scotland exceeded ten per cent.

1981 Formation of Social Democratic Party.

1982 Health Workers' strike.

1983 Labour again lost general election.

1984 Miners' strike.

EIGHTEENTH CENTURY
BEGINNINGS

1

The friendly society was the earliest form of organisation of working people. Hundreds of these societies—also termed benefit societies or box clubs—were formed in the eighteenth century. Most were purely local, drawing their members from a single village, town, or even street, often from a single local occupation, as illustrated by this plaque of the Friendly Society of Caulkers formed in 1791. Long before the coming of the Welfare State, friendly societies provided their members with some limited basic 'welfare' benefit— usually funeral benefit, that could save members or their families being cast into paupers' graves.

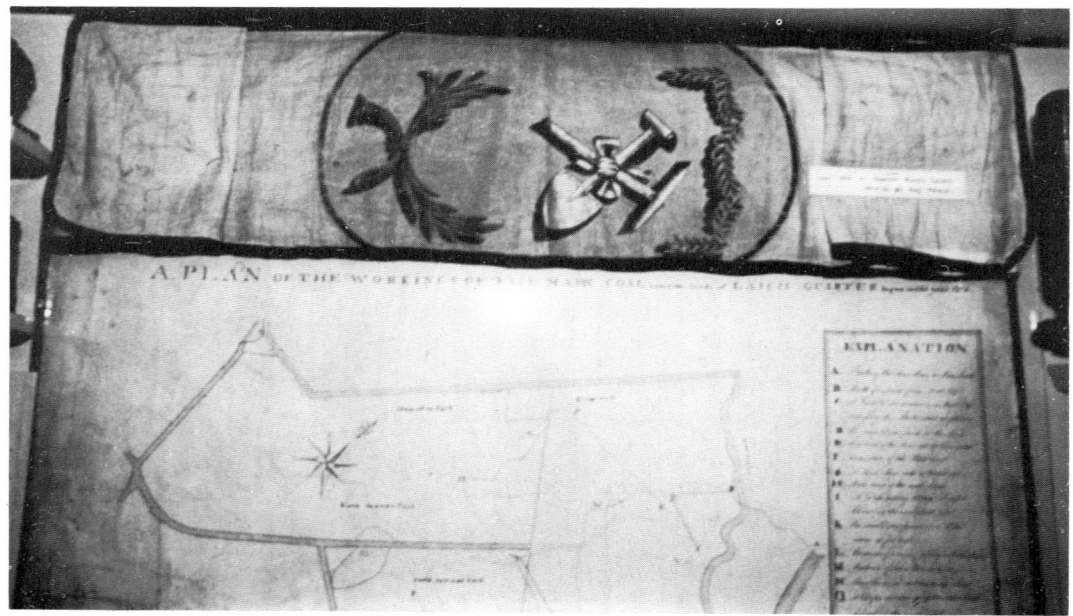

2

Workers in dangerous or unhealthy occupations, such as miners, fishermen, seamen, cotton-spinners or slaters, were sometimes excluded from membership of friendly societies for fear they became a burden on the funds. So miners and other 'dangerous trades' often formed their own friendly societies. This is a banneret of the Quarter Colliers Friendly Society in Lanarkshire, formed at the end of the eighteenth century.

OGLEFACE Friendly Society's HEARSE.

CONDITIONS on which the OGLEFACE FRIENDLY SOCIETY's HEARSE is Let out.

I. The Body of every Member of the Society, his Wife, or Widow; fhall be carried to their place of Interrment, by the Society's Hearfe, free of hire.

II. The Parents of Members entered before the 1ft of May 1793, and all the Children of every Member ftill unmarried, fhall have their Bodies carried by the Hearfe to their place of Interrment for the half of the hire payable by others.

III. When the Hearfe is let out to thofe who are not Members, nor entitled to the above Privileges, there fhall be Two Shillings and Sixpence paid, in name of Yoking-money: And Six-pence for every Mile that it travels from the place where it is kept, to the place of Interrment. And if it be not returned the fame day that it fets out, the Yoking and Mile Money fhall be charged as on the preceding day. The Money to be paid when the Hearfe is returned.

IV. If any Neceffitous Family fhall ftand in need of the Hearfe, by applying to the Hearfe-Keeper by a Line figned by two or three refpectable perfons, teftifying their neceffity; that Family fo applying, fhall have the Hearfe at that time for the Yoking-money, to the extent of Six Miles from the Hearfe-houfe. Thofe who fign the Line, fhall be good for damages.

V. If the Hearfe fhall be damaged when let out, the damage fhall be appraifed, and thofe who hired it fhall make it good.

VI. Whoever fhall hire out the Hearfe, (whether they be Members or not) fhall pay One Shilling to the Keeper for cleaning it.

A TABLE of the Computed Diftance of the different Places of Interrment, in the Neighbourhood, from the Hearfe-houfe of the OGLEFACE FRIENDLY SOCIETY at AVON-BRIDGE-END.

	Miles.	Qr.
To TORPHICHEN by the Straths,	3	3
To Ditto by Andrew's Yeards and the Wheat Acres,	4	1
To the Weft end of Ditto Parifh, and Eaft to Ditto Churchyard by Craigs,	10	
To MUIRAVONSIDE by Stand-burn and Tirdiff,	4	2
To Ditto by Torphichen,	8	
To Ditto by Boxten,	6	2
To Ditto by Grey-ridge,	5	
To BATHGATE by Torphichen,	6	
To Ditto by Bridge-houfe,	5	
To Ditto by Borbachly,	5	2
To the Old Church-yard always One Mile more.		
To WHITBURN by Wheat-acres or Hills,	6	
To SHOTTS by Craigs and Blairmucks,	8	2
To LINLITHGOW by Torphichen,	8	
To Ditto by Tirduff,	7	
To Ditto by Bathgate by Torphichen road,	11	1
To Ditto by Bathgate by Cairnnapple road,	10	
To FALKIRK by Glenburn,	6	2
To Ditto by Shieldhill,	7	3
To Ditto by Slamanan Kirk,	10	
To Ditto by Torphichen by Maddifton,	10	3
To SLAMANAN by Pirney Lodge,	3	3
To Ditto by Bulzingdale and Linhoufe,	4	
To WEST CALDER by Bathgate and Blackburn,	10	

The SOCIETY have agreed, that the above TABLE fhall be the Standard by which their HEARSE fhall be Let out in future.—And when the number of miles travelled by the Hearfe, cannot be counted by the above Table; that part of the journey that lies beyond the places fpecified above, fhall be left to the computation of the employers.

By Order of the OGLEFACE FRIENDLY SOCIETY,

3

A Stirlingshire friendly society with a hearse for hire.

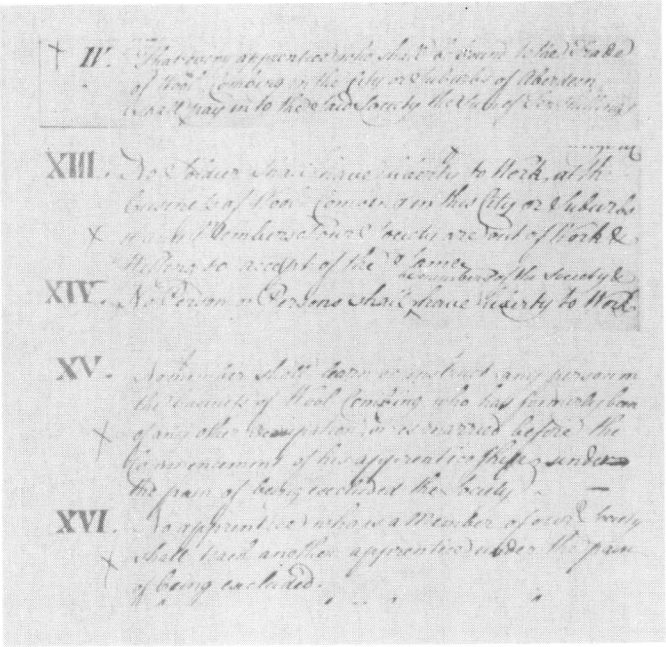

4

In the eighteenth century some friendly societies developed into trade unions, or combinations as they were usually termed. The Journeymen Woolcombers' Society of Aberdeen was a hybrid organisation, part friendly society, part trade union, as its rules of 1755 here show. The employers took the Society to court in 1760, claiming it . . . 'will prove means of caballing, drunkenness and destroying that just and necessary subordination which ought to subsist betwixt masters and journeymen and more especially betwixt masters and their apprentices'.

5

Printers were among workers — almost all skilled or craft — who formed unions in Scotland in the eighteenth century. This is a snuff mill presented in 1785 to the printers' chapel (union organisation) at Neill & Co. Ltd, Edinburgh.

THE Journeymen Masons in and about the city of Edinburgh, judging that they labour under the most severe hardships, have therefore thought proper to state their case in this public manner.

Above an hundred years ago, when the price of vivers, and every other necessary of life, was less than a fourth of what they presently sell at, the said Journeymen had their wages settled at one merk Scots *per diem*; and even this small sum, in the memory of the oldest of that trade, has been so hardly paid by the Masters, as that, of a Saturday night, after a poor man had wrought a whole week, and after waiting from the time he left work, 'till ten at night, in expectation of receiving 6 s. 8 d. his week's wages, he has been often dismissed home to his wife and family, by his Master, with only a shilling or eighteen pence to provide himself and them for a whole week.—— And now the Master masons having obtained an interlocutor of the Magistrates in their favour against the Journeymen, they are so elated, by means thereof, that (according to information) they have made a sort of law, enacting a penalty to be paid by every Master, who shall, in time coming, give any higher wages to the Journeymen employed by him, than the said one merk *per diem*. ——How far the said interlocutor of the Magistrates is well founded, or what title the said Master-masons have to make such laws, the Journeymen intend soon to submit, in a proper way, to the supreme court of the nation.

But, what is chiefly intended by this advertisement, is, to acquaint the public, as was formerly done, that the Journeymen masons are still willing to work at the moderate wages of 1 s. 3 d. per day during the summer, and 1 s. per day in winter, whereby all such gentlemen, carrying on buildings or Mason work of any kind, who please to employ them independent of any Master, will have a considerable gain upon each man's work in the week, and may assure themselves of having their buildings and work neatly and properly finished, according to their desire, and with as much expedition, if not greater, than if they employed any Master: And the Journeymen masons are resolved, one and all, to show the world that they are free men and not bond slaves, as the Masters would insinuate in their advertisement.

By authority of the Magistrates of Edinburgh, and by order of the Trustees appointed by act of parliament for carrying on the public works,

6

One of the earliest public collective statements by working men in Scotland: the Journeymen Stonemasons of Edinburgh explain their dispute with their employers, in 1764, over the rate and manner of payment of their wages. The masons are willing to bypass their employers and do work direct for customers at 1/3d. per day in summer and 1/- in winter. Some years later, in 1778, a producers' co-operative was established by Edinburgh building and furnishing workers during a wages dispute with their employers.

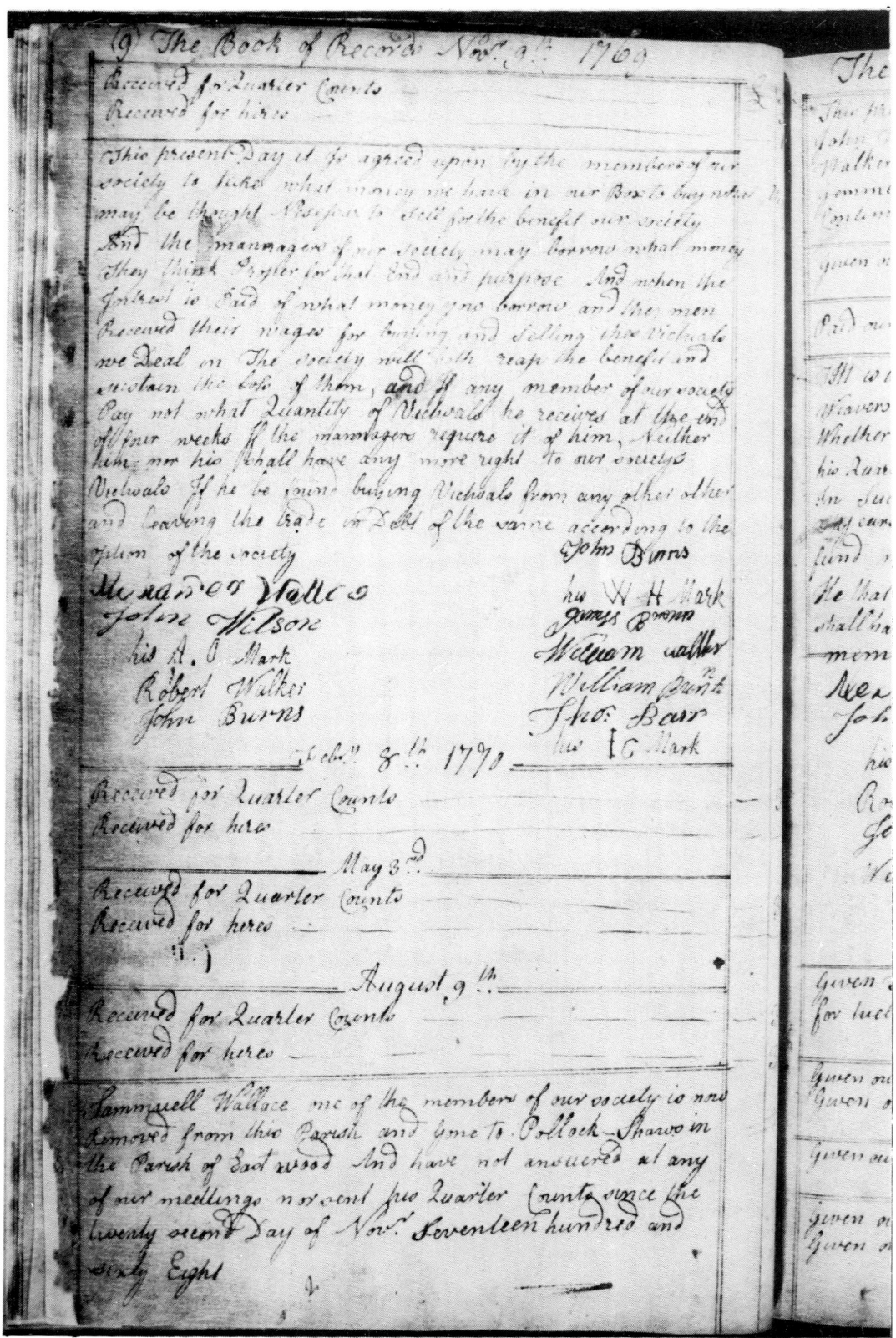

7

Minutes of the Fenwick Weavers' Society in Ayrshire, 9 November 1769. The Society at that meeting set up the first co-operative store in Britain. Several other co-operative stores were also founded before the end of the eighteenth century.

8

Society box of the Rothesay Cotton Mill society, formed in 1792. This Society seems to have developed further than either the Aberdeen Woolcombers or the Fenwick Weavers and to have been simultaneously a friendly society, a trade union, and also a co-operative society.

9

Disputes between workmen and employers became increasingly common in the eighteenth century, especially in the handicraft or skilled trades such as handloom weaving, tailoring, building. It was often from such disputes that trade unions, or combinations, emerged, even if the organisation was often ephemeral. This document seems to have been an instruction by the Glasgow journeymen blacksmiths in 1784 to a lawyer. Whether the men had a union is not clear, though collective organisation is certainly implied.

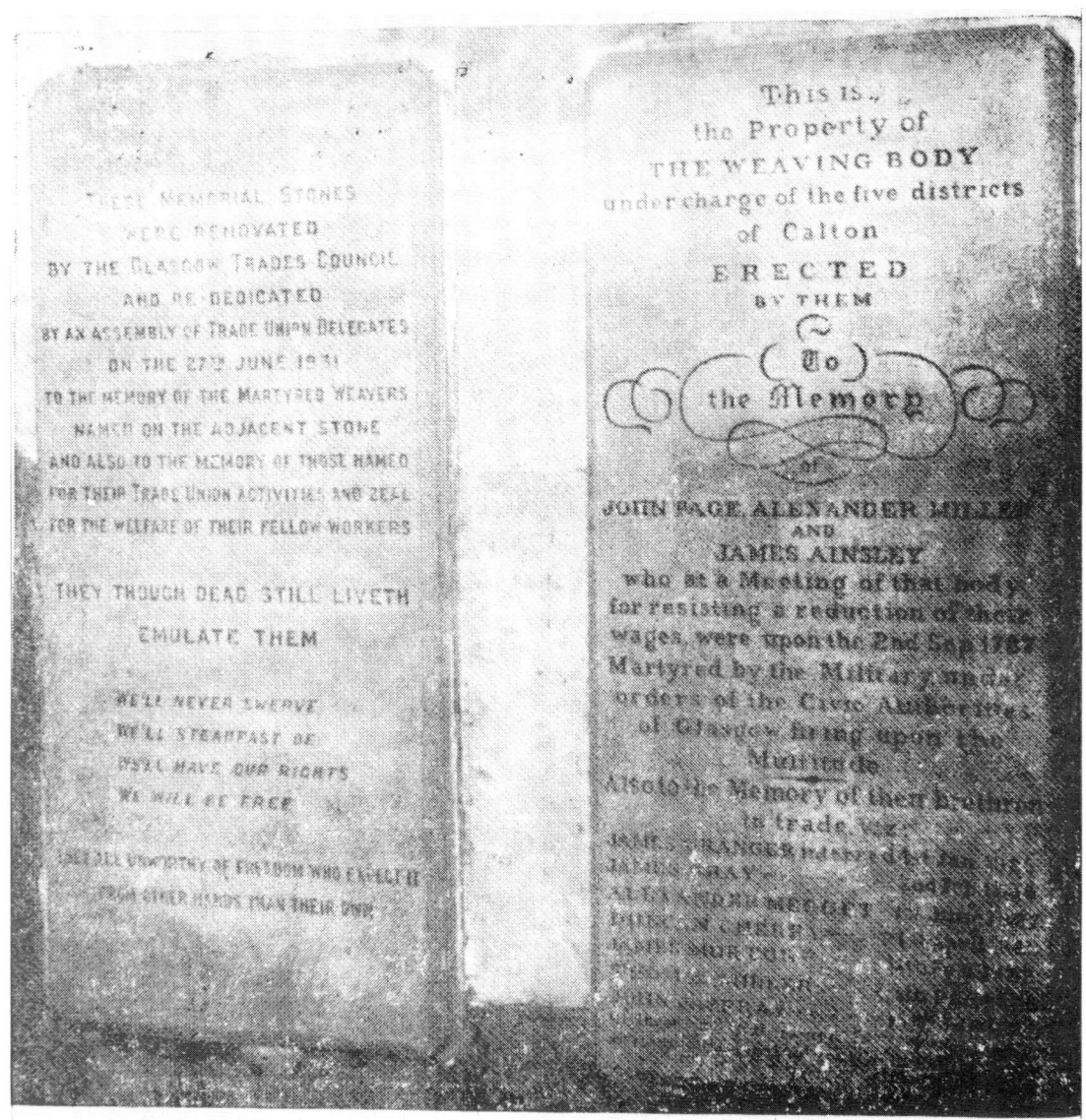

10

Violence was sometimes a feature of industrial relations in the eighteenth century. A strike by Glasgow weavers in 1787 against a reduction in their wages resulted in six being shot by troops called in by the authorities.

11

Seamen striking for an increase in wages at Aberdeen in 1792 unrigged ships going to sea and took possession of those loading or unloading cargoes, according to this letter from Lord Provost George Auldjo to the commander of the army in Scotland, General Lord Adam Gordon. The Lord Provost, who had the same day requested the Lord Advocate to send a warship to deal with the situation, asked General Lord Gordon in this letter to send troops.

12

Hawick Stockingmakers' flag, 1797—probably the oldest surviving trade union flag in
Scotland.

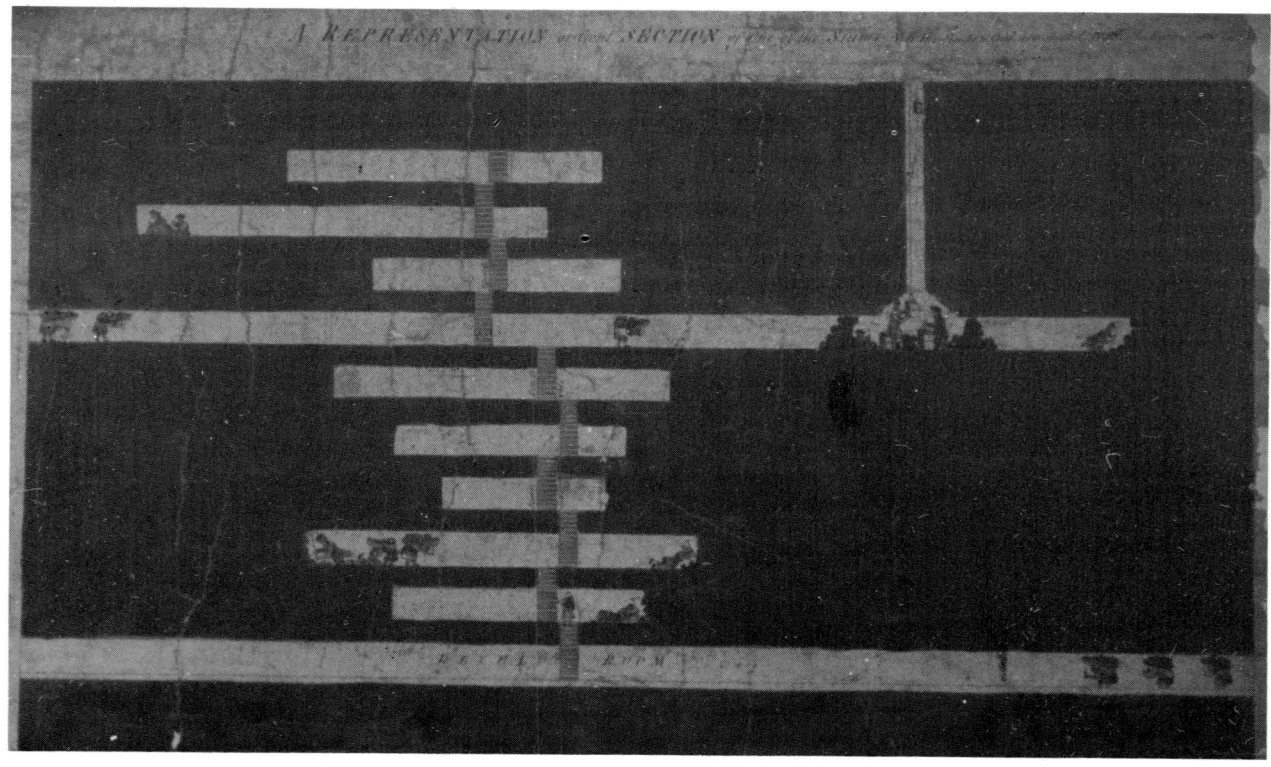

13

Forming trade unions in the eighteenth century was difficult enough for skilled workers;
it was even more so for the unskilled, such as farm workers or miners. Except in the case
of miners there is little evidence of combination among the unskilled before the early
nineteenth century. This sketch of mining at Gilmerton, Edinburgh, about 1786, shows
women coal bearers at work. Scots miners remained in a state of bondage or serfdom until
as late as 1799.

14

Warrant for the arrest of miner-serfs who had 'deserted' their work near Bo'ness in 1796.

SIR,   *Edinburgh, December* 27. 1797.

FOR fome time paſt, many of the Colliers in the neighbour-hood of Edinburgh, as well as in other Coal-works in Scotland, have refuſed to work, except for a few days in the week; and, of late, ſome of them have deferted their Works altogether, whereby there is at pre-ſent a great ſcarcity of Coals in that neighbourhood; and, as there is reaſon to believe that a combination has been entered into among many of the Colliers, for the purpofe of raiſing their wages, a meeting of ſome of the principal Coalmaſters was lately held with the Crown Lawyers, to conſider what ſteps ought to be taken for counteraﬁing their proceedings: But before coming to any determination, it was agreed to call a general meeting of the Coalmaſters of Scotland, in order to learn their ſentiments upon a matter in which all of them are fo deeply intereſted. It is therefore intreated, that you will, by yourſelf or proxy, attend ſuch meeting, within the Royal Exchange Coffeehouſe here, upon Wedneſday the 17th January 1798, at two o'clock afternoon.

P. S. Should any obſervations occur to you on the buſineſs pre-vious to the meeting, you will pleaſe communicate the ſame to Mr WEIR, under cover to LORD ADVOCATE, who was Convener of the laſt meeting.

15

A circular of December 1797 calling a general meeting of the coalmasters of Scotland to consider steps to deal with combinations of miners intent on increasing their wages. The reference in the postscript indicates the close co-operation of the government with the coalmasters. The circular is one of the scraps of evidence indicating an increasing tendency to combination among miners in the later decades of the eighteenth century.

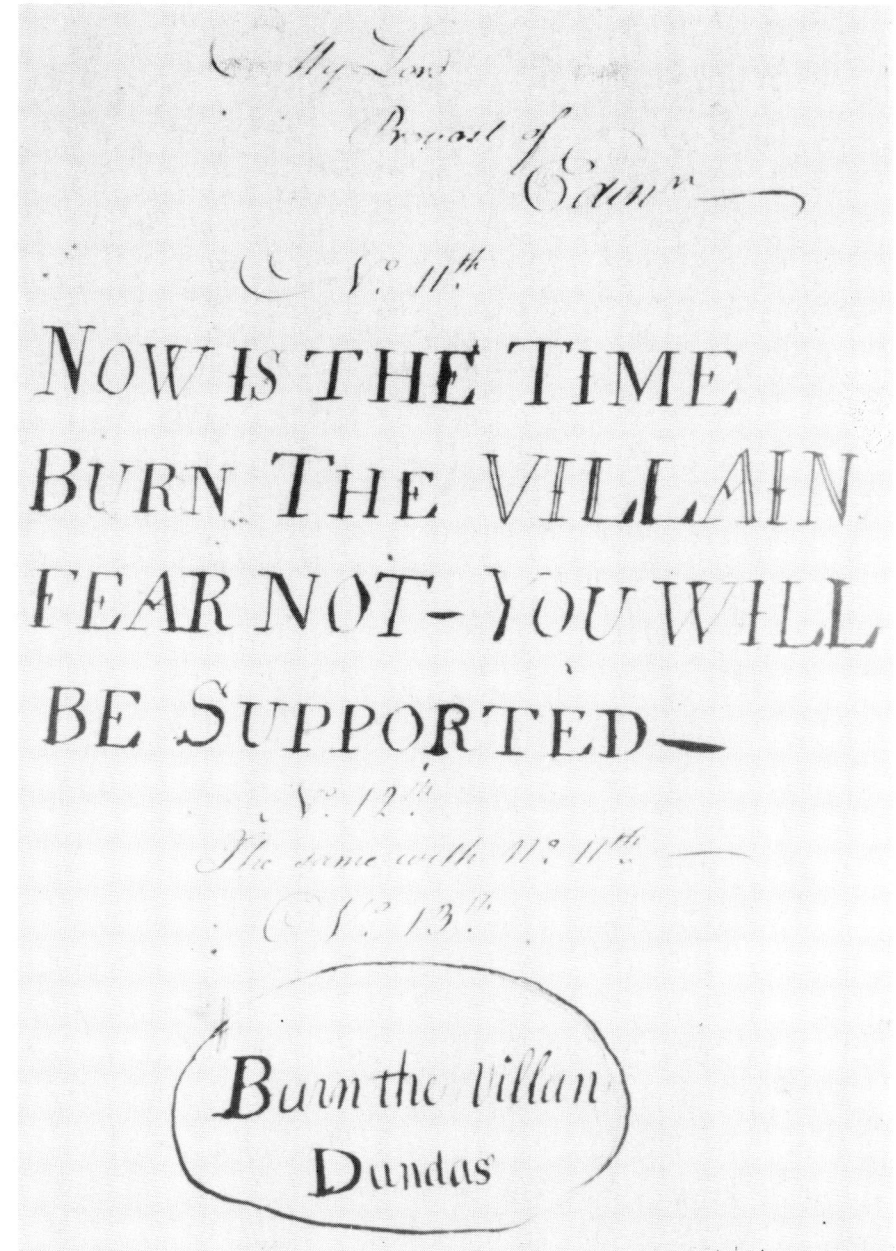

16

Rioting by the common people—the 'mob'—in eighteenth century Scotland was by no means uncommon and partly reflected their total exclusion from the right to vote in parliamentary or local elections. This placard was one of several pinned up in Edinburgh streets during the serious King's Birthday riot there in June 1792 against Henry Dundas, 'Harry the Ninth of Scotland', the powerful right hand man of the Tory prime minister William Pitt the Younger. The riot indicated rising political consciousness and demand for reform. Troops called out to quell the riot shot one man dead and wounded several others. One rioter was sentenced to fourteen years' transportation but was liberated almost at once.

FRIENDS OF THE CONSTITUTION AND OF THE PEOPLE.

THE two leading objects of this Society are, *First*, To Procure an Equal Representation of the People in Parliament, and a Shorter Duration of Parliamentary Delegation. *Secondly*, To Diffuse Useful Political Information.

In prosecution of these two important objects, a common contribution is requisite for defraying the expence of applications to Parliament, of advertisements, of printing cheap editions of good books, and of the various unforeseen contingencies which may occur.

The Friends of the People are the Friends of the Poor.

Upon subscribing our resolutions, each person shall pay Sixpence sterling.

He shall also pay Threepence quarterly.

The Secretary every six months shall lay before the Society a state of the receipt and expenditure.

There shall be Committees appointed in different districts for the purpose of admitting Members.

There shall be a General Committee of Direction, which shall sit once a week for the purpose of managing the affairs of the Society, and for receiving and inrolling the reports of the different Committees.

In proportion to the increase of the number of the members of this Society, and in relation to their local situation, it shall be in the power of this Society to form them into separate Societies.

These affiliated Societies shall in every respect be considered as branches of this one.

They shall act upon the same principles,

They shall have the same regulations,

They shall monthly transmit a written report of their number and proceedings to the Secretary.

Whenever this Society may call a General Convention, these Societies shall send Delegates, in proportion to their number.

No person shall be admitted a Member of this, or of our affiliated Societies, whose character cannot be vouched by at least one of the Committee to which he applies.

Every Member of this, or of our affiliated Societies, shall subscribe the following Declaration :

DECLARATION.

I shall be faithful to the British Constitution, as exhibited in our Statutes, and in the Books of our Law, consisting of a King, House of Lords, and House of Commons. Constitutionally I shall exert my utmost effort to procure a full, fair, and equal representation of the People in Parliament, and a shorter duration of Parliamentary Delegation. I shall discountenance, and endeavour to impress all sedition, riots, or disorder, which bad men may attempt to excite, under the pretence of Reform, and which others as bad may encourage in the view of preventing it. In applying to Parliament I shall know no other rule than that of the Constitution; and I shall endeavour to prevent any person from being admitted, or to remain a member of our Society, whose objects and designs may be unconstitutional.

17

Political interest and activity among working people in Scotland in the late eighteenth century was aroused above all by the French Revolution. Handloom weavers, blacksmiths, tailors, shoemakers and other working men joined the Societies of the Friends of the People formed in towns and villages in the Lowlands in 1792. The generally moderate nature of the demands of the Friends of the People is illustrated in this document of the Glasgow Society. But at the time most of the propertied class regarded such demands as subversive or seditious.

18

The leaders of the Friends of the People were mainly landed gentry or middle class professional men such as Revd. Thomas Fyshe Palmer (top), a Unitarian minister at Dundee, William Skirving (left), a small landowner, and Thomas Muir (right), an advocate. But the rank and file members came increasingly from the working people.

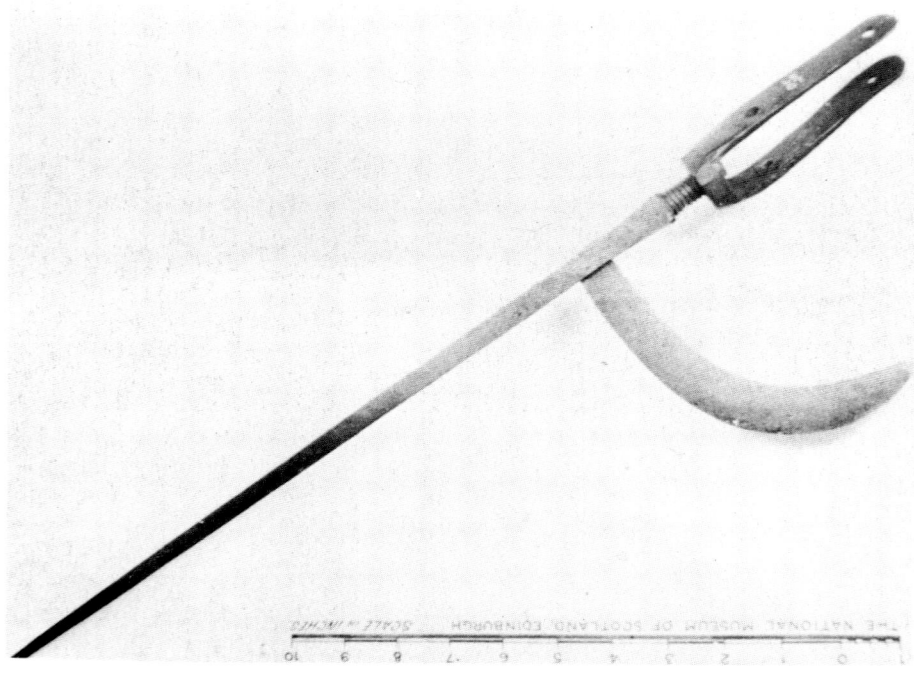

19

An anonymous letter to the authorities in Edinburgh in November 1792 from 'a soldier'
who says that all over Scotland the working men are 'poisoned with an enthusiastic rage
for ideal liberty'.

20

One of the pikes made for the so-called Pike Plot of May 1794 in Edinburgh, in which an
attempt was to be made by some radicals to seize power. The Plot was led by a former
Government spy, Robert Watt. He was convicted of treason and publicly hanged and
beheaded. The pikes were said to have been made by Robert Orrock, a blacksmith
member of the Friends of the People.

21

Monument to the 'Martyrs of 1793'—Muir, Palmer, Skirving, and the delegates from the London Corresponding Society, Joseph Gerrald and Maurice Margarot, to the British Convention of the Friends of the People. The monument was erected in the Calton Cemetery, Edinburgh, half a century after the 'Martyrs' were sentenced by the notorious judge Lord Braxfield to fourteen years' transportation (Palmer got a mere seven years) to the Australian penal settlements for sedition, i.e., for being leaders of the popular demand for political reform.

22

This letter to the Home Secretary from the Duke of Atholl at Dunkeld in November 1795 suggests connections between the political reformers in Scotland and trade unionism. The 'house of call' for tailors in London was a trade union centre where unemployed journeymen tailors called in search of work. E. P. Thompson in his book, *The Making of the English Working Class*, remarks that '. . . at any time before the 1840s it is a mistake to segregate in our minds political disaffection and industrial organisation'.

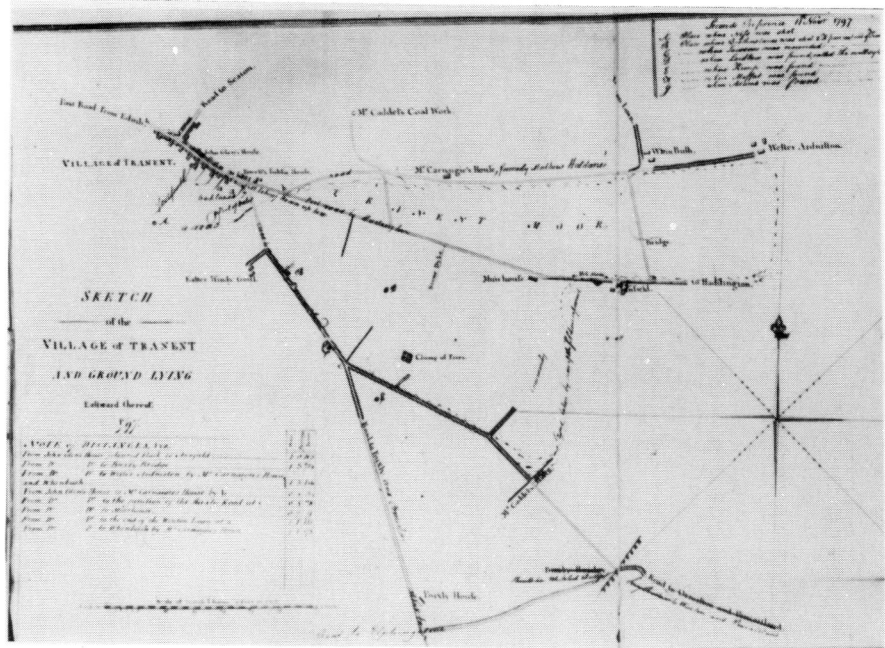

23

The Militia Act of 1797 aroused strong popular opposition in Scotland and serious riots took place in several places. The most serious was at Tranent in East Lothian on 29 August, when twelve working people, including a woman and a boy of fourteen, were killed by cavalry sent to repress the riot—one more death than at the Peterloo Massacre in 1819. This sketch of Tranent and area was made immediately after the riot.

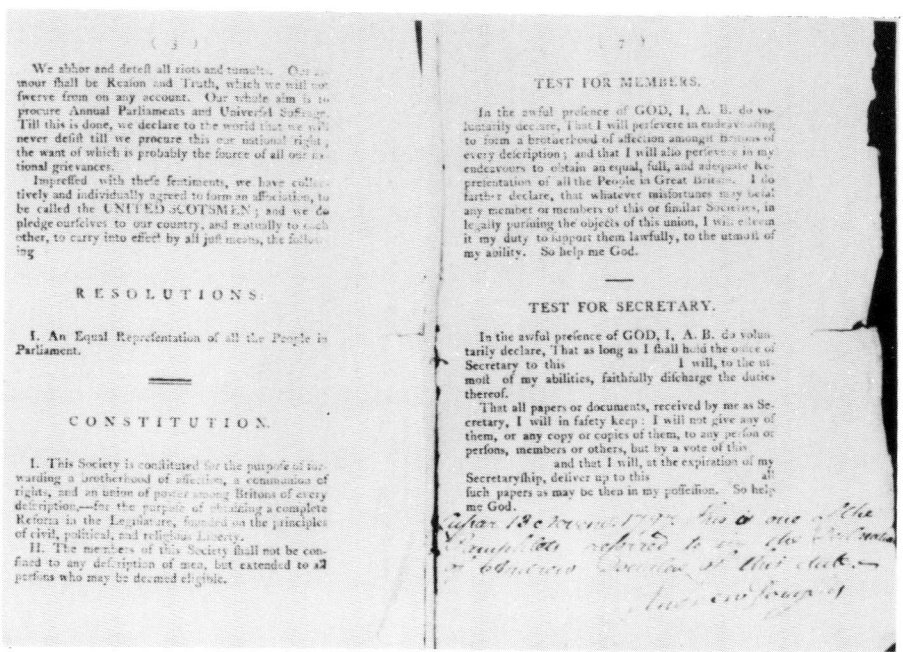

24

The United Scotsmen, a secret radical society formed in the later 1790s and modelled on the revolutionary United Irishmen, attracted some support from working people. The Society demanded universal suffrage and annual general elections to make Parliament more responsive to the wishes of the common people.

25

George Mealmaker, a Dundee radical handloom weaver, was a (perhaps the principal) leader of the United Scotsmen. Mealmaker had also been active in the Friends of the People in the earlier 1790s and had written the manifesto for which Revd. Thomas Fyshe Palmer was sentenced to transportation. Convicted himself of sedition in January 1798, Mealmaker was sentenced to fourteen years' transportation. After the suppression of the United Scotsmen radical agitation in Scotland largely died away until the end of the French Wars.

THE NINETEENTH CENTURY:
FIRST HALF

26

Highland Clearances had begun in the later eighteenth century and continued until almost the end of the nineteenth century. Many evicted Highlanders emigrated to North America; many others became part of the growing industrial working class in the factories or mines of the Lowlands or England. This is Strath Kildonan in Sutherland where occurred in 1813 one of a series of notorious clearances in the county.

27

A letter in August 1813 from the Lord Advocate to the Home Office concerning the sending of troops and ships to Sutherland to repress rioters against clearances.

REWARDS OF £50, £50, & £20

WHEREAS, JAMES M'EWAN, Carding Master, now or lately at Mr. Humphrie's Mill, Gorbals, and M'DOWAL PATE, Weaver in Piccadilly Street, Anderston, are accused of Treasonable Practices, and of taking and administering unlawful Oaths, and MOSES DAWSON, Bookseller, residing in High Street of Glasgow, is charged with Sedition, a REWARD is hereby offered to any one who may lodge the said persons in Glasgow Jail, or give such information as may enable that to be done, of FIFTY POUNDS STERLING, for each of the said James M'Ewan & M'Dowal Pate, and TWENTY POUNDS for the said Moses Dawson, to be paid on their being so lodged as aforesaid, by application to George Salmond, Writer and Procurator Fiscal, Glasgow.

The said James M'Ewan is about 38 years of age, about 5 feet 7½ inches in height, stout made, black complexioned and dark eyes, black hair and whiskers, was accustomed to wear a duffle great coat of an olive colour, and his hat a little to one side, he was sometime ago employed in Coalquay Mill, Tradestown, and taught dancing there.

M'Dowal Pate, is about 5 feet 6 inches high, thin made, broad chest, black hair, very black beard, sallow complexion, about 32 years of age, though he appears older, used to wear wide dark blue pantaloons and blue coat, and sometimes a coloured napkin about his neck, was accustomed to act as precentor in Mr. Neil Douglas's congregation.

Moses Dawson is an Irishman, and a hawking Bookseller from Belfast, staid lately in the house of Mr. Thomas Duncan, High Street, Glasgow, and left Glasgow about a fortnight ago.

Glasgow, 10th March, 1817.

28

Radical agitation and demand for reform revived in Scotland toward the end of the Napoleonic Wars and became much more widespread and intensive from 1815. Numerous arrests were made by the authorities, and several radicals were put on trial for sedition or, in the case of Andrew McKinlay, a weaver, treason. James M'Ewan and McDowall Pate were regarded as accomplices of McKinlay.

ADDRESS
TO THE
Inhabitants of Great Britain & Ireland;
FRIENDS AND COUNTRYMEN,

ROUSED from that torpid state in which WE have been sunk for so many years, We are at length compelled, from the extremity of our sufferings, and the contempt heaped upon our Petitions for redress, to assert our RIGHTS, at the hazard of our lives; and proclaim to the world the real motives, which (if not misrepresented by designing men, would have United all ranks), have reduced us to take up ARMS for the redress of our *Common Grievances.*

The numerous Public Meetings held throughout the Country has demonstrated to you, that the interests of all Classes are the same. That the protection of the Life and Property of the *Rich Man,* is the interest of the *Poor Man,* and in return, it is the interest of the Rich, to protect the poor from the iron grasp of DESPOTISM; for, when its victims are exhausted in the lower circles, there is no assurance but that its ravages will be continued in the upper: For once set in motion, it will continue to move till a succession of Victims fall.

Our principles are few, and founded on the basis of our CONSTITUTION, which were purchased with the DEAREST BLOOD of our ANCESTORS, and which we swear to transmit to posterity unsullied, or PERISH in the Attempt.—Equality of Rights (not of Property,) is the object for which we contend; and which we consider as the only security for our LIBERTIES and LIVES.

Let us show to the world that We are not that Lawless, Sanguinary Rabble, which our Oppressors would persuade the higher circles we are—but a BRAVE and GENEROUS PEOPLE, determined to be FREE, LIBERTY or DEATH is our *Motto,* and We have sworn to return home in *triumph*—or return *no more!*

SOLDIERS,

Shall YOU, Countrymen, bound by the sacred obligation of an Oath, to defend your Country and your King from enemies, whether foreign or domestic, plunge your BAYONETS into the bosoms of Fathers and Brothers, and at once sacrifice at the *Shrine of Military Despotism,* to the unrelenting Orders of a Cruel Faction, those feelings which you hold in common with the rest of mankind? SOLDIERS, Turn your eyes toward SPAIN, and there behold the happy effects resulting from the UNION of Soldiers and Citizens. Look to that quarter, and there behold the yoke of hated Despotism, broke by the Unanimous wish of the People and the Soldiery, happily accomplished without Bloodshed. And, shall You, who taught those Soldiers to fight the battles of LIBERTY, refuse to fight those of your own Country? Forbid it Heaven! Come, forward then at once, and Free your Country and your King, from the power of those that have held them *too, too* long in thraldom.

FRIENDS AND COUNTRYMEN, The eventful period has now arrived, where the Services of all will be required, for the forwarding of an object so universally wished, and so absolutely necessary. Come forward then, and assist those who have begun in the completion of so arduous a task, and support the laudable efforts, which we are about to make, to replace to BRITONS, those rights consecrated to them, by MAGNA CHARTA, and the BILL OF RIGHTS, and Sweep from our Shores, that Corruption which has degraded us below the dignity of Man.

Owing to the misrepresentations which have gone abroad with regard to our intentions, we think it indispensably necessary to DECLARE inviolable, all Public and Private Property. And, We hereby call upon all JUSTICES of the PEACE, and all others to suppress PILLAGE and PLUNDER, of every description; and to endeavour to secure those Guilty of such offences, that they may receive that Punishment, which such violation of Justice demand.

In the present state of affairs, and during the continuation of so momentous a struggle, we earnestly request of all to desist from their Labour, from and after this day, the FIRST OF APRIL; and attend wholly to the recovery of their Rights, and consider it as the duty of every man not to recommence until he is in possession of those Rights which distinguishes the FREEMAN from the SLAVE, viz: That of giving consent to the laws by which he is to be governed. We, therefore, recommend to the Proprietors of Public Works, and all others, to Stop the one, and Shut up the other, until order is restored, or we will be accountable for no damages which may be sustained; and which after this Public Intimation, they can have no claim to.

AND We hereby give notice to all those who shall be found carrying arms against those who intend to regenerate their Country, and restore its INHABITANTS to their NATIVE DIGNITY; We shall consider them as TRAITORS to their Country, and ENEMIES to their King, and treat them as such.

By order of the Committee of Organization,
for forming a PROVISIONAL GOVERNMENT.

GLASGOW, 1st April, 1820.

Britons.—God.—Justice.—The wishes of all good Men are with us.—Join together and make it one CAUSE, and the Nations of the EARTH shall hail the day, when the Standard of LIBERTY shall be raised on its *Native Soil.*

29

The post-War unrest and agitation culminated in April 1820 in the Radical War. This revolutionary proclamation was pinned up all over the West of Scotland and a general strike took place in Glasgow and the surrounding region.

BATTLE OF BONNYMUIR.

An Account of the Battle which took place at Bonnymuir, on Wednesday the 5th April, 1820, betwixt about 50 of the Radicals and a party of the Military; with the names of the 15 Radical prisoners.—Also, the names of those Killed and Wounded at Greenock, on Saturday the 8th.

KILSYTH, 5th APRIL 1820.

This morning a gentleman residing in this parish belonging to the Falkirk troop of Yeomanry Cavalry; left home to join his troop at Falkirk, and had proceeded a short way from his own house, when he came up with between 25 to 30 Radicals, all armed with pikes, muskets, and pistols, who stopped him and requested him to give up his arms, which he refused to do, and showed them a disposition to resist. They told him (at the same time presenting at him several pistols) that resistance would be vain, as they would kill him on the spot. He, however, got off retaining his arms and meeting with an Orderly from Kilsyth going with dispatches to Stirling, informed him it would be improper to proceed. They accordingly both returned to Kilsyth and reported, when the Commanding-Officer there ordered ten men and a serjeant from the 10th Hussars and as many of the Yeomanry Cavalry, to escort the Orderly and the other Gentleman on their several roads, and to endeavour to fall in with these armed Radicals if possible. The Radicals, in the interval, had been joined by a number more, who proceeded along the Canal Bank towards Bonny-muir, having taken several fowling-pieces and a pitch-fork from farmhouses in the neighbourhood of Bonnybridge.

The Cavalry, on their arrival at Loanhead, being informed of their proceedings, immediately went to Bonnymuir in search of the Radicals, and, on coming up with them, they showed a disposition to fight rather than fly: having taken their position behind an old dyke, they allowed the Cavalry to come within thirty yards of them, when they fired a volley; the Cavalry instantly charged, firing a few shots when going over the dyke; the Radicals received the charge with their pikes, and made all the resistance in their power, but they soon found themselves in a bad situation, and throwing away their arms, endeavoured to escape, when the Cavalry secured nineteen prisoners; three of whom are wounded, two remained on the field so badly wounded as not to be able to be carried to Stirling Castle, where the prisoners are lodged. Eight or ten of those who escaped are said to be wounded, and have not been able to go from the place where the affair happened. The whole number of the Radicals did not exceed forty or fifty. None of the Cavalry are severely wounded; two are slightly in the hand; and one horse severely wounded in three different places (since dead) and a number of horses slightly.

It is reported that the whole of the prisoners belong to Glasgow, except one of the name of Baird, said to be their leader, who lately resided at Condorrat. It is said that the whole had been drilling in the Calton Green of Glasgow this morning, that they left that place about four o'clock, and went over the country in a straggling way till they arrived at Bonnymuir, where they expected to be joined by a number from all parts of the country during this evening and to-morrow.

NAMES OF THE PRISONERS.

John Baird,	Andrew Hardie,
Thomas M'Culloch,	John Barr,
William Smith,	Benjamin Moir,
Allan Murphy,	Alexander Latimer,
Alexander Johnston,	Andrew White,
David Thomson,	James Wright,
Thomas Pink,	Robert Gray.
James Cleland,	

Saturday morning, about three o'clock, the prisoners were put on board a Steam Boat at Stirling, under the charge of a Macer of Justiciary, and a party of the 4th Veterans. They were landed at Newhaven, where six carriages were waiting for them to be conveyed to the Jail.

Names of the Killed and Wounded at Greenock.

Names.	Age.	Wounds	
Adam Clephane,	48	Under the groin.	Dead.
Archibald Drummond,	20	Shot dead through the Chest	Dead.
James Kerr,	17	Through the belly.	Dead.
John M'Whinnie,	65	Through shoulder and chest.	Dead.
Hugh Paterson,	14	Through the leg.	Leg amputated.
John Patrick,	38	Through the thigh.	Doing well.
David M'Bride,	14	Through the cheek and jaw.	Doing well.
A. M'Kinnon,	17	Through chest and arm.	Doubtful.
Catherine Turner,	65	Through the leg.	Leg amputated.
		The above in the Infirmary.	
John Boyce,	33	Through the belly.	Dead.
George Tillery,	25	Through the thigh.	Doing well.
Robert Spence,	11	Slightly in the foot.	Slightly.
William Lindsay,	15	Shot dead on the spot.	Dead.
James M'Gilp,	8	Ball in right thigh.	
Gilbert M'Arthur,	18	Through the left thigh.	Flesh wound
John Turner,	22	Through the calf of the leg.	Flesh wound.
Peter Cameron,	14	Through the right leg.	Flesh wound.
John Gunn,	24	Through calf of left leg.	

Printed for John Muir.

30

This contemporary broadside describes the Battle of Bonnymuir, when armed Radicals on their way to seize cannon at the Carron Iron Works at Falkirk were intercepted by troops. At Greenock the jail was stormed and Radical prisoners set free, at a cost of six killed, and a dozen others wounded.

STIRLING.

A Calendar of the Prisoners charged with High Treason, and to be tried under the special Commission to be holden at STIRLING, in and for the County of STIRLING, on Friday the 23d. day of June, 1820. before the Lords Commissioners named in the same Commission.

No.	NAMES AND DESIGNATIONS OF PRISONERS.	WHEN COMMITTED.	BY WHOM COMMITTED.
1	John Baird, Weaver in Condorrat		
2	Thomas M'Culloch, Stocking-weaver in Glasgow		
3	Andrew Hardie, Weaver there		
4	John Barr, Weaver in Condorrat		
5	William Smith, Weaver there		
6	Benjamin Moir, Labourer in Glasgow		
7	Allan Murchie, Blacksmith there		
8	Alexander Latimer, otherwise Lettimer, Weaver there		
9	Alexander Johnstone, Weaver there		
10	Andrew White, Bookbinder there	All on 5th April, 1820.	John Fraser Esquire, Sheriff Substitute of Stirlingshire.
11	David Thomson, Weaver there		
12	James Wright, Tailor there		
13	William Clackson, Alias Clarkson, Shoemaker there		
14	Thomas Pike, otherwise Pink, Muslin-Sindger there		
15	Robert Gray, Weaver there		
16	James Clelland, Smith there		
17	Alexander Hart, Cabinet-maker there		
18	Thomas M'Farlane, Weaver at Condorrat		
19	John M'Millan, Nailer in Camelon	7th April, 1820. Recommitted 9th June, 1820.	Alexander Dow, Esq. Sheriff Substitute of Stirlingshire. Charles Alexander Moir, Esquire of Leckie, one of the Justices of peace for Stirlingshire.
20	William Wright, Senior, Nailer there		
21	William Crawford, Weaver in Balfron		John Fraser, Esq. Sheriff Substitute of Stirlingshire.
22	Lewis Cameron, Weaver there	All on 10th April, 1820.	
23	James Wishart, Weaver there		
24	John M'Lintock, Weaver there		
25	William Wright, Junior, Nailer in Camelon		Thos. Spottiswood and Michael Stewart Nicolson, Esquire, two of the Justices of peace for Stirlingshire.
26	James Burt, Nailer there	All on 9th April, 1820.	
27	Andrew Grieve, Nailer there		
28	John Anderson, Weaver in St. Ninians	1st May, 1820.	Ranald Macdonald, Esq. Sheriff Depute of Stirlingshire.
29	Robert Wright, Junior,		Michael Stewart Nicolson, Esquire, one of the Justices of Peace for Stirlingshire.
30	Andrew Burt, Junior, — All Nailers in Camelon	11th May, 1820.	
31	Daniel Turner, Senior,		The said Michael Stewart Nicolson, Esquire, Charles Alexr. Moir, Esquire, one of the Justices of Peace of Stirlingshire.
32	James Dewar, Nailer there	11th May, 1820. Recommitted 12 June, 1820.	
33	Walter Bain, Stocking-maker in Falkirk	24th May, 1820.	Thos. Spottiswood, Esq. one of the Justices of Peace for Stirlingshire.
34	John Johnstone, Shoemaker there		
35	John Nicol, Weaver in Falkirk	30th May, 1820.	Charles Alexr. Moir, Esquire, one of the Justices of Peace for Stirlingshire.
36	James Aitken, Grocer or Merchant there		
37	Robert Gardner, Changekeeper in Kilsyth	2d June, 1820.	James Davidson, Esq. one the Justices of Peace of Stirlingshire.
38	Robert Vannan, Weaver there	7th June, 1820.	William Murray, Esq. one of the Justices of Peace of Stirlingshire.
39	James Aitken, Wright in Camelon	9th June, 1820.	Charles Alexr. Moir, Esq. one of the Justices of Peace of Stirlingshire.
40	Andrew Dawson, Nailer there		
41	John Shaw, Weaver in Kilsyth	11th June, 1820.	The said Charles Alexander Moir, Esq.

31

An official list of Radicals—almost without exception working men—captured at the Battle of Bonnymuir and charged with high treason.

Trials & Sentences.

A full and particular account of the Trials and sentences of the Radicals at Stirling, who received sentence yesterday; twenty two of whom are to be hanged, beheaded, and quartered on the 8th september, 1820.

STIRLING, JULY 18.

The Lords Commissioners appointed by the Special Commission of Oyer and Terminer, for trying all Treasons and Misprisons of Treason, committed within the counties of Stirling, Lanark, Dumbarton, Renfrew; and Ayr, opened their proceedings here on Thursday morning The following were the Lords Commissioners—The Lord President, Lord Justice Clerk, Lord Chief Baron, Lord Chief Commissioner of the Jury Court, Lord Hermand, Lord Gillies, Lord Pitmilly, Lord Succoth, and Lord Meadowbank. John Hullock, Esq. Serjeant at Law, assisted at the trials, and Mr. Thomas George Knapp, Clerk to the Arraigns of the Home Circuit in England, acted as Clerk to the Arraigns.

The Court was opened about nine o'clock, and in a few minutes was crowded with people. The Lord President then addressed the Court, after which the following prisoners were called to the bar:—

John Baird, weaver in Condorrat.
Thomas M'Culloch, stocking-weaver in Glasgow.
Andrew Hardie, weaver there.
John Barr, weaver in Condorrat.
William Smith, weaver there.
Benjamin Moir, labourer in Glasgow.
Allan Murchy, blacksmith there.
Alexander Latimer or Lettimer, weaver there.
Alexander Johnston, weaver there.
Andrew White, bookbinder there.
David Thomson, weaver there.
James Wright, tailor there.
William Clackson or Clarkson; shoemaker there.
Thomas Pike or Pink, muslin-singer there.
Robert Gray, weaver there.
James Clelland, smith there.
Alexander Hart, cabinet-maker there.
Thomas M'Farlane, weaver at Condorrat.

The indictment having been read over, (charging them with treason in four different counts) the prisoners severally pleaded Not Guilty. Hardie's trial was first proceeded in.

Mr. Jeffrey, in a long speech, insisted that Mr. Serjeant Hullock was not entitled to plead before the Court, he being an English Barrister. The objection was repelled.

The Lord Advocate then addressed the Jury, laying down the law of High Treason. The evidence went to connect the Bonnymuir business with the proposed Radical insurrection in the West of Scotland, Hardie having violently resisted a Magistrate in Glasgow, who wished to take down one of the posted Radical proclamations of the 1st of April. The evidence afterwards traced him, and about 24 more armed men, on their march from Castlecarry, where they got refreshment, and took a formal receipt for the reckoning, and from thence to Bonnymuir.

Mr. Jeffrey, for the pannel, addressed the Court at great length, he admitted that the prisoner was found in arms in a skirmish with the King's troops at Bonnymuir, but denied that this constituted the crime of High Treason. The Solicitor General replied.

At one o'clock on Friday, the Jury retired for 10 minutes, when they returned their verdict, finding him Guilty on the 1st count, for levying war; and also on the 4th, for compassing to levy war against the King, in order to compel him to change his measures.

FRIDAY, AUGUST 4.

This day, the Court met, and on the above-named persons being placed at the bar, the Lord President, after a most solemn address, said, the sentence of the law is—That you be drawn on a Hurdle to the place of execution, on the 8th September; and after being hanged by the neck till dead, that your heads be severed from your bodies, and your bodies to be cut in quarters, to be at the disposal of the King; and the Lord have mercy on your souls." The prisoners was then taken from the bar, without showing any signs of agitation. They were all recommended to mercy, except Baird and Hardie.

William Crawford, weaver in Balfron.
John Anderson, weaver in St. Ninian's.
John M'Millan, nailer in Camelon.
James Burt, nailer there.
Andrew Burt, jun. nailer there.
John Johnston, shoemaker in Falkirk.
James Aitken, grocer or merchant there.
James Aitken, wright in Camelon, and
Andrew Dawson, nailor there.

Were then put to the bar, charged with being concerned in the late Radical Rebellion, when four persons, viz.—William Crawford; John Anderson; John M'Millan and Andrew Dawson, received the same sentence as the above, but were recommended to mercy.

GLASGOW, PRINTED BY JOHN MUIR.

32

Trials of Radicals for treason were held in the summer of 1820 at Stirling, Glasgow, Dumbarton, Paisley and Ayr; and though many were sentenced to death in fact only three—Andrew Hardie, John Baird and James Wilson—were executed. The others had their sentences commuted to transportation to the Australian penal settlements.

33

The axe used and cloak worn by the executioner at the execution at Stirling in 1820 of two Radical weavers, John Baird and Andrew Hardie, for their part in the Radical War. A third weaver, James Wilson of Strathaven, was hanged in Glasgow.

TO THE WORKERS

AT

The Wellington Factory.

IN permitting you again to commence work, after the unprecedented Strike that took place here, from the intimidation created amongst you by the rebellious anonymous Address, of date the 1st April, I must call upon every honest man among you to assist me with your utmost information, to find out those persons, who by their personal threats to any individual employed in this work, deterred him from continuing his labour; and, I trust, none of you will, under false motives of honour, conceal the names of those who have been instrumental in getting you disgraced, by classing you in the ranks of a lawless banditti, who, under the mask of Reform, harboured only ideas of plunder and bloodshed, who, by their cunning and vile insinuations to the unsuspecting, got them unwarily to acquiesce in resolutions, and attend meetings, without inquiring or contemplating the ultimate intentions of the villains by whom they were, in a manner, led blindfold. For I rest satisfied, there is not one in twenty of those deceived individuals, who were infatuated to the length of procuring arms or pikes, but would have sooner plunged them into the hearts of their base leaders, than enlisted under their banners, had the real views of these factious guides been openly laid before them. Happily, the designs of these wicked rebels have failed, and in a manner which, considering the extent of numbers who had silently acquiesced in their proceedings, could hardly have been expected. Human Nature, however, prevailed, for when the hour came when their efficient strength was to burst forth, not one for a hundred that they expected, appeared at their summons. The eyes of their whole followers were then opened, and their cause deserted, when it became apparent that burning and bloodshed was to be the commencement of this pillaging system. Even had they been joined by the greatest number expected, it would not have been above the work of an hour for the strong Military Force collected here, to have sent them headlong to destruction—leaving behind the moanings of mothers for their sons, wailings of wives for their husbands, and the cries of children for their fathers, slain. When you return home this evening, thank God these distressing scenes have been averted, and you have not consented to the making the wife a widow, nor the child an orphan; and that the misguided have found out, before it was too late, the dupes they had been to a few designing scoundrels.

In congratulating you on this at present happy termination of a visionary delusion, I must call upon you for your assistance to prevent a recurrence of an evil likely to prove so disastrous; and I trust you will second me in so doing as far as lies in your power. Your comfort and happiness depend on it. And I must call upon you, 1st, Neither to pay nor subscribe money for any secret purpose whatever, nor in fact enter into any society, but what you would invite and wish your employer to be a member. 2d, If any sums are demanded of you by any person to assist in any purpose whatever, immediately to give your employer information on the subject. 3d, To give your employer information of any persons you may know who have been active in attending the late seditious meetings, or who have attended any of the drilling parties of the misnamed Radical Reformers; and if any of you have seen them at drill, particularly to give up the names of those who gave the word of command. 4th, To give up the names of all you know had pikes or unlawful weapons—the names of all who have asked you for money to subsist those delegates who have lived in idleness at the expense of the deluded, and brought the working classes into that infatuated frenzy, which they, luckily, now every day are getting the better of.

It is a duty you owe your Country—it is a duty you owe your Wives and Children—more, it is a duty you owe to Mankind, to give up the leaders and active abettors of this vile Confederacy. You need not be afraid of any harm happening to you for giving information—the illusion of intimidation has gone by, and all honest and industrious men are bound by their allegiance to the King and Constitution, to give up the names of Traitors, although they were their bosom friends; it is cowardice not to do it, for a purification is absolutely necessary for the security of the well disposed. The most conspicuous courage is that which will dare villany in every shape.—Listen no more to the disturbers of public peace and order, but by ridding this Work of them, and the Country, as far as in your power, live in future, industrious, content, and happy.

I hope it will be found that none of you will have acted in this nefarious business, so conspicuous a part as to come under the cognizance of the Civil Authorities; but trust that you have merely been silent spectators of a system, of the ultimate designs of which you were ignorant.

WELLINGTON FACTORY, 12th APRIL, 1820.

Printed at the Herald Office, Glasgow

34

An aftermath of the Radical War: a Glasgow factory employer's notice to his workers, 12 April 1820.

REFORM MEETING, RUTHERGLEN,

Saturday, Oct. 23d, 1819.

The morning was remarkably agreeable, slight frost, and plentiful sunshine. A little after breakfast, people were beginning to assemble round the hustings, erected on the Green, and by 12 o'clock, all the roads leading to this ancient and independent burgh were occupied with groups of persons, of every age and condition, wending their cheerful way thither.

A little before one o'clock, it was announced that the Union Societies were on the skirts of the Meeting, when lines through the crowd were instantly opened up, which enabled them to walk slowly to the hustings, their bands playing the " Dead March in Saul," where they delivered up their varied and elegant insignia. They consisted of the Glasgow Town-head, Calton, Bridgeton, Gorbals, Tradestown, Anderston, Pollockshaws, Cambuslang, and Kilbride Union Societies, bearing banners, with the following devices and inscriptions:—A woman, with a child in her arms, under the murderous sabre of a Manchester yeoman; motto, " Law, Blood for blood."—An ardent heart,

" Brave Britain's sons, why linger ye?
" Rise up, undaunted, and be free."

Tyranny falling under the arm of an ancient Caledonian— " So fall Tyranny."—Hands united: " Unite and be free." " Arise Britons and assert your rights;" reverse, " We shall be free."—" Remember Manchester."—A pole, bearing a cap of liberty, and poles, bearing a bundle of rods, tied with crape, emblematic of unity in Reform, and sympathy with their suffering brethren of Manchester.—" Taxation, without representation, is injustice;" reverse, the Rose, Thistle, and Shamrock blended,

" May the rose of England never blow,
" May the Thistle of Scotland never grow,
" May the harp of Erin never play,
" Till Hunt, the champion, gains the day."

" Hunt and Liberty," reverse, " No Luxuries," suspended from a stick across the pole of this flag, were inverted gill and half-mutchkin stoups, tea-pots, torn spleuchans, and broken tobacco pipes.—" Annual Parliaments, Universal Suffrage;" reverse, " United we stand, divided we fall."—" May the Tyrants of Great Britain now be brought to justice."— " Liberty or Despotism."—" We shall be free."—A spear, " Touch me not;" reverse, " Cartwright's Bill."—" Rights of Man," &c. &c.

Before the business of the Meeting was commenced, the bands played, " God save the King;" during which, all those on the hustings stood up, uncovered: " Rule Britannia" and " Scots wha hae wi'Wallace bled," immediately succeeded.

The cap of liberty was placed on the President's head, amid the cheers of the multitude, and the pealing of national airs. Mr PATTISON, on being called, unanimously to the Chair, requested that the Meeting would be attentive and orderly. It was, he said, the first time he had appeared before such a numerous and intelligent assembly, which might account for oratorical inaccuracies—the imperious

35

The *Spirit of the Union*, a Radical newspaper, described by the authorities as 'a revolutionary periodical', was published in Glasgow in 1819-20. Its editor, Gilbert MacLeod, was convicted of publishing seditious articles and sentenced to five years' transportation to Botany Bay. The paper here reports a huge demonstration by Radicals at Rutherglen, that demanded universal suffrage and annual general elections.

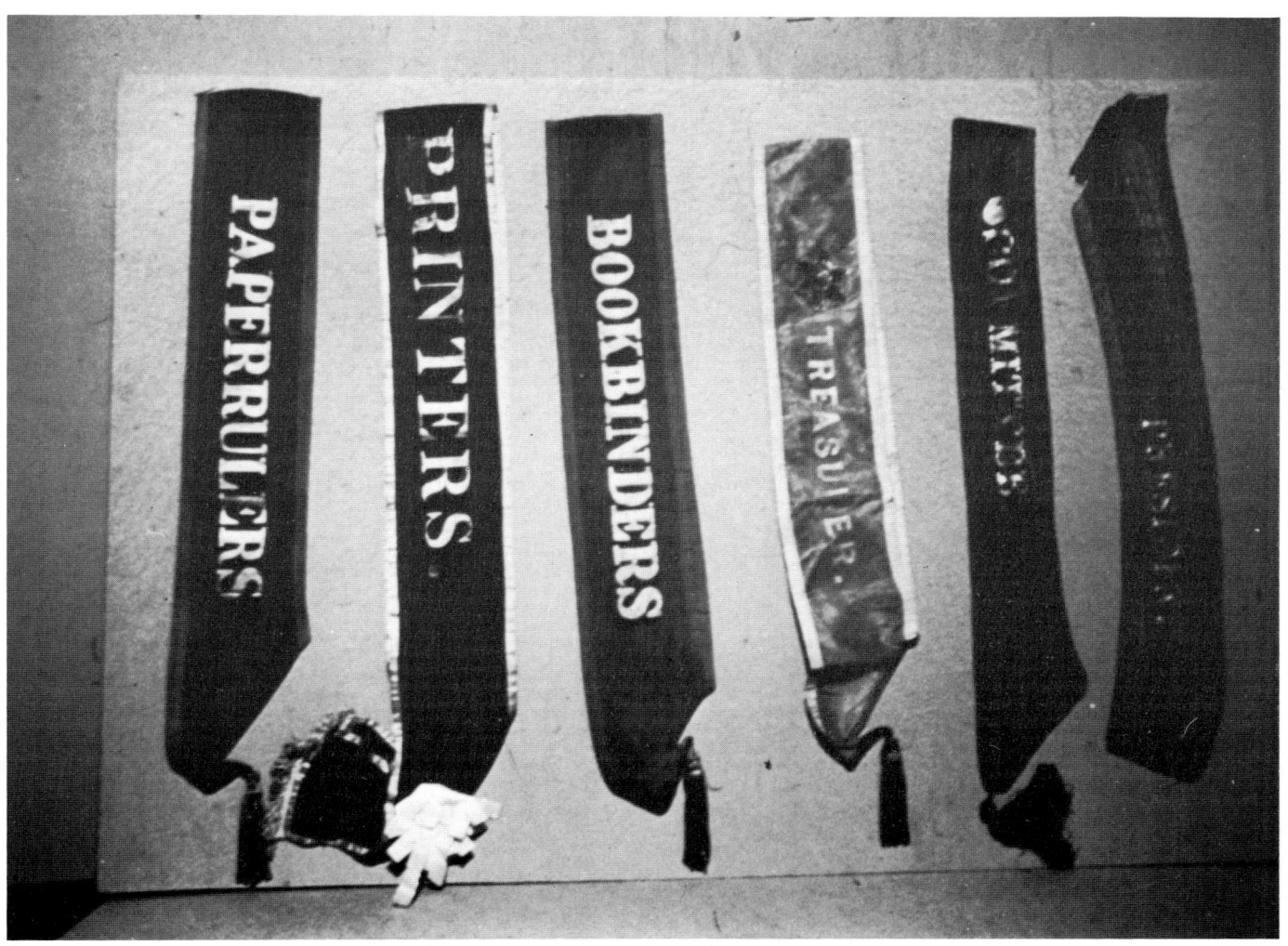

36

The early years of the nineteenth century were also an important and often dramatic period in the development of trade unionism in Scotland. In the two preceding centuries the state had exercised, through local Justices of the Peace, the power to regulate wage rates, apprenticeship, and other conditions of labour. But the spread of *laissez faire* philosophy during the later eighteenth century made regulation by the state increasingly a dead letter. The Edinburgh Journeymen Printers—whose later cermonial sashes are shown above, along with several of those of the city Bookbinders' union—were one of the last groups of working men in Britain to succeed in having their wages fixed by law, in an Interlocutor or judgement granted by the Court of Session in 1804.

37

Membership card of the Greenock Coopers' Society, 1811. The Anti-Combination Laws passed by Parliament in 1799 and 1800 were not implemented in Scotland and until 1812-13 prosecution of combinations seems to have taken place only when they became involved in violence.

38

Snuff horn presented to the printers' chapel of the *Edinburgh Evening Courant* in 1813. Skilled or craft unions in particular seem not to have been prosecuted if they did not press employers too closely for improved wages or conditions.

39

An early nineteenth century banner of the Airdrie Weavers' Society.

40

The emblem of the Glasgow Cotton Spinners' Union. Formed about 1806 it later became
the leading union in Scotland until it was broken by a great crisis in 1837-8.

PROCLAMATION

BY THE

SHERIFF

OF THE

County of Renfrew.

Whereas information has been received, that certain evil-disposed persons have, of late, unwarrantably interrupted a number of OPERATIVE WEAVERS in the City of Glasgow, and in its neighbourhood, bordering upon, and within this County, in the peaceable exercise of their trade, and have, by threats and intimidation, compelled them to desist from their work; AND WHEREAS information has also been received, that certain evil-disposed persons have attempted to intimidate different PUBLIC CARRIERS, for the purpose of preventing them from conveying to a distance any Materials for Weaving: The SHERIFF of RENFREWSHIRE, THEREFORE, and for the protection of the great body of industrious and well-disposed OPERATIVE WEAVERS residing within this County, in the lawful prosecution of their business, for the support of themselves and families: AND ALSO, for the conviction and punishment of the persons who may be guilty, GIVES this Public Intimation, that these proceedings are illegal, of a Criminal Nature, and highly punishable; and that any person or persons who may be guilty of such conduct, within this County, will be apprehended and brought to punishment, as disturbers of the Public Peace.

Paisley, **20th November 1812.**

J. Neilson, printer

The Justices of the Peace, for the Lower Ward of Lanarkshire, having, of this date, published an explanation of their Interlocutor of the 10th current, wherein they find, and declare, " That all webs taken out " to weave, prior to said 10th Nov. current, at a certain price per ell, specified in the Tickets accompany- " ing each web, in terms of the Weaver's act, must be wrought out at the prices mentioned in these " Tickets. Such contracts between the Weavers and Manufacturers being by no means affected by the " sentence of the 10th current."

The Committee for managing the process on the part of the Weavers, conceive that the aforesaid sentence and explanation having been passed, in consequence of a note given in to the Justices by the Manufacturers of Glasgow, which note was not intimated to the Weavers' Procurator, or any of their Managing Committee, is therefore *irregular.*

And, with all due deference to the above sentence of the Justices, said Committee are of opinion, that whatever proportion of the webs in the loom were unfinished at the date of the decision of the Justices on the aforesaid 10th of Nov. are, by the laws of this country, affected; and the contract, as marked in the tickets (if a contract it can be called), rendered null and nugatory by said decision, because the Interlocutor that fixes and declares the weavers' Table to be moderate and reasonable, at the same time virtually condemns any lower rate of payment as unfair, unreasonable, and therefore *illegal.*

If, therefore, the law ordains that the weaving of twenty-one yards of muslin ought to be paid with as many shillings, can it be supposed that the same law will punish a weaver for refusing to perform that quantity of labour for two-thirds of that sum; and to demand this of a weaver, must, to all intents and purposes, be unjust. The weaver cannot compel the manufacturer to employ him at the rates fixed by the Justices; it must therefore be absurd to suppose, that the manufacturer can compel him to do his work for less. On these grounds the Committee are satisfied, that a weaver has it in his option, whether he will or will not finish the remainder of the web, taken at the low price prior to the decision of the Justices, without the advance; and cannot help holding this opinion till the parties be heard, and a contrary judgment pronounced in the regular course of law.

Glasgow, 28th *Nov.* 1812.

D. *M'Kenzie, Printer.*

JOHN WILSON,
WM. M'KIMMIE,
JAMES JOHNSTON,
A. RICHMOND,
THOMAS SMITH.

41

Between 1780 and 1830 the number of handloom weavers in Scotland more than trebled. They were the largest single group of manufacturing industrial workers. Probably influenced by the success eight years earlier of the Edinburgh journeymen printers, the handloom weavers took court action in 1812 to persuade the Justices of the Peace in Glasgow to fix a reasonable rate of wages. The weavers did obtain a judgement from the Court of Session that it was within the competence of the JPs to fix wage rates; but as the judgement omitted any compulsion either on the JPs to fix rates or on employers to pay those that might be fixed, the Glasgow employers continued to pay less than the rate that the weavers had established as 'moderate and reasonable'. The weavers then went on strike all over Scotland. The strike, supported by some 40,000 weavers, was centred on Glasgow and the West of Scotland, but spread as far as Aberdeen. It was the biggest strike until then in Scotland. The alarm felt by the authorities is indicated by the first of the two documents above—the proclamation by the Sheriff of Renfrewshire. The second document is a statement by the Committee of the operative weavers of Glasgow—among them Alexander Richmond, who later became a police spy and *agent provocateur.*

PROCLAMATION

597

By the Sheriff of the County of Lanark, the Magistrates of Glasgow, and the Justices of the Peace for the Lower Ward of Lanarkshire.

WHEREAS, certain information has been received, that, nothwithstanding the Proclamation of the 16th November last, great numbers of OPERATIVE COTTON WEAVERS, pretending to have instructions and powers from other Operative Weavers in the City of Glasgow and Suburbs, and in other towns and Villages in the County of Lanark, have held VARIOUS MEETINGS, for the purpose of exciting and maintaining a GENERAL COMBINATION AMONG THE OPERATIVE COTTON WEAVERS IN SCOTLAND, to enforce an advance of the Rates or Prices of Weaving by illegal means: And WHEREAS, certain information has also been received, that numerous bodies, or bands, of people, have, for the said illegal purpose, and in prosecution of the plans adopted at the said Meetings, gone about intimidating, by threats of violence, great numbers of peaceable and well-disposed persons engaged in the Cotton Manufacture, and have thereby succeeded in preventing the said persons from exercising their lawful Trade, and reduced them to a state of poverty and distress; And WHEREAS, information has likewise been received, that the said bodies, or bands, of people have, for the accomplishment of their unwarrantable objects, proceeded even to acts of personal injury, destruction of property, and open outrage, in manifest Breach of the Public Peace, the SHERIFF of LANARKSHIRE, the MAGISTRATES of GLASGOW, and the JUSTICES of the PEACE for the LOWER WARD of LANARKSHIRE, HEREBY INTIMATE, that they can no longer refrain from exercising the powers, with which they are by Law invested, for the protection of His Majesty's peaceable and well-disposed Subjects, and have determined, by the most vigorous and effectual measures, to suppress all such illegal Meetings, plans of Combination, and violent and outrageous proceedings, and to bring to immediate Trial, and condign Punishment, all such violators of the Laws of their Country: And they hereby offer a

REWARD OF TWENTY POUNDS STERLING,

to any person, or persons, other than the parties concerned, who shall, within fourteen days from this date, give such information, as may lead to the apprehension and conviction of such heinous Offenders: FARTHER, the Sheriff, Magistrates and Justices deem it their duty thus publicly to put the Well-disposed Operative Weavers on their guard against frequenting such illegal Assemblies in future; and hereby intimate to them, that, if, after this notice, they shall be found attending any such Meetings, they will expose themselves to criminal prosecution, and will have themselves to blame for the consequences.

And WHEREAS, it is notorious, that numbers of OPERATIVE WEAVERS have, for sometime past, been in the practice of calling at the Houses of the Inhabitants of this City and Suburbs, and of other parts of the County, and of attempting by solicitation, to obtain Sums of Money for the purpose of supporting themselves and their Brethren in wilful idleness, and of promoting the objects of their illegal Combination, The SHERIFF, MAGISTRATES and JUSTICES feel themselves called upon, in the discharge of their public duty, to declare, that men, who, although in health and able to procure work, thus obstinately persist in idleness, and degrade themselves to the rank of Public Beggars, have no claim whatever to the maintenance, provided by law, for the industrious Poor, who are, by age, or disease, disabled from working: and instead of being objects of compassion and charity, are guilty of an illegal act: And the SHERIFF, MAGISTRATES and JUSTICES therefore, hereby admonish the Inhabitants, in general, that those persons, who comply with the unreasonable demands of such Mendicants, instead of fulfilling a duty, contribute to the support of the idle and disorderly, encourage proceedings illegal in themselves, and highly prejudicial to the welfare of the Country, and assist in enabling a few designing men, still farther to mislead their deluded Brethren.

COURT-HALL, GLASGOW, 14th Dec. 1812.

Printed in the Courier Office.

42

The weavers' strike seems to have been remarkably peaceable, but the local magistrates and government claimed that the weavers were turning to violence.

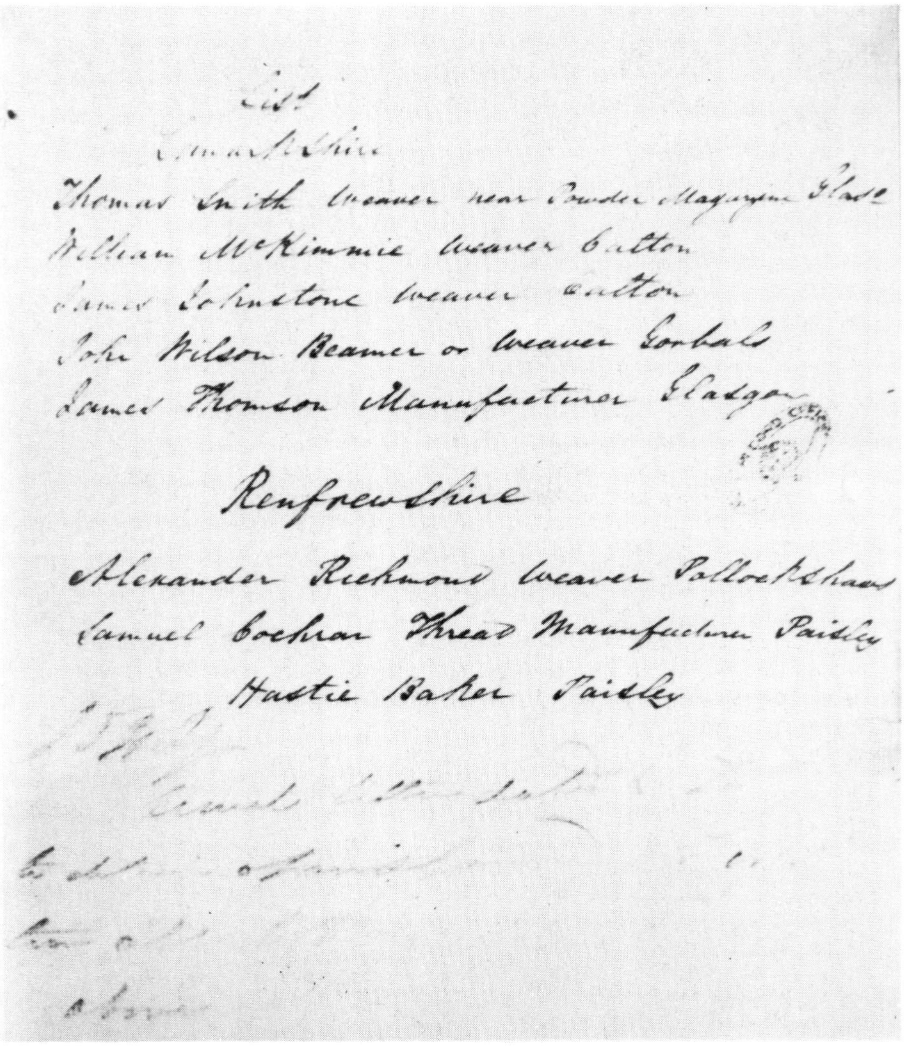

List

Lanarkshire

Thomas Smith weaver near Powder Magazine Glass

William McKimmie weaver Calton

James Johnstone weaver Calton

John Wilson Beamer or weaver Gorbals

James Thomson Manufacturer Glasgow

Renfrewshire

Alexander Richmond weaver Pollockshaws

Samuel Cochran Thread Manufacturer Paisley

Hastie Baker Paisley

43

Fear by the authorities that the strike had political or revolutionary significance was probably the explanation for the opening of letters addressed to the strike leaders, including Alexander Richmond.

WILLIAM M'KIMMIE weaver, presently or lately residing in Kirk Street, Calton of Glasgow; THOMAS SMITH weaver, presently or lately residing in Galloway Society's land, at or near the powder magazine of Glasgow; JAMES JOHNSTON weaver, presently or lately residing in Crossloan Street, Calton of Glasgow; CHARLES CHRISTIE weaver, presently or lately residing in Rotten-row Street of Glasgow; JAMES GRANGER weaver or beamer, presently or lately residing in Rotten-row Street of Glasgow; You are indicted and accused, at the instance of ARCHIBALD COLQUHOUN of Killermont, his Majesty's Advocate for his Majesty's interest: THAT WHEREAS, by the laws of this and of every other well governed realm, ILLEGAL COMBINATION or CONSPIRACY, and particularly ILLEGAL COMBINATION or CONSPIRACY among many thousands of workmen or artificers, to compel their masters or employers to raise their wages, or the prices of their work or labour—by striking work in a body, or in great numbers, and in different parts of the country, at one, or nearly at one and the same time;—by supporting those workmen who so strike work, and stand out against their masters or employers, with money subscribed, collected, or borrowed for that purpose, and by the interposition of the joint credit of the persons so combining or conspiring, or of some of their number;—by preventing workmen willing to work at wages or prices different from, or lower than those demanded by the workmen or artificers so combining or conspiring, from so working, by either masterfully depriving them of the possession of machinery or implements necessary for carrying on their work, or by improperly excluding them from, or denying them the use of the same, is a crime of an heinous nature, and severely punishable, MORE ESPECIALLY when committed by intimidating by means of threats, abuse, or violence, workmen so willing to work from so working, and by extorting money for the aforesaid purpose: YET TRUE IT IS AND OF VERITY, that You the said William M'Kimmie, Thomas Smith, James Johnston, Charles Christie, and James Granger, are all and each, or one or other of You, guilty actors or actor, or art and part, of the said crime, aggravated as aforesaid: IN SO FAR AS, some time in the year 1809, or in 1810, or in 1811, or in 1812, many thousands of Operative Cotton Weavers, resident in various villages, towns, or places of Scotland, did, within the city of Glasgow, or elsewhere to the Public Prosecutor unknown, illegally and feloniously combine or conspire together, for the purpose of compelling their masters or employers to raise their wages, or the prices of their work or labour: And, time and place foresaid, the said Operative Cotton Weavers, so combining or conspiring, were formed into, or acted as a body or general Association; which general Associa-

A   tion

44

After three months the weavers' funds were exhausted and they were forced to end their strike. Immediately afterwards fourteen of the weavers' union leaders were indicted for illegal combination. Four fled before trial and three others were not tried; but the remaining seven were sentenced to terms in prison of up to eighteen months. The weavers' union was broken. The strikers returned to the old low rates of wages. Control over the ratio of apprentices to journeymen was lost: the trade became swamped. The old wage-fixing and apprenticeship legislation for all working men and women was repealed by the government. As a result of this highly significant strike trade unionism itself was now declared unlawful in Scotland—and remained so until 1824.

45

Banner of the Edinburgh Journeymen Bookbinders. They formed their union in 1822, despite the unlawfulness of all trade unions, and had the support of many local bookbinding employers who feared the spread of unapprenticed labour that threatened to lower craft standards and hence possibly endanger the very existence of the trade.

46

Although this banner dates from later in the nineteenth century, the Glasgow Typographical Society was founded in 1817 during the years when trade unionism was unlawful.

AN ADDRESS TO THE COLLIERS OF AYRSHIRE AT
THE FORMATION OF THE COLLIERS' ASSOCIATION
IN 1824, PRINTED AT KILMARNOCK IN 1824 BY H.
CRAWFORD, BOOKSELLER, AND NOW REPRINTED
FOR DISTRIBUTION AMONG THE DELEGATES OF
THE AYRSHIRE MINERS' UNION.

By the exertions of a number of intelligent individuals, and the liberal policy of the present Administration with regard to trading, upwards of thirty Acts of Parliament, the remains of Gothic barbarism and feudal tyranny, known by the name of Combination Laws, have been swept from the Statute Book. These laws, while they did not prevent the masters from regulating the wages of labour, punished with great severity mechanics who were convicted of combining for a rise of wages. Under these circumstances, it is the opinion of a number of intelligent men, masters as well as others, that this is the proper time to check several abuses which have gradually crept into the trade; and that, at a meeting of the operative colliers, held in Kilmarnock upon Monday, the 25th October, 1824, twenty-seven works being met, it was their opinion it would be highly expedient to associate for the general good of the trade, and that a committee be appointed to call the attention of all the colliers in Ayrshire, that some new Regulations respecting the mode of taking in neutral men into their works be adopted. Were an association formed and strictly adhered to a number of abuses that are now in practice would soon be abolished; and it surely will not be considered either unjust or unreasonable to adopt measures for self-defence, when the trade of a collier is considered an useful, and must be allowed a laborious avocation. Upon these grounds, therefore, we mean to make out a few Articles for our future guidance; but we admit that nothing but the united efforts of the general body will be sufficient to carry our Articles into effect.

Thus far, brethren, have we done our duty by endeavouring to call your attention to some of the advantages which may be derived from a consolidated union, conducted upon moderate and

47

A miners' union, despite prohibition by law, had existed in 1817 in Lanarkshire and Ayrshire. But the repeal of the Combination Laws, and also the ending of the illegality of unions under Scots Common Law, in 1824 was immediately followed by the formation of this Ayrshire colliers' union. There was in fact a considerable outburst of trade union organisation and activity between the mid-1820s and later 1830s.

IMPORTANT

STRIKE, OF THE MAID SERVANTS

OF EDINBURGH

Just Published, upon good Authority, an account of the Meeting of the Maid Servants of Edinburgh, which took place on Friday last, and who have formed themselves into an Union Society, for the purpose of making a general Strike for a rise of wages at the ensuing Term; with a Copy of 12 Resolutions formed by the Chairwoman, and Office-bearers.

Taken from the Evening Post, of Saturday last.

We understand that it is contemplated by ' The Maid Servant Union Society' of this City, to make a 'strike' on the 14th of next month, with a view of obtaining higher wages; and really after perusing the resolution of that respectable feminine institution, we hesitate not to confess that they have strong grounds for standing out. The following are the resolutions:—

1—As labour is voluntary, wages should be liberal.

2—As maids are generally delicate, both in regard to constitution and feeling, lenity, sympathy, and kindly feelings ought to be exercised towards them.

3—That of late years the perquisites which custom and long usage had converted into "Vesty Rights," have been decreasing, and in many cases withdrawn.

4—That Sundays being days of rest, these days are to be entirely at the disposal of maid-servants—no questions asked.

5—That mistress's old clothes have ever been, and must continue to be the property of maid-servants, and that when a gown or any other piece of dress has been worn a sufficient time, it must be considered as old clothes.

6—That in case of any difference of opinion between the mistress and the maid about the condemnation of the dress—the servants of the house and those of the two adjoining houses to be appointed Judges.

7—The hares and rabbit skins, kitchenfee, fat, dripping, shall continue to be considered the property of the cook, and no skinned hare or rabbit to enter the house.

8—That no young women under 16 shall be allowed to take service, and that no wages shall be under L2 10s, the half year, and L1 1s, for tea money; those taking less to be considered KNOB STICKS, and treated accordingly.

9—That in consequence of the late strike among the silk manufacturers at Lyons, the price of that indispensable article has risen to a great height, and that this circumstance, coupled with the exorbitant prices of furs and tooth powder, has obliged the Union to resolve on demanding a higher rate of wages.

10—That after the 14th of May, the wages should and must be advanced 25 per cent.—that is, those who engaged at L4 must now insist upon L5, the half year—tea money to remain as it is until the arrival of the free tea trade, when a change may be deemed necessary of which due notice will be given.

11—That in the event of mistresses refusing to comply with this small advance, the maids are to strike work, and refuse to serve those who will not go into these resolutions. Joseph Hume's Act will protect the maids should they be brought before the Justice of Peace (generally known as M'Farlane,) Court.

12—That each maid servant shall be supplied by the Union with a copy of the above resolutions, to be hung up in the kitchen along with the Police Regulations, that all concerned may see them.

FORFES, PRINTER, RATTRRY'S COURT, COWGATE.

48

A satiric contemporary comment on the upsurge of trade unionism following the repeal of the Combination Laws.

49

Robert Owen (1771-1858), regarded as the founder of British socialism and co-operation, acquired the cotton mills at New Lanark in 1799 and remained a partner until 1828. His experiments in enlightened industrial paternalism there, and his writings and work in England and America, inspired the foundation of utopian communities, such as that at Orbiston, Lanarkshire, in 1825-28. But, as already noted, co-operative societies existed in Scotland before Owen (his conception of co-operation was much grander than the local consumers' society); and if he were a socialist he was distinctly the utopian sort. He, or his ideas, attracted devoted followers in Scotland some of whom, such as Alexander Campbell, a Glasgow joiner, played an active part in working class movements.

50

The mills at New Lanark, in the early nineteenth century.

51

Working class radicals and trade unionists strongly supported the agitation behind the passing of the Reform Bill of 1832.

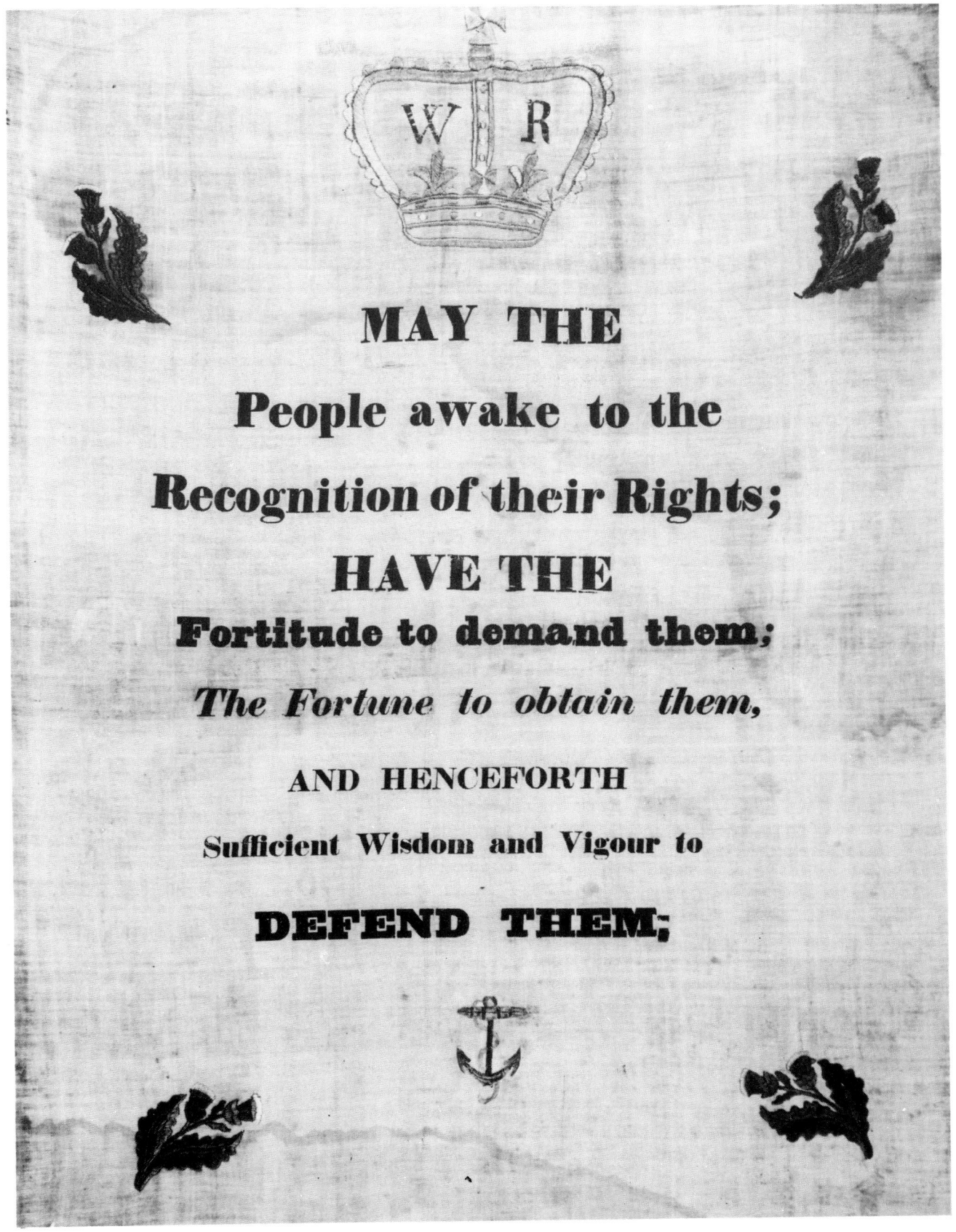

52

A Paisley 1832 Reform banner.

53

An Edinburgh working men's 1832 Reform Bill banner showing a Tory anti-Reformer, Professor John Wilson (whose *nom de plume* was Christopher North), receiving a ducking.

54

A banner of the Edinburgh carpenters and joiners' union carried in the 1832 Reform Bill demonstrations.

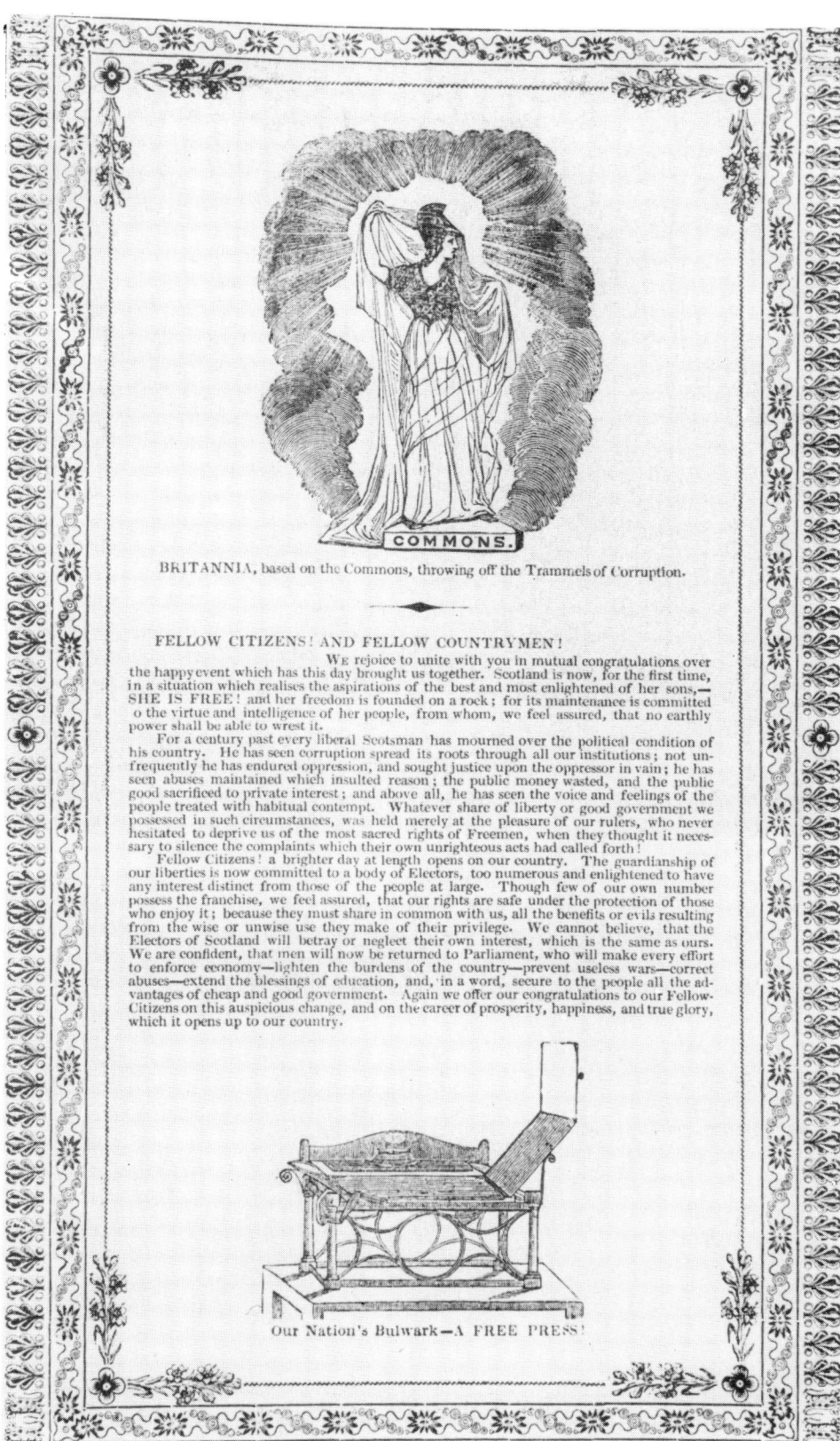

BRITANNIA, based on the Commons, throwing off the Trammels of Corruption.

FELLOW CITIZENS! AND FELLOW COUNTRYMEN!

WE rejoice to unite with you in mutual congratulations over the happy event which has this day brought us together. Scotland is now, for the first time, in a situation which realises the aspirations of the best and most enlightened of her sons,— SHE IS FREE! and her freedom is founded on a rock; for its maintenance is committed to the virtue and intelligence of her people, from whom, we feel assured, that no earthly power shall be able to wrest it.

For a century past every liberal Scotsman has mourned over the political condition of his country. He has seen corruption spread its roots through all our institutions; not unfrequently he has endured oppression, and sought justice upon the oppressor in vain; he has seen abuses maintained which insulted reason; the public money wasted, and the public good sacrificed to private interest; and above all, he has seen the voice and feelings of the people treated with habitual contempt. Whatever share of liberty or good government we possessed in such circumstances, was held merely at the pleasure of our rulers, who never hesitated to deprive us of the most sacred rights of Freemen, when they thought it necessary to silence the complaints which their own unrighteous acts had called forth!

Fellow Citizens! a brighter day at length opens on our country. The guardianship of our liberties is now committed to a body of Electors, too numerous and enlightened to have any interest distinct from those of the people at large. Though few of our own number possess the franchise, we feel assured, that our rights are safe under the protection of those who enjoy it; because they must share in common with us, all the benefits or evils resulting from the wise or unwise use they make of their privilege. We cannot believe, that the Electors of Scotland will betray or neglect their own interest, which is the same as ours. We are confident, that men will now be returned to Parliament, who will make every effort to enforce economy—lighten the burdens of the country—prevent useless wars—correct abuses—extend the blessings of education, and, in a word, secure to the people all the advantages of cheap and good government. Again we offer our congratulations to our Fellow-Citizens on this auspicious change, and on the career of prosperity, happiness, and true glory, which it opens up to our country.

Our Nation's Bulwark—A FREE PRESS!

55

This leaflet was run off by Edinburgh journeymen printers and distributed among the spectators lining the streets during the Grand Reform Bill procession on 10 August 1832.

56

Kirkintilloch Waterside weavers' Reform banner, 1832. The French Revolutionary cap of liberty and the scales of justice indicated how the struggle for the Reform Bill aroused political excitement among working people like that of the 1790s though on a much wider scale.

Working Classes.

PUBLIC MEETING,

SKINNER'S HALL, HIGH STREET.---On TUESDAY, July 2, 1833.

It being now so clear as to admit of no dispute that the *Parliamentary Reform Bill* is, in point of Practical Effect, and as regards the diminution of the *Public Burdens, and relief of General Distress,* a mere Mockery ; it being, also, equally clear that the *present,* like the *former* House of Commons has been chiefly *constituted* as regards its *Election,* by the same sinister means, and consists, as regards its composition, of the same *all monopolizing aristocratic body,* ignorant of, insensible to, and incapable of Representing and of Legislating for the Condition, Interests, and Feelings of the *People,* as well as interested in Public Prodigality.

The Committee of the Working Classes deeply regret that the Compromise of their Political Rights, into which the *People* entered in favour of the Whiggish Paltry Measure of Parliamentary Reform, on condition, and for the sake of obtaining the early removal of all Monopolies, Corruptions and Abuses should have been made on their parts. Still more do they regret that such conditions should be so shamefully forgotten on the part of Earl Grey and his Creatures. The Committee therefore feel that a most important Duty remains to be discharged. They feel that the Practical Relief for the sake of which the People were parties to this compromise being now refused and withheld, they have sufficient room not only for deep disappointment but for bitter indignation. The Rival Factions, Whig and Tory, have United ! These political Cormorants are entered into an open coalition to uphold all those abuses whose extinction was the *pretended* object of the Whiggish tiny, puisne, milk and water Reform Bill.

The MERCHANT COMPANY of this City must cease to control the Election. That body has dared to saddle *the People* with Two obnoxious Whigs ! To this the Tories never presumed ! Away then with the dictation of the Merchant Company. Away with the assumed consequence of that *dependent* body.

The Committee of the Working Classes would not wish it to be supposed that they are anxious to exclude the Merchant Company from having a voice in the Election.—By no means, but they are anxious to see that no undue influence or any unworthy dictation be practised. The Committee are of opinion that all should have a voice in the Election of *their* Representatives. That there should be no Taxation without Representation. All the Community should be Represented for all have an interest in the State. All pay taxes direct and indirect. America proves that the most extensive suffrage carries with it the most extensive good. The Merchant Company should bear in remembrance that the greater the resources of the Working Classes the greater the profits of every Shopkeeper or Trader, and the more beneficial upon every link of Society. This is the secret of national prosperity. The branches of the oak can never flourish without a sound and healthy root. The Upper and Middle ranks of life can never flourish whilst the industrious and labouring classes are lost in wretchedness and want. The all wise Creator has made Man to depend on his fellow-man. Let us therefore have an efficient representative system of Government—the *bona fide* representation of every person *possessing* or *producing* wealth—of every adult capable of engaging in rational voluntary transactions, and of course of being influenced by the laws made—the *bona fide* representation of every *tax-paying* adult ; in short, let all unfurl the Flag of Public Liberty, entire and perfect, and call for UNIVERSAL SUFFRAGE, and for TRIENNIAL PARLIAMENTS, and VOTE BY BALLOT !

In pursuance of these views, the Committee give notice that a *Public Meeting of the Working Classes* will be held in the SKINNER'S Hall, High Street, on Tuesday, July 2, 1833, at 7 o'clock, p. m. to Petition Parliament for THE RIGHTS OF THE PEOPLE !

Admittance One Penny. [MURDOCH, Printer, 44, Cowgate.]

57

Despite the intense agitation the Reform Bill gave nothing to the working class: it remained disfranchised. Some of the bitterness felt by working people is reflected in this Edinburgh broadside. Working class agitation for reform continued, however, and revived massively with the formation of the Chartist movement in the later 1830s.

58

Consumers' retail co-operation was spreading simultaneously with the rise of working class consciousness and the development of trade unionism in the 1820s and '30s. This is a later painting of the members of the Board of the Brechin Co-operative Society, founded in 1833. Sometimes local co-operative societies were formed to enable members to escape from truck—the obligation to buy from employers' company stores—and from adulterated food sold by private shopkeepers.

No. 1.   Price 2d.

HERALD

TO

THE TRADES' ADVOCATE,

AND

CO-OPERATIVE JOURNAL.

Ignorance is the base of all Despotism and Misery.
Knowledge is the very soul of Liberty and Happiness.

FELLOW LABOURERS,

      THE greatest numbers of you are now, through the lowness of wages, reduced to such a state of indifference to your interests, as scarcely to hold out any prospect of being able to raise you from your present apathy, while others

59

Working class radical and trade union papers began to appear in Scotland soon after the Napoleonic Wars. *The Herald to the Trades Advocate*, 1830-31, was the organ of the Glasgow United Committee of Trades—a kind of trades council—and was probably edited by the trade unionist and Owenite Alexander Campbell. *The Liberator*, edited by John Tait, was succeeded in 1836 by the *New Liberator*, edited by Tait's friend the Chartist Dr John Taylor; and that in turn was followed by the *Monthly Liberator*, a Chartist paper, in 1838-39.

60

The 1830s were a lively decade in the history of trade unionism in Scotland. Women began to organise. Very little is known about this Female Weavers' Society.

"1. That it is the opinion of this meeting, that from and after the term of Martinmas next, the hours of labour should be reduced to ten hours in summer and eight hours in winter.

"2. That while this meeting is of the opinion that the above hours are as much as the human frame can bear with a due regard to its physical and mental powers, yet, as the seasons are beyond human control, this meeting, having no wish to injure their masters' property or neglect the bounties of Providence, the persons composing it resolve —

"3. That in seed-time, hay-making, and harvest, they will work extra hours whenever the masters require them, provided they be remunerated, according to the rate of day-labourers, for every hour beyond the stipulated agreement.

"4. That in order to carry the above resolutions into effect, an Association shall be formed, and a committee appointed, to promote by every legal and constitutional means, the object which we have in view, until it reach the 'consummation so devoutly to be wished for.'"

61

Resolutions carried at a meeting of 600 ploughmen at Inchture in the Carse of Gowrie at the Whitsun term in 1834. It seems very likely that the union formed, along with one or two others set up then by farm servants in Perthshire, quickly collapsed. But it is one of the earliest known attempts by farm servants at trade unionism in Scotland.

62

Membership emblem of the Scottish Iron Moulders' Union, 1831. The Iron Moulders became an important Scottish union in the nineteenth and into the twentieth century.

Miller's Monument.

THE COMMITTEE of MANAGEMENT have to return their thanks to the SUBSCRIBERS who have so readily come forward to raise a MONUMENT to perpetuate the remembrance of the extraordinary circumstances attending the cruel murder of GEORGE MILLER at Maryhill. They likewise request that the outlying sheets and proceeds may be sent in as early as possible. After defraying the expense incurred, the overplus is to be paid over for the benefit of the Widow.

BY ORDER OF THE COMMITTEE.

Glasgow, 28th May, 1834.

63

The struggle to form or maintain unions in the face of lock-outs, employment of non-unionists or blacklegs (usually termed knobs or knobsticks at that time), reductions in wages, and other difficulties, sometimes led to violence. This extract from *The Liberator* newspaper of May 1834 reports the erection of a monument to a trade unionist murdered during the calico-printers' strike of that year in the West of Scotland.

64

The five leaders of the Glasgow Cottonspinners' Union whose trial in 1838 for serious crimes, including murder, became a *cause celebre*. The case corresponded in some ways to that four years earlier of the Tolpuddle Martyrs, although the charges against the Cottonspinners were far more serious. The jury unanimously found nine of the twelve charges not proven; the three charges found proven—conspiracy to keep up wages and assaults at two factories in Glasgow—were by a majority of one only. The five men were sentenced to seven years' transportation. They spent three years on the prison hulks at Woolwich on the Thames then they were pardoned. The men were Hacket and Hunter (top), McNeil and McLean (left), and Gibb (right).

SIR,

At a numerous MEETING of the COMMITTEES of UNITED TRADES, held on Tuesday Evening, 29th inst., in the UNIVERSALIST'S CHAPEL, we were appointed to invite one DELEGATE from each Trade, to form a Committee of Enquiry into the conduct of the Authorities here, relative to the seizure and imprisonment of the COTTONSPINNERS' COMMITTEE, and to report the same to a public meeting of the Operatives of Glasgow; your Trade is therefore earnestly requested to send their Representative to the first meeting, to be held in Mr. SMITH'S HOUSE, Black Boy Close, Gallowgate, on Tuesday Evening next, 5th September, at 8 o'clock.

We are, Sir,

Yours, Respectfully,

WILLIAM PATTISON.
JOHN M'KECHNIE.
JAMES WALKER.
ALEX. CAMPBELL, Convener

31st August 1837.

65

The Cottonspinners' trial arose out of the shooting of a blackleg or 'knobstick' in Glasgow during a major strike by the Cottonspinners against reduction in wages. Support for the five accused was general throughout the organised working class movement in Scotland, as this leaflet implies. The Cottonspinners' Union, until then the most powerful in Scotland, was broken by the struggle of 1837-38 and the sentencing of its leaders. The United Trades Committee was a kind of early Trades Council formed or re-formed to co-ordinate the rally by many other unions in support of the Cottonspinners. The whole episode contributed to the support for Chartism in Scotland and for what seem to have been the closer connections there than in England between unions and the Chartists.

66

Banner (double-sided) of the Biggar Weavers' Society in the 1830s.

WITHIN GIBB'S INN,
STIRLING 5TH MAY, 1837.

At a Meeting of the Woollen Manufacturers in this District, held here this day, present :—

Messrs Stevenson and Marshall, Stirling.
James Dick,   -   - do.
Robert Smith,   -   - do.
Thomas Gillies   -   do.
Andrew Miller,   - - Tillicoultry
Andrew Walker,   do.
Robt. Archibald and Sons, do.
James Dawson,   -   do.
John Archibald,   -   do.
J. and D. Paton,   -   do.
J. and G. Walker, -   do.
William Archibald, Keilarsbrae.

Messrs William Drysdale, Menstry
Andrew Archibald   do.
Robert Walker, Devonside.
David Muir,   do.
J. and W. Archibald,   Alva.
William Drysdale, junr. do.
John Dawson   -   do.
Wm. Drysdale and Sons, do.
Donald M'Laren, Blackford.
John Gilchrist, Deany
John Paton, Alloa.
John Tod, Kier.

Mr JAMES DAWSON, IN THE CHAIR.

It was moved and carried unanimously, with the exception of one dissenting voice, that in consequence of the coercive measures adopted by the Union of Shawl Weavers in this District, this Meeting agree to discharge every Weaver, or any other person in their employment, connected with said Union, on and after MONDAY the Fifteenth current, unless they relinquish their connection with the above Union.—The Meeting also recommend the other Manufacturers in this District, not present, to adopt the measures.

It was also moved and carried unanimously that the above Resolution be printed, and hung up in the various Mills and Weaving Shops of all the Manufacturers present.

J. LOTHIAN, PRINTER AND STATIONER.

67

A reflection of the bitter class struggles of the period.

REWARD

OF

20 Sovereigns.

WHEREAS late on the Evening of Sunday, or early this Morning, some evil and malicious Person or Persons CUT and DESTROYED the ROPES at one of the Pits of *Wellwood Colliery*; and also DESTROYED part of the Machinery of the Steam Engine thereat; a REWARD of £20 is hereby offered to any Person, who, within fourteen days after this date, shall give such information to the Procurator Fiscal as will lead to the conviction of the Offenders.

DUNFERMLINE, Monday, 1st *May*, 1837.

J. Miller and Son, Printers.

68

Bitterness against wage reductions, long hours, dangerous working conditions, employment of non-union labour (in some industries, including coal, sometimes that of poverty stricken Irish immigrants), was occasionally expressed in industrial sabotage.

69

Two of the famous Six Points of the People's Charter proclaimed on this later banner of the Edinburgh bookbinders' union. The Chartist movement carried working class consciousness, organisation and activity to a new height in the decade 1838-48.

70

Some Chartist newspapers published in Scotland.

ADDRESS

BY THE

DUMFRIES AND MAXWELLTOWN WORKING-MEN'S ASSOCIATION,

TO THE

WORKING CLASSES

OF

DUMFRIES, MAXWELLTON, GASTOWN, SANQUHAR, ANNAN, LOCHMABEN, LOCKERBY,
ECCLEFECHAN, GATEHOUSE, CASTLE-DOUGLAS, &c.

ROBBED, ENSLAVED, OPPRESSED, BROTHERS AND SISTERS :—
GOD, the Father of all, gave unto his children the earth for a general inheritance, and he endowed them also with wisdom to choose good, and avoid evil.—To *no* class of men did he, like a partial step-father, grant large portions of that earth, or endow *that* class with *superior* wisdom.—Nevertheless, a class of men called Whig and Tory aristocrats, composed of a few thousand lords and squires, priests and lawyers, call themselves the only wise and good men, and denounce the millions of their fellow-men as "the swinish multitude." That class, in former days, *robbed* our forefathers of the land of Britain, leaving them, and us their posterity, not even ground for a grave.—That class, like blood-thirsty fiends, murdered, in unjust and unprovoked, wars, hundreds of thousands of our fathers, and rejoiced amidst the groans of the dying, and the tears of widows and of orphans. That class, to carry on these horrid wars, borrowed Six hundred millions of money, and instead of mortgaging and pawning the lands of which they had robbed us, they mortgaged the bodies of us, and of our children in security of that enormous debt ; and our sweat and blood have to pay 30 millions as the interest thereof. That class, not content with robbing us of the land, murdering our forefathers and mortgaging our bodies, compel us also to spend our sweat and blood to pay them in taxes, tythes, and stipends, upwards of 30 millions more every year that they may inhabit palaces, and wear purple and fine linen, and fare sumptuously every day ;—while all the time, they turn up their noses at us, and call us "the mob," "the rabble," "the unwashed," "the swinish multitude," and tell us to stand from between the wind and their nobility, lest the smell of our sweat offend their nostrils. Thus are we forced to pay 1s. for 6d. worth of bread ; 1s. for 6d. worth of soap ; 1s. for 6d. worth of sugar ; 4s. for 1s. worth of tea ; and 8s. for 1s. worth of snuff or tobacco ;—in every thing we are taxed, from the swaddling band to the winding sheet ;—the light of heaven itself is taxed, and so would the air and the water if these remorseless monsters could contrive how to do it.—In short, from every hard-won shilling which the industrious man makes, these greedy fiends extorts eight pence,—so that, from a farmer or shop-keeper, who, with unspeakable care and anxiety, makes £75 a-year, they extort £50 ; if an operative or labouring man makes £24, they extort £16.—Thus, while that class lives to oppress and plunder, we live to toil, and toil to live, starve, and be insulted. Good God, is this the peace on earth and good will among men which angels sung at thy advent : is this the practice of thy divine rule, of *doing to others as we would they should do unto us ?* How long shall the land groan with injustice ! How long shall heartless tyrants beat thy people to pieces, and grind the faces of the poor !

To you, suffering Brothers and Sisters, who are already sunk in the lowest depths of human misery, nothing need we urge, for already has the iron entered your souls, and the rankling wound is continually bleeding !—But to you Brothers and Sisters who are not plunged so deep, we would with fervour ask,—know you not that in England when the poor have neither work nor meat, and so are forced to seek parish aid, that they are fed on *skilly* and resined food ;—the kind husband is separated from the loving wife—the child is torn from the mother's bosom,—and when they die their bodies are given to be mangled on the doctor's dissecting table ? Know you not that even in this town, already the industrious are robbed for Poor-Rates, while the poor are starved ? Know you not that multitudes of your brethren who once made 26s. 6d., can only make for a week's toil of 14 hours a-day, the miserable pittance of 5s. 6d. to support a wife and family ? Know you not that *your* wages too, sooner or later, must come down, and that as all your children cannot be of your trade, some of them *must* welter in the general mass of human wretchedness ? Have you, therefore, no hearts to feel for others, or for yourselves, or for your children ? Know you not also, that when many of your Brothers and Sisters are starving for a mouthful of the coarsest food, or are glad to live on the sea-weed of the shore,—that to please a whim of our virgin Queen, the House of Commons, the representatives of the £10 voters, without a single objection, granted £70,000 to rebuild a set of stables,—while not a fraction has been granted to relieve the starvation of the people, or even a single feeling of pity expressed for their heart-rending situation !

Brothers and Sisters, our righteous object is to exercise the right which God gave us, but which that class who stole our land and mortgaged our bodies, have also stolen from us :—it is the right to have a voice in appointing men to make laws and lay on taxes, so that our greivances may be redressed, and peace and prosperity may cause the hearts of all to rejoice.

But our tyrants say because we are poor we have no wisdom, and hence they trample our petitions under their feet, and laugh at our afflictions, while their advocates, the Newspapers of this town ;—the Herald, and these pretended friends of justice M·Diarmid of the Courier, and Harkness of the Times, the imposer and swallower of the Poor-Rates, abuse and misrepresent us, and do all they can to poison the minds of the public against us. But our cause is founded on eternal truth and justice, and must prevail.—Liberty and justice is our watch-word. Britain free or a desert, is our stern determination.—Brothers and Sisters, "now's the day and now's the hour."—British slaves, the day of our freedom draweth nigh,—the glad sounds of liberty are pealing through the length and breadth of the land,—we are millions, our oppressors are but as a handful, and before the breath of a united people they will be blown as chaff before the wind !

Up then, and be doing, and soon will tyranny, discontent, and human wretchedness be for ever banished from the British Isles :—

Wha wad be a *traitor* knave,
Wha sae base as be a *slave,*
Wha wad fill a *coward's* grave ?
Britons shall be free !

71

A Chartist leaflet of 1839.

RULES
OF THE
PERTH
Chartist Association.

AT a Meeting of the Committee, held in the *Chronicle* Office, on *Friday, the 19th Nov.* 1841, the following RESOLUTIONS were unanimously agreed to :—

1st,—That the Name of the Association shall be " THE PERTH CHARTIST ASSOCIATION."

2d,—That the object of the Association shall be to obtain the enactment of the CHARTER, which they pledge themselves to endeavour to effect by all Legal, Peaceful, and Constitutional means, and by these alone—holding themselves entirely aloof from, and discouraging all persons or parties who advocate or adopt illegal and violent measures themselves, or countenance them in others ; and for this purpose, the Association shall consider every Member who either himself advocates illegal and violent measures, or countenances their advocacy or adoption by others, as no longer belonging to the Association—his expulsion following as a matter of course ; and in order that this provision may be more generally known, and better attended to, they resolve that this rule shall be read over at all Meetings called by the Association.

3d,—That the Association shall consist of all those who agree to its Regulations, and receive a Ticket of Membership, for which they shall pay the sum of Threepence.

4th,—That the business of the Association shall be conducted by a President and Managing Committee of Thirty, to be appointed by the Association at their Annual Meeting in December, and of Two Vice-Presidents, a Treasurer, and Two Secretaries, who shall be chosen by the Committee from their own numbers.

☞ *TICKETS of Membership may be had by applying at the* CHRONICLE *Office.*

R. BAXTER, PRINTER, PERTH.

72

73

Monument to Dr John Taylor (1805-42), in Russell Street burial ground, Ayr. Taylor was one of the outstanding leaders of the Chartists.

TO THE ELECTORS

AND

NON-ELECTORS

OF THE COUNTY OF

ROXBURGH.

GENTLEMEN,

I have been invited by a great many Reformers of your County, to present myself as a Candidate at your coming Election. Most cheerfully do I comply with your request. In doing so, I shall fearlessly advocate the rights of the people against those who from ignorance, prejudice, and pride oppose them. I shall assert the high claims of principle in opposition to expediency. I shall denounce the injustice, partiality, and tyranny of those who, whilst raising their voice against certain monopolies, are resolved to perpetuate the worst and blackest of them all--a monopoly of freedom and of power, in defiance of the just claims of all men to equal civil and political privileges. The following are some of the great objects I shall support:

I. ADULT MALE SUFFRAGE.

2. ANNUAL PARLIAMENTS, EQUAL REPRESENTATION, and the PAYMENT of MEMBERS.

3. A vast reduction in the expenditure of Government.

4. Direct Taxation only, exacted from Property by a graduated scale.

5. Free Trade in all things throughout the world.

6. Freedom to speak and write on all subjects, Civil, Political, and Religious.

7. Freedom of Religion to all Sects and Parties, giving state supremacy to none.

8. The Education of the whole people under the control of Parish Boards chosen by the Electors.

These, Gentlemen, are my principles, and they are those of a great many of yourselves. Need I say, then, that I shall rejoice to see you give them triumphant support in the face of their foes at the approaching ELECTION.

I am, Gentlemen, your obedient servant,

JOHN FRASER.

Edinburgh, July 2, 1841.

74

Election poster of John Fraser, a leading Scots Chartist and editor of the *True Scotsman*, at the General Election of 1841 in Roxburghshire. The Chartists put up candidates at elections but usually withdrew after making speeches at the hustings and securing a majority in the show of hands. The number of working men with the right to vote was so small before 1867-68 that it was not considered worthwhile by the Chartist candidates to go to the poll. Fraser himself withdrew from the election of 1841 a few days before polling.

EXTRAORDINARY MEETING.
NATIONAL STRIKE
FOR THE
CHARTER.

At the GREAT DELEGATE MEETING, held in the School-Room, Pullar's Close, on the evening of Friday the 19th instant, it was decidedly ascertained that the vast numbers of workmen, of all the Trades in Dundee, represented by the assembled Delegates, with the exception of a very few workmen, agreed to STRIKE for the PEOPLE's CHARTER.—In accordance with the will of the Delegates,

A PUBLIC MEETING
WILL BE HELD
ON THE MAGDALEN YARD GREEN,
THIS EVENING, AT HALF-PAST SIX O'CLOCK,

For the purpose of consulting the whole of the people in regard to the means which ought to be adopted for carrying their will into operation.

THE VOICE OF THE PEOPLE IS THE VOICE OF GOD.

A Collection will be made to Defray Expenses.

BY ORDER OF THE DELEGATES.

Dundee, August 20, 1842.

PRINTED AT THE CHRONICLE OFFICE, DUNDEE.

75

A Dundee Chartist poster in 1842 at the time of the proposed general strike to achieve the People's Charter. Along with 1839 and 1848 the year 1842 was one of the high tides of Chartism.

76

Robert Cranston (1815-92), a leading Edinburgh Chartist. Like many other Scots Chartists Cranston was a temperance supporter. He founded a chain of temperance hotels and later became a town councillor and bailie.

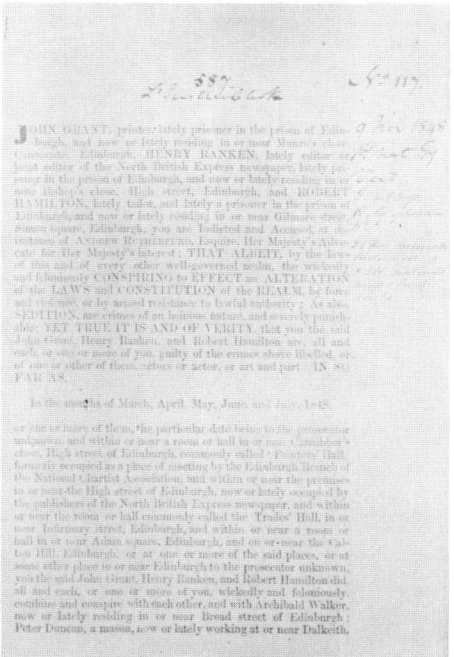

77

Chartism reached its third and final crisis in 1848, when the petition for the Six Points was again presented to Parliament and again rejected. The authorities swooped on leading Chartists in Edinburgh, Glasgow, and Greenock, and two—Henry Ranken, an upholsterer and editor of the Chartist newspaper *North British Express*, and Robert Hamilton, a tailor—were sentenced to four months' imprisonment for sedition. This is part of the indictment against them.

78

One of several initiatives local Chartists took was to form co-operative stores. These were established at, among other places, Leith, Galashiels, Hawick, Greenock, Tillicoultry, Dalkeith, and Coupar-Angus. This is a sketch of the first shop, in Silver Street, of the Hawick Chartist Provision Store, formed in 1839. Since then Co-operation in Hawick has had a continuous history.

OLD CHARTISTS' FESTIVAL.—This festival came off on Thursday evening, in Lamb's Hotel, Reform Street. Councillor Gray occupied the chair. Among those present we observed several old veterans who have taken part in most of the imperial and local questions which have agitated the public mind for the last thirty years, and who seemed to be yet anxious to take some part in those of the future. The Chairman opened the meeting with an appropriate address, rehearsing the reminiscences of the past. The meeting was afterwards addressed by Messrs Drummond, Bruce, Whitton, Blair, &c. The proceedings were enlivened during the evening. Several excellent songs were sung by a gentleman from Glasgow and others. After having enjoyed a happy evening, the company sang " Auld Lang Syne," and, resolving to meet again at some future day, separated.

... ..eutenant. Dec. 24, 1873

THE CHARTIST MOVEMENT.—A number of gentlemen who took part in the Chartist movement during its early days, met last night in Mathers' Hotel, Crichton Street, for the purpose of considering the propriety of holding a reunion of all who were similarly engaged, and who might be desirous of enjoying an evening's reminiscences of the events in which they performed a part. It was unanimously resolved to hold such reunion, and a meeting is to be held on an early day for the purpose of taking the necessary steps to carry the resolution into effect.

79

The Chartist movement petered out after 1848 but many Chartists remained active in radical political groups, trade unions, and co-operative societies in Scotland for many years afterward. These reunions of Dundee Chartists took place in 1873-74.

THE NINETEENTH CENTURY:
SECOND HALF

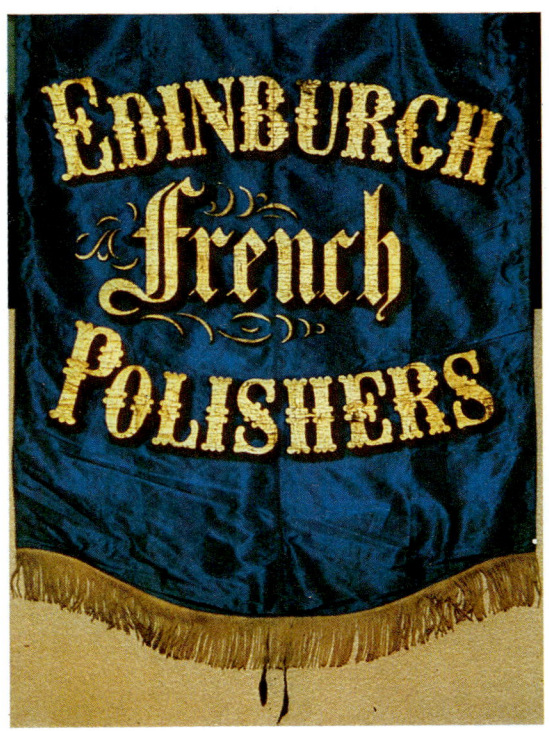

80

Trade unionmism expanded considerably in Scotland in the third quarter of the nineteenth century. Many new unions—mainly of skilled workers, such as upholsterers, carpenters and joiners, blacksmiths, shipwrights and French Polishers—were formed or re-formed.

81

82

83

Banner of the Aberdeen Branch of the Blacksmiths' union. Formed in 1857 in Scotland, the union soon opened branches in England and provided an uncommon case of an originally Scottish union becoming a United Kingdom organisation.

84

The Associated Carpenters and Joiners of Scotland was formed in 1861, a year after the formation in England of the 'New Model' Amalgamated Society of Carpenters and Joiners. Within a few years each Society had formed branches on the other side of the Border. The two unions amalgamated in 1911.

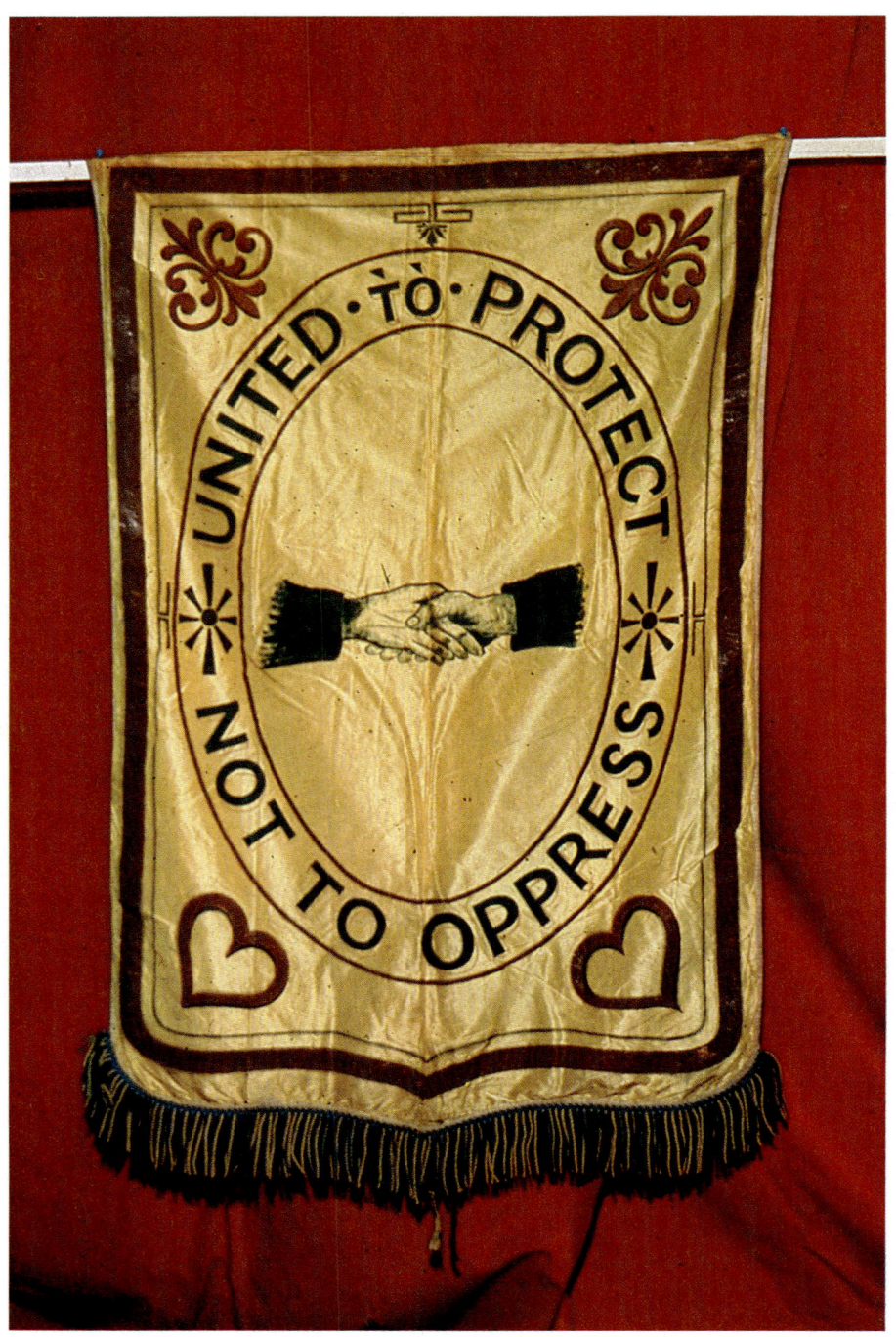

85

A banner that illustrates the often defensive attitude of unions in the third quarter of the nineteenth century. This banner, belonging to an unidentified union, was rescued from a dustbin in Edinburgh a few years ago.

[ADVERTISEMENT.]

NINE HOURS' MOVEMENT.

The Operative Masons of Dundee, fearing the struggle that is before them, would call upon their brethren in neighbouring towns and country to refrain from accepting engagements in Dundee to fill up the place of those who may be out on strike, and they would also appeal to all interested in the movement to render them assistance, by means of subscriptions, which will be thankfully received in their name by David Gibb, the Secretary, at Mr Skene's coffee-house, Crichton Street, Dundee.

The Operative Masons also take this opportunity of contradicting a report, which they understand has been spread by the employers, to the effect that they are demanding ten hours' pay for nine hours' work. This is not the case; they only ask nine hours' pay for their daily work of nine hours.

BY ORDER OF COMMITTEE.

Dundee, Feb. 14, 1862.

86

The stonemasons had re-established a united Scottish union in 1852. The widespread use of stone in building in Scotland made the union one of the more important craft societies. Pressure by the building and other craft unions for a nine hours' day was one of the features of the 1860s and '70s.

87

Alexander Campbell (1796-1870), one of the most active leaders of trade unionism, co-operation and working class radical journalism in Scotland in the nineteenth century. Campbell, a joiner by trade, was originally a missionary for the ideas of Robert Owen, and claimed to be the originator of the idea of dividend on purchase that was taken up from 1844 by the founders of the modern Co-operative movement, the Rochdale Pioneers. In the early 1830s Campbell had often contributed to the Glasgow trade union paper, *Herald to the Trades Advocate*, and was probably its editor. In the third quarter of the century, Campbell was a reporter, later editor for a time, for the main working class newspaper in Scotland, the *Glasgow Sentinel* (1850-77). He was also associated with Glasgow Trades Council, founded in 1858, and was an active leader of demands for women's suffrage and for reform of the Master and Servant Laws.

Glasgow 30th April 1858
Candleriggs Street —

Met Messrs Bennet, McKay, McInnes Bunyan, Little, Smith, Cumming and Blair when it was agreed to call a preliminary meeting of all those from various trades the parties present were acquainted with on Friday evening 7th May at 8 oclock in the Democratic Rooms Nelson Street for the purpose of forming a central Committee of one or more delegates from the various Trades in the City of Glasgow, to watch over the interests of the Working classes, and at present consider the sufferings of those who were out of employment and adopt some means for relieving the same X

In accordance with the above resolution a meeting took place on Friday evening 7th May in Above Rooms. Present Messrs Bunyan Cumming & Dunn at ½ past 8 no other parts making their aperance the reporters 4 in number who were present were requested to retire and that they would be furnished with a report of the proceeding (should the parties come forward) by Mr Cumming. after they retired Mr Cumming stated that Mr Bennet could not get attending that night but that he would be agreeable to any reasonable proposal or resolution they might come to. Mr Bunyan

88

The first minutes of Glasgow Trades Council, founded in 1858. Permanent trades councils—local organisations composed of trade union delegates—began to be formed in Scotland from the mid-nineteenth century. The earliest seems to have been that of Edinburgh, formed about 1853; Dundee trades council was formed about 1861 and re-formed in 1867, Aberdeen in 1868, Greenock was formed about 1859 and re-formed in 1872, and Kirkcaldy in 1873. By the end of the century there were about fifteen trades councils in Scotland.

PARLIAMENTARY REFORM.

The following is a copy of the political reform address read at last meeting of Council:—

To the Working Men of the United Kingdom.

FELLOW-COUNTRYMEN,—In the prosecution of our three-fold object, viz., the Moral, Social, and Political elevation of the Working Classes, we venture to call your attention to the important matter of Parliamentary Reform, in the hope that you may be induced to put forth your energies once more for the attainment of that share of political power which is our due. Since the fervour of the Chartist agitation extorted from the then Government the admission that the time was come when the working classes ought to be placed on the electoral roll, there has been a gradual decrease in earnestness in pressing our claims on the notice of Parliament.

Evidently the people have trusted too implicitly those who made such admission, for they have waited patiently, almost silently, for the promised boon. Our silence has been misconstrued into a lack of interest in the movement; hence the enemies of Reform have successfully argued that the people did not want to be enfranchised. Two Reform Bills have been thrust out on this account chiefly. The two great parties in the House of Commons are each pledged to an extension of the franchise, yet neither of them do it. One says, you give too much; the other says, you give too little; and thus they squabble, while the people look tamely on as if they had no interest in the matter in dispute. We have now a Government which came into office charged with the duty of amending the representation of the people. We have seen how they have discharged that duty. After one miserable attempt they have, to all appearance, abandoned the question entirely. True, we are promised a bill next session—we were promised one last session too. Our experience of the First Lord does not warrant us in relying implicitly on his pledges, yet we feel satisfied that he will not withhold a right when demanded by a well expressed popular opinion; he is too sagacious to do that. To urge you to express in a manner not to be mistaken your opinion in the matter of political right, is the object of the present address. No measure of Reform will be final that does not embrace Manhood Suffrage, with a residential qualification, along with other important changes. But can we reasonably expect that the present Parliament would pass such a bill? We think not. What shall we do, then? Shall we wait until we can bully the present electors into electing a Parliament that will concede our full claim? What we would suggest is, that we push for what is now attainable, and occupy that as so much vantage ground to help us on to greater victories. Let us then push Government to fulfil their pledge in the ensuing Session of Parliament—declare to them our just claims and our determination to achieve the same. They are pledged to a Five Pound Franchise for Burghs and Ten Pounds for Counties, and if we only show that we are in earnest it is certain that no less liberal measure would satisfy the House of Commons.

We would respectfully, yet confidently, declare that the various Trades' Societies of the country are the best existing machinery for carrying out a successful movement of this kind. We are aware that many are opposed to trades' meetings being mixed with politics; we cannot coincide with such views so long as Trades' Societies are amenable to the law. There are several matters in law that affect them, such as those relating to combinations of workmen and the Inequality of the law of master and servant; also how many times have they been baffled in the attempt to establish Councils of Conciliation and Arbitration? By what means are three measures to be rectified or obtained but by the possession of political power?—the want of which affects the whole labouring class. If these things be true, how can it be that working men, in their associated capacity, ought not to entertain politics? All objections can, however, be overcome by special trade meetings on the subject. We conclude by submitting our plan of action, which is, that all Trades' Councils, Trades' Societies, and such like Associated Bodies, at once memorialise Government to fulfil their pledge in the ensuing Session of Parliament; after which let a monster National Petition be got up for presentation to Parliament on the day of its opening, in favour of a comprehensive measure of Reform, or, should it be deemed a wiser course to send petitions from various parties, let that be done. We most cordially invite the expression of your opinions on the course proposed as to a National Petition to Parliament, and most earnestly urge all to memorialise Government without delay to redeem their pledge.

We are, your Fellow-Countrymen,
GLASGOW COUNCIL OF UNITED TRADES.
GEORGE NEWTON, President.
MATTHEW LAWRENCE, Secy.

Glasgow, 23rd October, 1861.
Bell Hotel, 68 Trongate.

89

Trades councils played a particularly important role in trade unionism in Scotland. They helped co-ordinate activities of local unions or branches, and not least they took a lead in political activities. This *Address* by Glasgow Trades Council in 1861 is an example of the latter—an appeal to working men throughout the United Kingdom to demand political reform.

90

Banner of the Leith Joiners' union branch, carried in the Second Reform Bill agitation of 1866-67. The agitation arose out of a revival of political interest among working people generated by such international events as the American Civil War, the unification of Italy, and the Polish Revolt of 1863, but also more immediately from the economic recession and unemployment of 1866.

91

An Edinburgh Bookbinders' union banner of 1866-67. Despite the attempts by the Conservative leader Disraeli to capture the loyalty of working men, most politically involved workers in Scotland supported the radical wing of the Liberal Party.

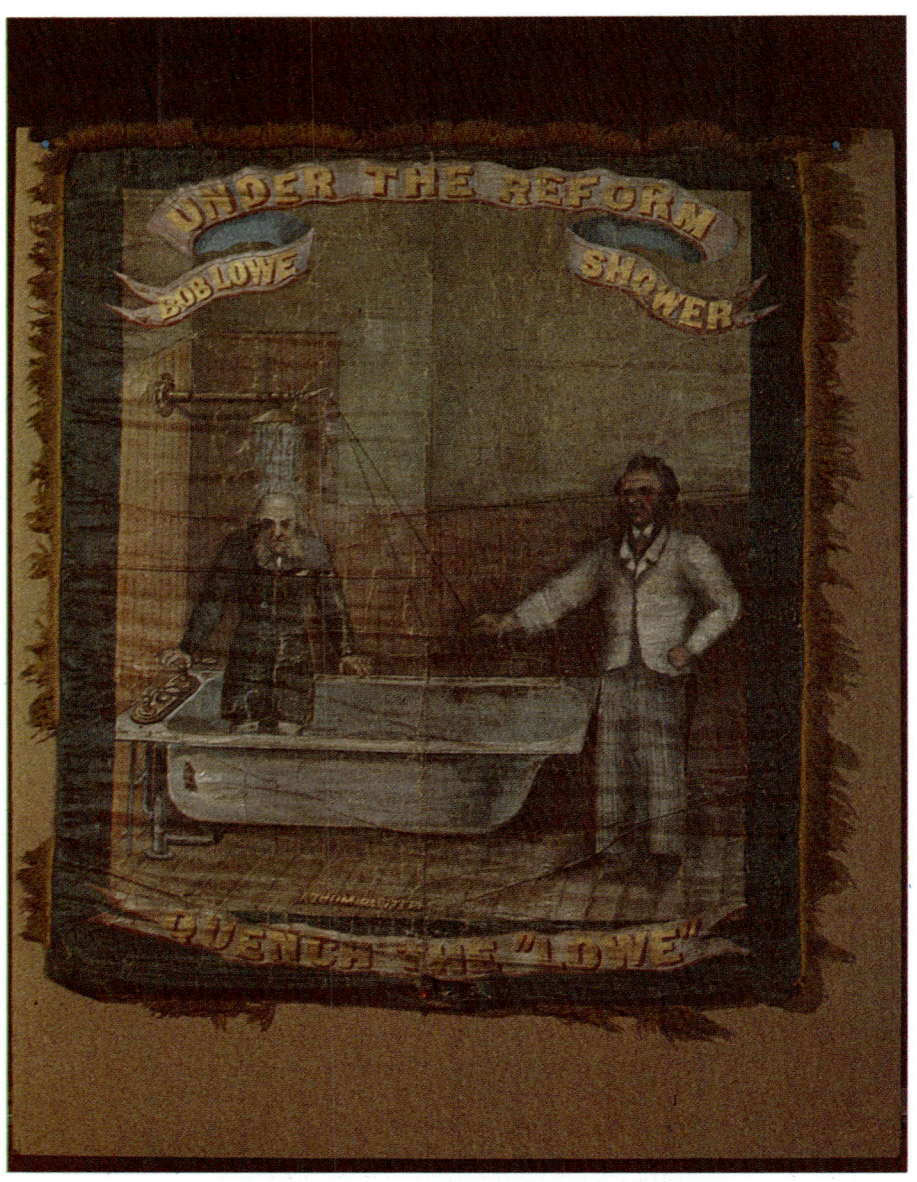

92

The Second Reform Act of 1867-68 gave the right to vote to many urban workers, though the secret ballot was not achieved until 1872. This Edinburgh Tinplate Workers' union banner depicts Robert Lowe, a leading Liberal opposed to the extension of the franchise to the masses, being ducked for his reactionary views. It may be the maker of this banner was inspired by that at No. 53 above carried in the 1832 Reform agitation.

93

Another banner of the Edinburgh Tinplate Workers' union of the early 1870s. Labour law became a major source of agitation between 1863 and 1875. The Master and Servant Acts, which regulated contracts of employment, were grossly biased against working people and prosecutions for breach of contract were numerous. From time to time conspiracy law was also used against trade unions—a notorious case in 1872 involved the London gas stokers.

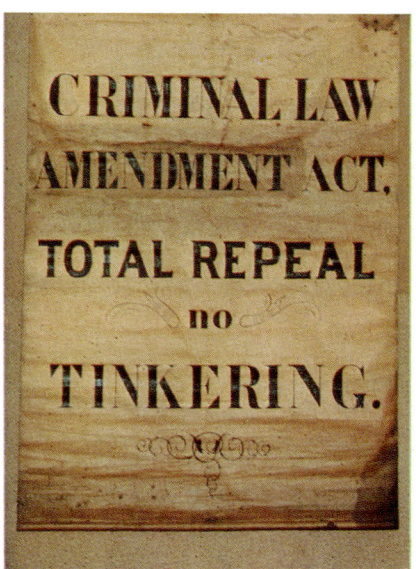

94

Another source of grievance and agitation among trade unionists was the Criminal Law Amendment Act, passed by Gladstone's Liberal government in 1871. The Act made picketing, and therefore effective strike action, difficult and led to several greatly resented prosecutions of trade unionists. In the hope of winning support from the newly enfranchised urban workers Disraeli's Conservative government in 1875 repealed the Act and replaced it with the Conspiracy and Protection of Property Act. This made some concession to peaceful picketing and debarred use of conspiracy law in industrial disputes so long as nothing otherwise criminal was involved. This banner was carried by the Edinburgh Tinplate Workers' Society in the agitations of 1871-75 over labour law.

95

In the 1860s and '70s, the movement for shorter hours—a constant aim of organised labour—also gained new successes. In 1861 the Edinburgh Operative Stonemasons had become the first building workers in Britain to win the nine hours' day (51 or 54 hours' week); and by the end of that decade almost all stonemasons throughout Scotland had won it. In the early 1870s many other skilled workers—engineers, moulders, blacksmiths, cabinet-makers, printers and bookbinders—had won the nine hours' day. This banneret of the Edinburgh carpenters' and joiners' union dates from those years.

96

The mid-19th century was a period when the appalling state of working class housing in Scotland also became a source of agitation. The winning of the franchise by many urban workers in 1867 led central and local government to begin to concern itself with improved housing. This photograph, of a close at No. 118 High Street, was among those taken by Thomas Annan between 1868 and 1877 of some working class housing in Glasgow.

97

Working class slum housing in Dundee.

98

Miners' housing remained notoriously bad until well into the twentieth century. This photograph of the late nineteenth century shows miners' rows at Low Quarter, Lanarkshire, built two hundred years earlier.

99

Working men sometimes formed co-operative building associations to provide improved housing. One example was the Edinburgh Co-operative Building Company, formed in 1861, which built these houses for skilled workers at 'The Colonies', Stockbridge, as well as similar schemes at Dalry, Shandon, and Abbeyhill. But working class housing in Scotland remained seriously overcrowded—25 per cent of Glasgow's population of 511,000 in 1881 was living in one-room and 45 per cent in two-roomed houses—and a major source of grievance until at least the middle of the twentieth century.

100

From the 1860s Co-operation began to expand in Scotland. By 1868 it was estimated there were over 130 Co-operative societies. In that year was formed the Scottish Co-operative Wholesale Society. By the end of the century it had become a major productive and distributive organisation. The S.C.W.S.'s original premises at Madeira Court, Glasgow, are shown here.

101

Another initiative taken by Co-operators was the formation in 1869 of the United Co-operative Baking Society, whose original premises at Coburg Street, Glasgow, are shown here, along with the larger premises at St James Street to which the Society moved within a year.

102

William Maxwell, President of the Scottish Wholesale Society from 1881 to 1908, was one of the outstanding leaders of Co-operation in Scotland in the later nineteenth century.

103

By the second half of the nineteenth century the number and memberships of friendly societies had also increased considerably. Benefits tended to widen to include cover for sickness and accidents and also medical attendance. This banner of a Midlothian society presents some of the symbols of the functions and aspirations of friendly societies—the tree of life, the horn of plenty. The crossed pick and spade are reminders that Oxenford was on the edge of the Lothian coalfield.

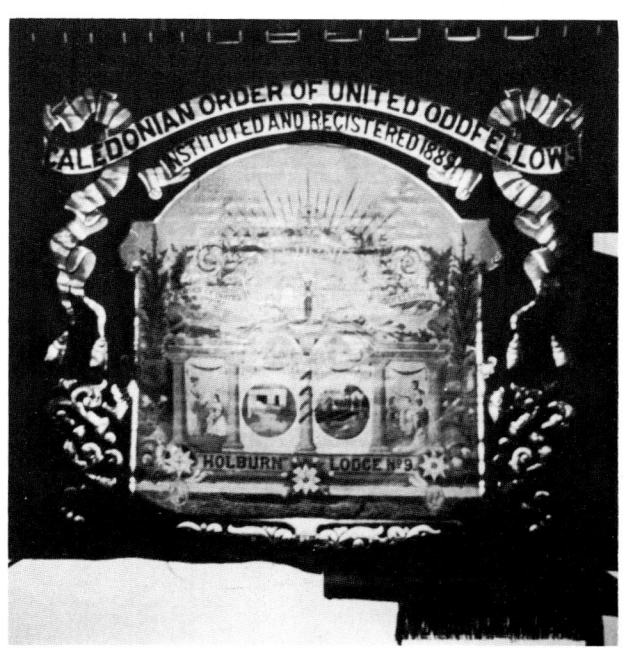

104

From the early nineteenth century great national or 'affiliated' Orders of friendly societies developed—Oddfellows, Foresters, Free Gardeners, Shepherds, and others. These had larger memberships and financial resources than the old purely local societies, and usually offered a wider range of benefits. Although the coming of the Welfare State in the twentieth century superseded many of their funcions some friendly societies continued to exist.

105

Most friendly societies ran social activities, such as an annual parade or gala day. This photograph shows members of the Ancient Order of Foresters, Juniper Green Branch, Edinburgh, about 1890.

106

Alexander McDonald (1821-81), who first went down the pits in Lanarkshire at the age of nine, became a leader of miners' unionism in Scotland and then, from 1863, in Britain as a whole. McDonald was one of the two first 'working men' to be elected an M.P.—for Stafford, in 1874.

THE BLANTYRE COLLIERY EXPLOSION, NEAR GLASGOW CALLING FOR VOLUNTEERS FOR THE EXPLORING PARTIES

107

The notoriously difficult and dangerous conditions endured by the coalminers and their severe exploitation by the coalowners made continuity in union organisation difficult before the last quarter of the nineteenth century. This contemporary engraving depicts the scene at the pithead—the calling for volunteers for the rescue party—after the catastrophic underground explosion at Blantyre Colliery, Lanarkshire, in October 1877 that cost 207 miners their lives.

108

Paddy, an itinerant farm labourer in the Borders, about 1870. Farm workers were among the unskilled workers who attempted in the 'boom' years of the later 1860s and early '70s to organise unions. A Farm Servants' Protection Association formed at Slateford, Edinburgh, in 1865 lasted for some seven years, and other local unions were set up for a short time in Kinross, Forfar, Perth, Kincardine, Stirling, Clackmannan, Peebles, Roxburgh, Berwick and East Lothian. Here and there wages were consequently pushed up and the movement probably helped establish a normal working day in agriculture. It also seems to have brought the end of the bondager system on many farms.

109

The bondager system was one where the male farm worker had to provide a woman worker for a stated number of days' work in the year. The system survived into the twentieth century. Here bondagers and male farm workers pose for the camera during harvest threshing at Rutherford near Selkirk in 1898-99.

110

Joseph Hope, General Secretary of the Amalgamated Society of Railway Servants for Scotland, a union formed in 1872. Railwaymen, like farm servants, had long hours of labour and, like farm servants and miners, often lived in tied housing.

TO THE TRADE UNIONISTS OF SCOTLAND.

FELLOW-WORKMEN,

The GLASGOW UNITED TRADES' COUNCIL would earnestly and respectfully call your attention to a subject that has been at various times under consideration, very notably in 1858 and in 1862, viz., The propriety and expediency of establishing a Confederation of the various Trade organisations throughout Scotland, having a Central Board for direct communication, with the view of strengthening and extending the interests of Trade Unionists. Since the last mentioned date, some important changes have taken place regarding the social and political position of Working Men. Principally by their own exertions, they succeeded in obtaining the repeal of an Act, a barbarous relic of the old feudal system, an Act that ordained that for a simple breach of contract, a workman could be dragged to prison as a felon; whereas for a similar refusal on the part of an employer, he was treated as a debtor at civil law, and only held liable for arrears of wages. At the time referred to, the generality of working men were mere political nonentities; now, however, a large proportion of this class being in possession of the franchise, if so disposed, they can use their municipal and parliamentary influence with some degree of benefit to themselves. Again, the influence of Trades Unions having been felt to be a power in this country, Government has at length acknowledged their thorough legitimacy, by a feeble attempt to legislate specially for them, instead of treating them simply as any other lawful association. Only a few years ago, the legalising of Trades Unions would have been treated as absurd; it is now an accomplished fact, and the members must not again be compelled to look through such a long vista of years without further improvement. As a consequence of the advanced position of the industrial classes, cases are not now rare where the employers evince a disposition, or at least make the concession, to meet the workmen in conference to adjust disputes. This is a leading novelty of the age; many, however, prefer the old plan, treating the working classes simply as material, although holding an eminent position in the producing power of the nation, they should have no right or voice in the management or disposition of profits, on the ground that the employers have the risk and responsibility to bear, and that they alone should regulate the working hours and fix the price of labour. So much for the arrogance of capital. Capital and labour have been called by some industrial and social reformers twin sisters; some one has gone further and said they were the father and child, as capital was simply the product of labour. It is then only the ignorance of the toiling masses, combined with the want of faith in each other, that gives capital the Herculean power and the lion's share. One of the largest employers of labour in England, in giving evidence before the National Congress for the Promotion of Social Science, said, that trades that were not organised got a very poor share of the profits of capital and labour combined, and the ratio of profit was just in accordance with the perfection of the organisation that existed in any particular trade. It would be well that every working man pondered over that statement. In conclusion, the action taken by employers, in not confining their bonds of unity to any particular locality, demands some action on the part of workmen. The question of concentrating our various ramifications ought to be warmly taken up. Our mutual dependence and identification of interests has long been a settled conviction, and it now becomes a necessity to recognise and act upon that conviction—the circumstances of our brother workmen everywhere being a question of vital importance to us. The trade societies that simply protected local interests will be found to be inadequate to meet the demands of the future. The disposition of employers to unite for the purpose of frustrating the just demands of labour, the concentration of capital, coupled with the application of machinery to be confronted, a general organisation of skilled labour becomes absolutely requisite.

The primary object of this institution is to levy a small sum on each trade, according to its numerical strength, for the purpose of supplementing the aliment of those who have already a protective fund, and generally assisting trades in the throes of a lock-out, or a strike that could not be averted without loss and degradation, instead of as at present depending partly if not wholly upon eleemosynary aid.

You are requested to send representatives to a meeting, to be held in TONTINE HOTEL, Glasgow, at 10 A.M., on *Tuesday, the 11th June,* for the purpose of drawing up and confirming Rules for the constitution and government of the Confederation, and the Branches of National Associations having their centre in Glasgow, will please communicate their views to their respective Boards, so that Delegates may be appointed here with full instructions. The names of all Delegates to be sent to the Subscriber on or before *Tuesday, the 28th May.*

On behalf of the Council,

I am, yours very respectfully,

CHARLES LANG, SECRETARY.

TONTINE HOTEL, TRONGATE,
GLASGOW, 6th April, 1872.

111

This attempt in 1872 to form a confederation of unions in Scotland foundered in the following year, when the larger unions refused to support it. By the time the confederation collapsed Britain was about to be plunged into a lengthy period of industrial depression.

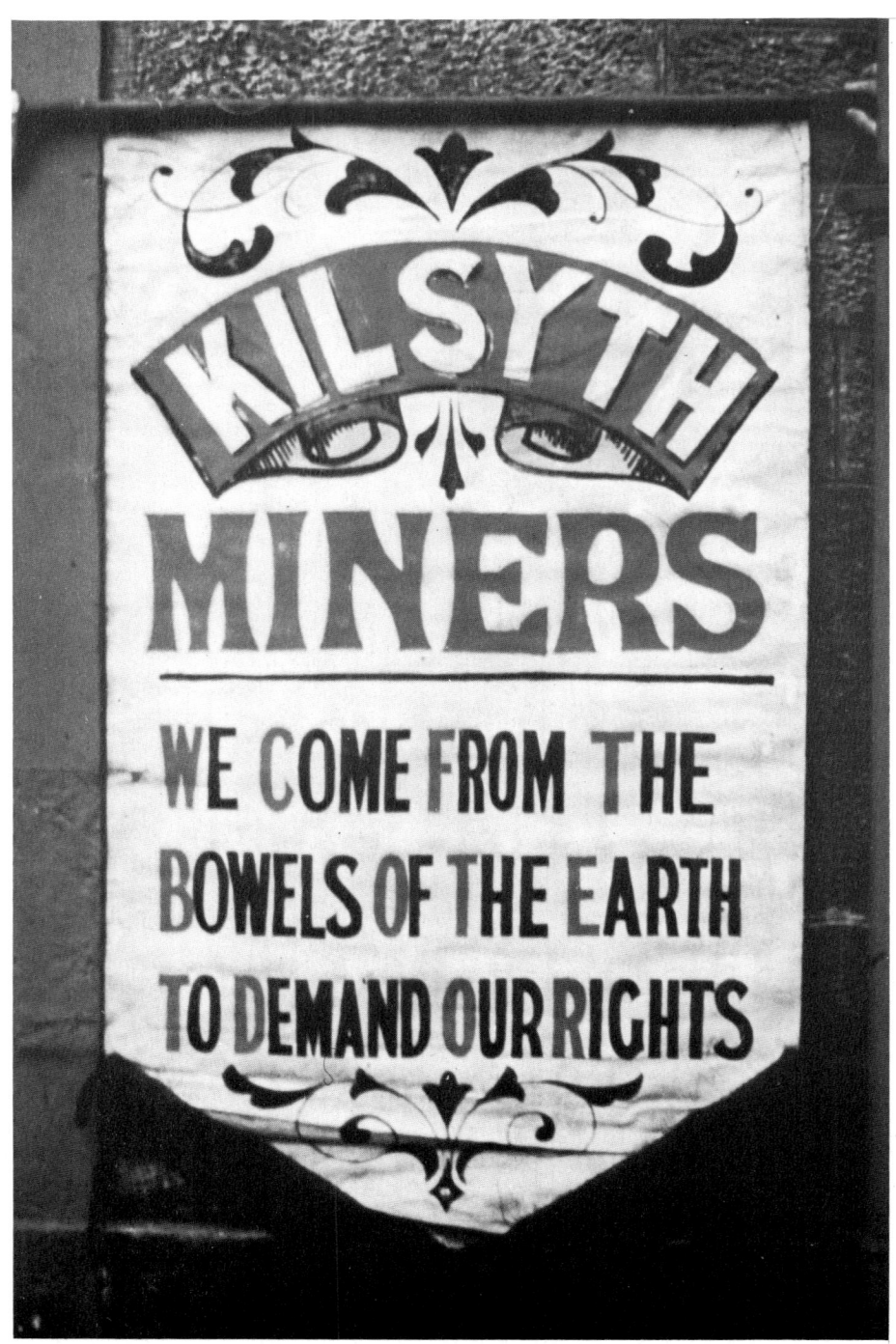

112

The industrial depression, although it undermined or overwhelmed some labour organisations, aroused—especially in the 1880s—important new movements. One achievement was the right to vote gained in the Third Reform Bill of 1884 by many male workers previously without it, such as many miners and farm servants. This banneret was carried in the agitation for the Bill.

114

113

114

Part of the Franchise demonstration in Glasgow in 1884.

115

Banner of the Hawick Stockingmakers, 1884. The Marquis of Salisbury was the leader of
the Conservative Party from 1881 to 1902.

116

Banner of the Peebles tailors, carried in the 1884 Reform agitation, and depicting Gladstone, the Liberal prime minister. Although the industrial depression of the 1870s and 1880s destroyed the belief of some workers in the 'inevitability of progress' under *laissez faire* capitalism, many continued to support the Liberals.

117

Demonstration by Aberdeen trade unionists, in favour of the Reform Bill, 1884.

118

Highland Land League meeting at Bettyhill, Sutherland. The League was formed in 1883
when serious agricultural depression, demands by the crofters for rent reductions and
more land, and evictions had led to the Crofters' War or Highland Land War.

119

The Crofters' War was marked by rent strikes and conflicts with the police, such as the Battle of the Braes in Skye in 1882, and the sending of a gunboat with marines to the isles. Here police and marines seize crofters at Aignish Farm, near Stornoway, on 9 January 1888.

120

Links between Irish and Highland land agitations are illustrated by this ticket. Michael Davitt was leader of the Irish Land League, supported land nationalisation, and had links with the labour movement in Britain.

THE LABOUR CANDIDATE FOR CATHCART

121

A crofters' leader who had for some years close connections with the labour movement was Dr Gavin Brown Clark, seen here electioneering in later years. Clark was elected Crofters' M.P. for Caithness in 1885 and held the seat till 1900. As an Advanced Radical he had been associated with the First International Working Men's Association and became a founder-member of the Scottish Labour Party formed in 1888 by Keir Hardie.

BUCHANAN'S HOTEL,
114 HIGH STREET, *30th March 1885.*

GENTLEMEN,

We beg to intimate to you that the following Resolution has been passed by the EDINBURGH UNITED TRADES' COUNCIL, viz. :—

"That, in the opinion of this Council, the great change which is being effected in the constitution of the country by the passing of the Franchise and Redistribution Bills renders the present a most opportune time for one of the Divisions of this City to return a *bona-fide* Working Man to Parliament ; and with the prospect that in the coming Parliament domestic and social questions must occupy to a very large extent the attention of the Legislature, this Council is of opinion that the return of a Working Man would strengthen and enrich the thought of Parliament. The wants of the industrial class can be most efficiently represented by a man who, by being a participator in, knows the circumstances of, his own class. This Council therefore resolves to make arrangements to secure the return of such a member for one of the Divisions, and to support him while in Parliament. For this purpose, that all the trades of the city be requested to appoint representatives to form a general committee to give practical effect to this Resolution."

In order to give practical effect to that Resolution, we beg most cordially to invite Representatives from your Trade for the purpose of organising an Association to secure the return of a *bona-fide* Working Man, and supporting him while in Parliament, Meeting to be held in BUCHANAN'S HALL, on the *Afternoon of Saturday, 11th April 1885,* at Five o'clock.

If your Trade does not meet before that date, will you kindly make an appointment *ad interim,* as it is absolutely necessary to take immediate action, with the view of securing the co-operation of the Parliamentary Committee of the Central Division, that being the Division which, from its large working-class electorate, is the most likely to return a Working-Man Representative.

Note.—It is to be distinctly understood that we, as a Council, do not arrogate any power in the matter, nor do we intend to drift into an electioneering machine. We have only taken the initiative, as being to a large extent representative of the organised Trades of the city, and once the matter is fairly set agoing, it will be left entirely in the hands of the Association to appoint its own office-bearers, and carry the matter to a successful issue.

We are, GENTLEMEN,

In name of the Council,

Yours very faithfully,

A. C. TELFER, *President.*
NEIL M'LEAN, *Secretary.*

122

Independent working class mass political organisation had faded away with the decline of Chartism after 1848. But there had been several attempts before the late 1880s to secure representation of labour by working men both in Parliament and local government: Aberdeen Trades Council, for example, in 1884 had two of its members elected as Labour candidates to the town council. Edinburgh Trades Council, which in 1869 and 1870 had put up its own candidates (unsuccessfully) in the municipal elections, indicates in this circular the growing concern to return working men to Parliament.

123

Membership card of the Scottish Labour Party, formed in 1888 after the mid-Lanark by-election in which Keir Hardie had stood unsuccessfully as an independent Labour candidate. The Scottish Labour Party was not socialist but an independent working class radical party among whose demands were nationalisation of land and minerals and railways, an eight hours day and payment of M.P.s.

124

Keir Hardie. Hardie was a leader not only of the Scottish Labour Party but also of the
Independent Labour Party formed in 1893, into which the Scottish Party amalgamated,
and of the Labour Party after its formation in 1900.

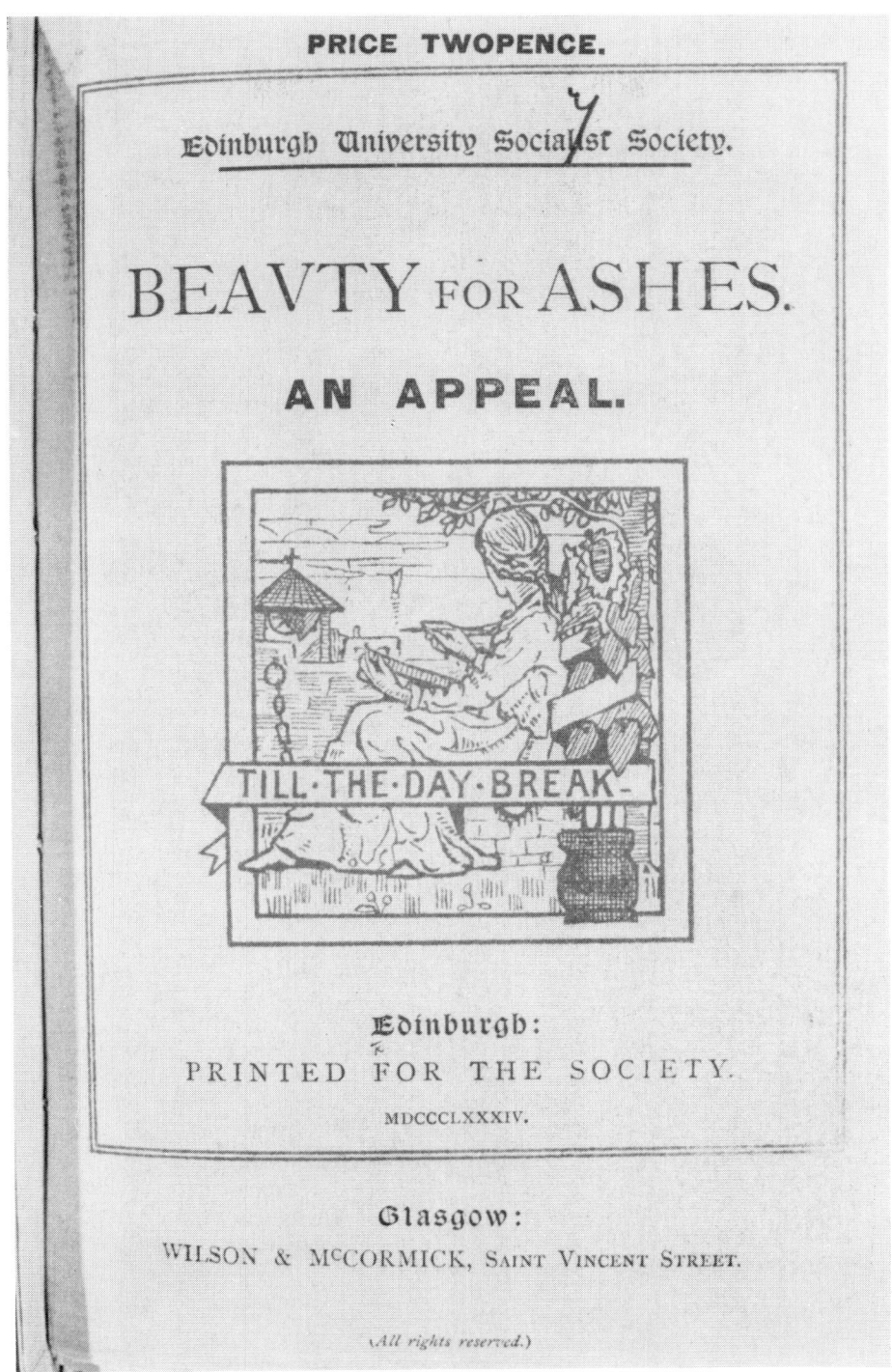

PRICE TWOPENCE.

Edinburgh University Socialist Society.

BEAVTY FOR ASHES.

AN APPEAL.

TILL·THE·DAY·BREAK·

Edinburgh:
PRINTED FOR THE SOCIETY.

MDCCCLXXXIV.

Glasgow:
WILSON & McCORMICK, SAINT VINCENT STREET.

125

Edinburgh University Socialist Society was one of the first organisations in Scotland
formed by the socialist revival of the 1880s.

126

Some continental socialist refugees contributed to the socialist revival in Scotland. Andreas Scheu, an Austrian socialist, lived and worked in Edinburgh for some years.

127

The photograph above left shows Bruce Glasier seated (left) and Keir Hardie standing. The photograph on the right is of J.L. Mahon. Both Glasier and Mahon were Scottish leaders of the socialist revival. Glasier, originally a member of the Social Democratic Federation, the first Marxist party in Britain, formed in 1881-84 and of which a Glasgow Branch was established in 1884, became a close associate of Keir Hardie and, like him, a leader of the Independent Labour Party. Mahon, an engineer, along with Andreas Scheu, an Austrian refugee socialist, founded in Edinburgh in 1884 the Scottish Land and Labour League, which affiliated to the Social Democratic Federation.

128

William Morris, artist, poet, socialist. Morris founded the Socialist League in 1884 as a breakaway from the Social Democratic Federation led by H.M. Hyndman. Several leading Scots socialists, including Glasier and Mahon, supported Morris against Hyndman in the split with the S.D.F.

PROSPECTUS.

A SOCIALIST PAPER FOR ABERDEEN AND THE NORTH.

THE WORKERS' HERALD.

WITH ten local newspapers—morning, evening, and weekly—one might expect that all shades of opinion in Aberdeen would be adequately represented and voiced. But " there is a sea below the sea." The *Journal* may stand for Conservatism—the Landed Interest—the good old-fashioned people who believe that this is the best of all possible worlds if everybody would but do

the Duty of Man according to Mrs. Grundy ;

the *Free Press* may serve the commercial Thugs of Liberal Unionism ; the *Northern Daily News* may be the *beau ideal* of a newspaper to those who worship the Gladstone-Morley-Harcourt party of plausible platitudes. *Bon-Accord* may satisfy north-country jokers, young and old, and *Figaro* meet the needs of cynics, musical people, and those who seek to cultivate the intellect by the reading of advertisements ! The *Express* is "solid," respectable, Philistine ; the *Gazette* is lively and gossipy, but a party paper, and the paper of the wrong party ; the *People's Journal* is good enough for those who require a paper, not to lead public opinion, but to follow at a safe distance

the clearly-distinguishable " set " of the current.

Each and all of these papers are owned by capitalists, written by men with capitalistic sympathies, supported by capitalist advertisers, and are for those reasons opposed to labour's new demands.

The thousands of Trades Unionists and Socialists that there are in Aberdeen and the surrounding district have no organ. The *Northern Daily News*, which some expected to be the last word of journalistic enterprise in the city, hesitates at giving its voice explicitly for Land Nationalization, is unsound on the Eight Hours Question, and, like the *People's Journal*, puts Liberalism first and Labour a long way after. It asks us to believe that the Liberal ticket is the Labour ticket ; that

the political creed

of the Mundellas, the Crombies, and the Earl of Aberdeen ought to be the political creed of Mundella's sweated laceworkers, Crombie's sweated tweedworkers, and Lord Aberdeen's rack-rented crofters.

To those who want a paper which does not depend for its existence on advertisements from the exploiters of labour ; to those who see the Liberal Party to be a party of capitalists chiefly and of lawyers and landlords for the rest, and who realise what that means ; to those who believe that Universal Suffrage, Payment of Members, Shorter Parliaments, and Home Rule all round are simply means to an end, and who regard that end as being shorter hours,

the wealth of the world for those who make it,

and the ultimate conquest of the land and the other means of production—to all such

THE WORKERS' HERALD

will be the journalistic mouthpiece and mentor in Aberdeen.

THE WORKERS' HERALD will advocate and elucidate Socialism ; but as steps in the evolution of society towards the Socialistic goal, and as palliatives of existing social evils, the *W. H.* will seek to further the following measures :—Statutory Limitation of the Hours of Labour, the Nationalization of Land, Mines, and Railways, the starting of Municipal Workshops and Stores, the Building and Letting of Houses by Town and County Councils, Municipalization of Cab-Hiring, Tramways, and Public Houses, Home Rule to all sections of the Empire, Disestablishment and Disendowment of State Churches, Abolition of Standing Armies, Formation of a National Citizen Force, Adult Suffrage, Payment of Members, Abolition of the Monarchy and the House of Lords, and any other measures or methods, whether evolutionary or revolutionary, which experience may dictate.

15 ST. NICHOLAS STREET,
ABERDEEN, NOV., 1891.

To all who have anything interesting to say on questions of public importance, and who can observe the proprieties of discussion, the columns of the *W. H.* will be open.

THE WORKERS' HERALD will be a weekly to begin with ; but if Irish and Continental towns are able to maintain their Socialist and Radical bi-weeklies and even dailies, there is no good reason why a politically-phenomenal city like Aberdeen, with a population of 120,000, with 7000 organised workers, with a Socialist organisation which can dispose of hundreds of copies of a London paper at street corners in a week, with

abundance of news to give and an eager desire to get it

—there is, we say, no good reason why THE WORKERS' HERALD should not in time become a daily.

Besides being only a weekly, the new paper will not be as large a sheet as some of the capitalist papers you get already for your penny. But the brown coin will not be disbursed for pages upon pages of advertisements, for London and New York prices, for lists of local stocks and shares, for the figures which " cod and halibut fetched to-day," for weather reports, court summaries, agricultural news, or London betting. You pay a penny for your programme when you go to the theatre, and if you are interested in sport you spend a halfpenny late at night on a *Despatch* or *Telegraph* for the sake of the little bit of sporting intelligence which it contains for you. THE WORKERS' HERALD will be

full of the sort of thing you want it for.

A large portion of the *W. H.* will NOT be taken up with flunkeyish stories in which working men are taught to admire and imitate the follies and the snobbery of their " betters " ; stories in which the boy hero is introduced to your notice in humble circumstances, grows up a proud, clever, handsome young man, is one day discovered to be the son of an earl, and is able thenceforth to live upon other folks' labour. As if the sons of working men were never handsome, talented, or high-spirited !

THE WORKERS' HERALD will be a paper owned by workers, largely written by workers *for* workers ; but its

Literary Staff,

which will be numerous, will be composed of all sorts and conditions of men except bad ones and dull ones. Among the contributors we expect to have WILLIAM MORRIS, R. B. CUNNINGHAME-GRAHAM, M.P., JOHN MORRISON DAVIDSON, GEORGE BERNARD SHAW, J. BRUCE GLASIER, " GRACCHUS," ANDREAS SCHEU, RAYMOND UNWIN, and the Rev. ALEXANDER WEBSTER. Smartly written local articles will appear from the pens of local men. The *W. H.* will contain a large quantity of general news bearing on the Labour Movement which does not find its way into the ordinary papers.

What *The Star, The Daily Chronicle, Reynolds's Newspaper*, and *Justice* are to London and the South,

that and something more

THE WORKERS' HERALD will be to Aberdeen and the North. It will be lively, condensed, and always abreast of the times. It will be well printed, on good paper, with bold headings and sub-headings, showing at a glance what it contains. It will be got up with a due regard to the shortness of life. the necessity for saving time, and the number of events and subjects bearing on the Social Question about which intelligent persons want to know.

The price will be one penny. The publication day will be Friday. The paper will be delivered weekly in town for 1s. a quarter of 13 weeks, and will be sent inland by post for 1s. 6d., payable in advance.

The Committee of the Aberdeen Socialist Society.

129

Aberdeen Socialist Society was founded in 1887 by J.L. Mahon and a local activist, James Leatham, and published *The Workers' Herald* in 1891-92, the first socialist newspaper in Scotland.

130

The Scottish Labour Party formed by Keir Hardie in 1888 failed to win any seats in Parliament nor did it attract mass support from the trade unions. Aberdeen Trades Council called a conference in 1891 that led to the formation a year later of the Scottish United Trades Councils Labour Party which was intended to give independent labour representation firm support among the unions, without being a rival to the Scottish Labour Party. The secretary of this new Party was R. Chisholm Robertson (above), a Stirlingshire miners' leader who was something of a rival of Keir Hardie.

GLASGOW FABIAN SOCIETY
◆ ◆ ◆ ◆

LECTURES IN THE SHEPHERD'S HALL, 25 BATH ST.
ON FIRST AND THIRD THURSDAYS OF EACH MONTH
AT 8. P.M. ◆ ◆ ◆ ◆

1903.

Oct. 2 **George Bernard Shaw—**
" Is Free Trade Alive or Dead ?"

,, 15 **John Clark—**
" Educational Ideal from a Rational Standpoint."

Nov. 5 **Rev. James Forrest—**
" Social Democracy in Byron, Shelley and Burns."

,, 19 **Alex. Gilchrist—**
" Anatomy of House Rent." *(Lantern Illustrations).*

Dec. 3 **Bailie George Mitchell—**
" Glasgow's Educational Endowments.'

,, 17 **W. R. Lester, M.A.—**
" Karl Marx and Henry George : a Comparison."

1904.

Jan. 7 OPEN.

,, 21 **Tom Jones M.A.—**
" Imperialism and Empire."

Feb. 4 **S. Horsfall Turner, M.A.—**
" Municipal Trading."

,, 18 OPEN.

Mar. 3 **Fra. H. Newbery—**
" Instincts in Civic Art Life."

,, 17 **Alex. M'Kendrick—**
" Heredity and Environment as Factors in Social Development."

Apr. 7 **Robt. Pollok—**
" An Experiment in Housing."

131

The Fabian Society was another socialist organisation formed in the 1880s, with George Bernard Shaw and Sidney and Beatrice Webb among its leaders. Like the Independent Labour Party, the Fabians were reformist, in contrast to the revolutionary Social Democratic Federation and Socialist League. This syllabus of the Glasgow Society appears to be one of the earliest surviving records of Scottish Fabians.

THE
LABOUR LEAFLET.

Compiled by R. DEMPSTER.

No. 1.   6 Copies 1d., Postage ½d.

LABOUR is the source of all wealth, "therefore all wealth belongs to labour," and recently when labour integrity was at its best, it was found by economists and statisticians, that the estimated gross or total annual income of all the folk in Great Britain and Ireland came to something like £1,500,000,000.

THE MILLIONS of folk who do the manual labour, or in other words, men and women, boys and girls, who do the laborious and physical toil, which go such a long way in creating the above annual wealth, only receive somewhere distributive as a gross amount over all, about £300,000,000 per annum, out of the total amount created by the labour advantages which should be for the good of all.

THE EMPLOYERS of folk who labour, and those who live by mental or brain work, to them it may be assumed that they get, or rather in ordinary instances retain, an amount no less than £100,000,000.

TO ARCHITECTURAL WORK, the genius' mental and physical skill, another £100,000,000 may be assumed to them who do such useful duties, which should be a benefit to other labouring folks, but which is too much grasped to advantage of idleness by capitalists or idle scoundrels.

TO PROFITS in honest businesses of distribution etc., say another £100,000,000, and to DISHONEST PROFITMONGERS, and sweaters of labour, say £50,000,000 this still leaves yet £650,000,000 unaccounted for, or over one half of the total value of labour going to daylight or LEGALIZED ROBBERS, or in other words to those whom no truthful person could look upon as ought else but drones or slugs who do nothing at all for it. A few thousands of persons by privilege of law enjoy a life of idle and extravagant luxury, while the millions who by their mental and physical labour and skill combined, create the whole amount referred to, continue under tyranny and ill paid labour, the majority in poverty, and large numbers in utter misery and destitution, CAUSED BY THE DRONES having all political privilege, etc.

THE CONDITION OF SOCIETY—thus illustrated, the pulse of it as felt, or is felt by all honest thinking persons, to millions is much worse than chattel slavery could now be, or in instances was, ought therefore to be revolutionised or changed the opposite way about, namely from unsocialism to a condition of Socialism ; or to put the injunctions of St. Paul, "That if any would not work, neither should they eat"; or, "Let him that stole, steal no more, but rather let him labour."

SOCIALISM as said——"Should be the hope and aspiration of every honest man and woman, whether brain or hand worker, but the fear and dread of the wilfully idle," and added thereto "of all who are dishonest either in thought, word or deed.'

SOCIALISM may be defined "an art," or rather "a social and scientific ideal," when realized will result in a "Condition of Society," with privileges of law, etc., in which that amount of labour value, over one half (£650,000,000) of our annual income of wealth, would go not to drones and slugs, but to the exchequer of labour instead. SOCIALISM does not mean disorder, confusion or violence, etc., as stated by the opponents of it, but it means the complete opposite.

Issued under the auspices of the Ploughmen's Club and the Socialist Union.
Address, R. DEMPSTER, Morn Street, Alyth, N.B.

132

The spread of socialist ideas in late nineteenth century Scotland is illustrated by this leaflet issued by the Alyth Ploughmen's Club and Socialist Union in Perthshire, probably about 1888.

133

James Connolly, the Irish socialist born in Edinburgh in 1868 and executed by the British authorities for his part in the Easter Rising in Dublin in 1916. The Irish struggle, often an issue of great importance in Scottish labour history, was particularly so in the late nineteenth and early twentieth centuries.

THE
LABOUR CHRONICLE

A LOCAL ORGAN OF DEMOCRATIC SOCIALISM

The great appear great to us because we are on our knees; let us rise.—CAMILLE DESMOULINS.

No. 1.   EDINBURGH, OCTOBER 15, 1894.   ONE HALFPENNY.

About Ourselves.

IN a first issue, some words of introduction to the public may not unnaturally be expected.

The Labour Chronicle will be devoted to questions affecting the welfare of the people—questions which every working-man and working-woman ought to be, and, we believe, are, not unwilling to understand.

The principles it will contend for are those held by its proprietors, the local branches of the Independent Labour Party and the Scottish Socialist Federation, and which have two years in succession received the emphatic endorsement of the Trades Union Congress.

In short, *The Labour Chronicle* will expound and defend the principles of Social Democracy, of Collectivism, in their application to national and municipal life.

As a local paper, it will give the most searching criticism of our local public councils and boards. Their misdeeds and mismanagement will be mercilessly laid bare, and all members of such bodies who do not strive for the realisation of the Socialist ideal will find their policy attacked in these columns, and no effort on our part spared to turn them out of office in order to make room for better representatives of the people.

Purity of public life will be insisted upon, and jobbery promptly exposed ; but corruption and venality cannot be got rid of until men whose whole career is guided by " business " principles, by the false morality of commercialism, are cleared out.

The Labour Chronicle will advocate the public ownership and management of the land, the mines, and all the means of production and distribution, such as railways, shipping, factories, workshops, &c.

The working-classes have now a very great measure of political freedom, but they have not gained even a small degree of industrial freedom. They have considerable political power, and can, despite the drawbacks of not having election expenses and the salaries of members of public bodies paid by the State, control the political machine if they choose. But in matters industrial they are helpless in the hands of their employers. The capitalists impose almost any conditions of pay and work they please, owing to the weakness of the workers as individuals, and even as organised trades. The only cure is for them to use their political power and convert as quickly as possible the various trades and industries from private into public concerns, so that the actual workers themselves will have control of the conditions of their industrial life.

But until the working-people have fully realized this, industrial undertakings will be managed for private profit by employers, armed with well-nigh despotic powers over their employees.

To mitigate the evils of this system, which we are working to abolish, *The Labour Chronicle* will, with due regard to the law of libel, make the public acquainted with working-class grievances, with cases of exceptional capitalist injustice and tyranny, and cases of the evasion of the legal regulations of industry by local firms. Information of the usual, but nevertheless shameful, cases of over-working and under-payment will also be given. And as it is to be hoped the fear of publicity will have a wholesome and restraining influence on local petty tyrants, trade unionists and others are invited to let us know of bad cases. Full inquiry will be made, and steps taken to put a stop to the flagrant abuse of the power of capital.

Unlike the capitalist press, we do not fear the wrath of evil-doers, who may be brought to book. Our existence *does not depend on capitalist patronage.* The *Chronicle* relies wholly on the support of the workers.

The gross misrepresentations from which the Collectivists suffer at the hands of the local press, and the unfair suppression of their side of the case when offered by correspondents, has made it imperative that the movement should have an organ of its own, unfettered by capitalist control.

The work that lies before us is onerous, but we undertake it with joy and hope. We strive to hasten the time when poverty and overwork, riches and idleness, will no longer exist ; but when comfort and leisure and culture will be at the command of all.

And we know that the future is ours.

What We Think.

IT must not be imagined that the quotation which appears under the title of this paper has any reference to the recent acrobatic performance of Lord Provost Russell and his henchmen at Balmoral. That was but a fitting finish to their term of office.

It *is* a little surprising, though, that a " Radical Council " should have such a record of snobbish " presentations," of shameless betrayals of trust, and of neglect of those questions which are vital to the welfare and happiness of the people of Edinburgh, as this one has.

About twelve months ago, the members of the present Council, bursting with zeal for the well-being of the workers, took a census of the unemployed, and finding that there were only a little over *twelve hundred*, thanked God " this was not exceptional," and—did nothing.

Were these twelve hundred, with their wives and children, not as surely " made in the image of God," and as deserving of considerate, brotherly treatment as the Duke and Duchess of York, whom the Council went out of its way to present with an article of senseless luxury—at the city's expense ?

When the be-titled Provost and his precious colleagues squandered over seventy pounds in going to Balmoral to congratulate a rich old woman on the birth of a grandchild, were there no starving children in the collier homes of the Lothians, or even in the slum tenements of their own city ?

Were not the people in some parts of St Cuthbert's and St George's Wards, in the houses under £5 in rental, dying at the rate of 50·5 and 40·5 per 1000 ; while the average for the city was only 18 per 1000 ? And was not a large and densely-populated part of his Lordship's Ward unfit for human habitation, by reason of noise and dirt and obnoxious smells ? And all that the councillors have done in the matter is to fly a proposed Fountainbridge improvement scheme for a few weeks before the election as a kite to catch the working-class votes for the Right Honourable the Lord Provost.

If the workers are foolish enough to trust him again, when a sturdy democrat like Mr Blaikie is in the field, and may be had for the voting, they may rest assured they will be fooled just as long as they are willing.

There is surely sufficient manliness and independence of character among Scottish workmen to make them despise the men who have toadied in their name for the sake of royal favour ; who have betrayed the city to the Railway Company out of cowardice, or worse; who have squandered money in senseless luxury and held it in when it was needed for popular welfare ; and who now come forward with smooth words and glib professions of undying faithfulness to the public good.

We believe that the day is not far distant when the Balmoral Radicalism of Messrs M'Crae and Russell, and the smug respectability of the Merchant Company jobbers, will alike be unknown in the Council Chambers.

Throughout the length and breadth of the land the workers are smashing their party chains, and rallying to the flag of Independent Labour. In Edinburgh, as elsewhere, the revolt of Labour grows apace. " Forward ! " say we. " God defend the right ! "

134

Labour Chronicle was the organ of the Scottish Socialist Federation, formed in 1888 to co-ordinate the work of the various socialist groups and the Scottish Labour Party. The first secretary of the Federation was John Leslie, another Irish-Scot and a close associate of James Connolly.

THE FIRST NATIONAL COUNCIL OF THE I.L.P.
Back Row (left to right) A. Field, J. Kennedy, J. Lister (Treasurer).
Centre Row (left to right) G. S. Christie, J. W. Buttery, Joseph Burgess, W. H. Drew, E. Aveling, Alf Settle.
W. Johnson, W. Small, Chisholm Roberton, George Carson.
Seated (left to right) Pete Curran, Shaw Maxwell (Secretary), K. St. John Conway.

135

The Independent Labour Party, founded in 1893, absorbed the Scottish Labour Party and became the largest of the socialist parties. Its first National Council met at Glasgow that year and included William Small, a leader of the Lanarkshire Miners' Union; J. Shaw Maxwell, a leader of the Scottish Labour Party; Chisholm Robertson, leader of the Stirlingshire miners; and George Carson, a tinplate worker and a leader of the Scottish Labour Party who also became secretary of Glasgow Trades Council and of the Scottish Trades Union Congress. For the following half century Scotland remained one of the strongest bases of the Independent Labour Party.

136

Craft unions survived, despite some casualties, the industrial depression of the 1870s and '80s that had contributed so greatly to the revival of socialism. Nor was unionism of the unskilled destroyed by the severity of the depression, though many of the organisations formed in the 'boom' period in the late 1860s and early '70s were swept away. By the later 1880s, however, there began a great revival of unskilled workers' unionism—the 'New Unionism'. The London dockers' strike of 1889, and the successful strikes of Bryant & May match girls and of the gas stokers in London, marked the rise of a new militancy that made trade unionism a mass movement which, despite numerous setbacks, it has never ceased to be since that time.

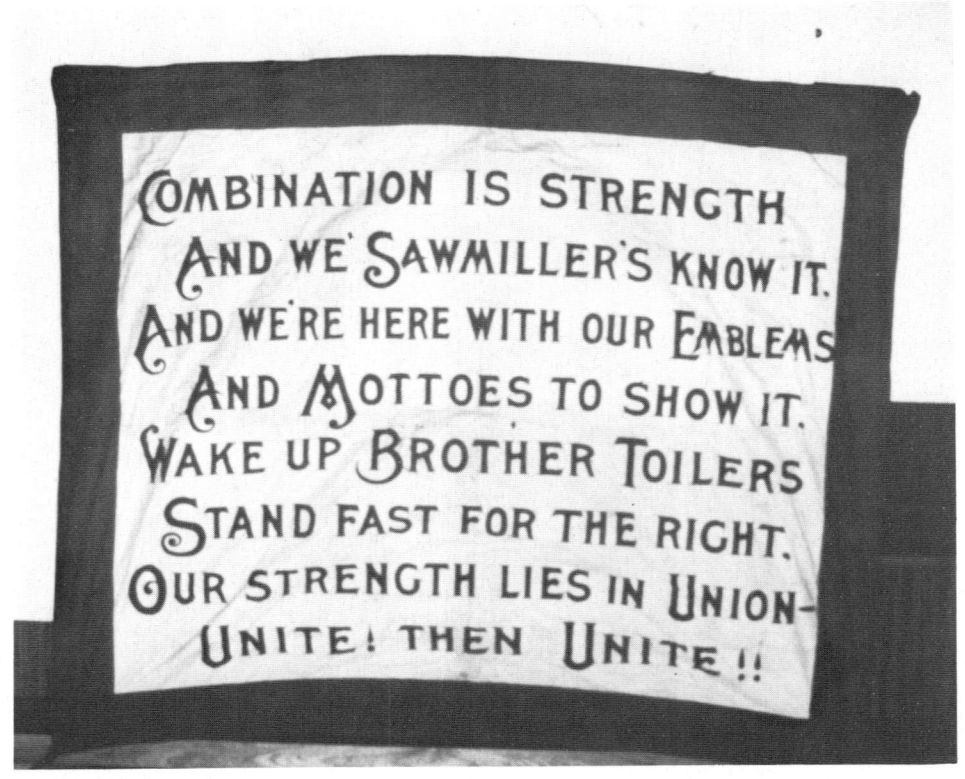

137

Banner of the Aberdeen Sawmillers.

138

Miners at Slamannan, Stirlingshire. The formation of the Miners' Federation of Great Britain in 1889 marked a big step forward in mining trade unionism, though county mining unions remained in Scotland as elsewhere in Britain until almost the middle of the twentieth century.

139

The Executive Board of the Fife and Kinross Miners' Association at the end of the
nineteenth century. In 1870, as the result of a sit-down strike, the Fife miners had been
the first in Europe to win an eight-hours day.

140

Robert Smillie, leader of the Lanarkshire miners and of the Scottish Miners' Federation established in 1894. The Federation, which changed its title in 1914 to National Union of Scottish Mine Workers, embraced all the miners' county unions in Scotland until their reorganisation in 1945 into the National Union of Mineworkers (Scottish Area).

141

Seamen, like coalminers, faced many dangers at work. The National Amalgamated
Sailors and Firemen's Union was formed in 1887. This is the membership emblem of
Charles Bickon of the Leith Branch.

142

Sowing seed by hand on a farm at Lilliesleaf, Roxburghshire, at the end of the nineteenth century. Their conditions of work—isolation from other workers, employment in fairly small units, paternalism, deference, tied housing, low wages, etc.—had made it very difficult for farm workers in Scotland to establish unions.

AUGUST, 1927. 317 The Scottish Farm Servant.

A Voice from the Past

" Manifesto to the Farm Servants of Scotland: ' United we stand, divided we fall '

RETHREN,—The time has now come for action. Too long have we stood idly by, indifferent to our interests as a class. The Farm Servants' Union affords an opportunity to all workers connected with the land to unite their energies in securing for themselves a position worthy of their manhood. Individual effort has always and everywhere failed. By combination and organisation only can we hope to gain deliverance from a system inimical at once to freedom and to social, moral and intellectual improvement. That system speaks to us with a living force, when we consider our housing and sleeping accommodation, our dietary and bothy arrangements, as well as the wages paid for our hire. For years we have endured these hardships or accommodated ourselves to them without remonstrance, the outcome being the maintenance of a privileged class ' who toil not, neither do they spin,' while, on the other hand, *we* have had to toil and labour, in season and out of season, for a bare existence. It is thus clearly our duty to put our hands to the plough and resolve not to turn back until we have made the crooked path straight and the rough places plain, if not for our own, for our children's feet.

The last question concerns us deeply. Our own happiness, and that of the industrial classes in the towns and cities throughout the country, depends on its solution. It is necessary, therefore, to have our minds set upon the right principles, so that when these come to be applied, they shall operate, not for us as a class, but for the good of the whole nation. Our enfranchisement has made us a potent political power in the commonwealth Numerically speaking, no other class occupies such a unique position. The weapon put into our hands, if used intelligently and determinedly, is able to cleave and to smash all systems that monopolise. This is specially true in relation to our Land System, as from it all

material blessings flow, and no mere handful of men should be permitted to appropriate God's gifts to the human family. On us rests a heavy responsibility. Will we discharge it faithfully? The artisan classes are deeply interested in our movement, anxious that we should ally them in the onward march of progress.

Many other subjects demand our attention, but these, we think, are fully covered by the objects as stated in the book of rules. We commend them to your kindly consideration and support, so that our Union may become a living power for good to us all.

The Exec. of the S.F.S.U.

JAS. C. THOMSON, Gen. Secy.,
58 Shiprow, Aberdeen."

In 1887

The above letter was issued in 1887 by the original Scottish Farm Servants' Union, which later became the Ploughmen's Federal Union of Scotland. It was reprinted in the " Scottish Farm Servant " of August, 1913, to show what were the ideas that animated the minds of those who were before us. Older readers of this journal will remember the manifesto, but many of our younger members may not have seen it. It will be good for them to realise what the force was behind those who began organisation amongst the farm workers in Scotland. It was not the force of selfishness, but the impelling desire to make conditions better for others.

In 1927

It is forty years since the manifesto was written and published. Conditions have bettered considerably in these forty years, and many of the hardships endured by the pioneers of our movement have disappeared. Our younger members have not had to fight for many of the rights they enjoy, and some of them tend to forget the strenuous fight put up in the past to secure the conditions we have to-day. It is useful to remember those who began the fight and those who worked without seeing the fruits of their labour. When we are faced, as we are this year, with a curtailment of our freedom as Trades Unionists, it is well to realise that we, as well as those who began our movement, have a heavy responsibility, and to make up our minds to discharge it faithfully.

Lothian Harvesters' Strike—continued.

that these threats could not be passed over, so he sent " an express " to the commanding officer of the press gang at Leith, and at dead of night, when the harvester of independent mind was sound asleep, an armed party of the press gang crept silently up (guided no doubt by " the respectable farmer ") and carried him off. They employed him, it is stated, " in the service of his country, without allowing him to use threatenings against any other than the common enemy."

Another Little War

Now, if something like that could be done to-day, would'nt agriculture flourish? Perhaps some of our leading agricultural bodies will take the matter up with the government; and there's not a member of the present government who would refuse. All that's needed is to start a war, then conscript every farm servant who does not cheerfully accept the lowest wage he is offered.

R. N. D.

143

Further attempts to form unions were made by farm servants in the 1880s and '90s. This manifesto was issued by the Scottish Farm Servants', Carters' and General Labourers' Union, formed in 1885, that merged ten years later into the Scottish Ploughmen's Federal Union.

144

'Feeing Saturday' at Arbroath, about 1900. The feeing marts, held in the open street once or twice a year in several towns in each county, such as Arbroath, Turriff, Cupar, Earlston, were where a great many farm workers were hired. A later Scottish farm workers' leader, Joseph F. Duncan, described feeing marts as 'simply a relic of barbarism'.

The Scottish Farm Servant.   NOVEMBER, 1915.

Don't Throw Yourself Away Too Cheap!

Big Money Can Be Got For The Asking.

Here are some of the bargains made at the October Hirings. They are not exceptional bargains, but have been got by many men who had the pluck to ask for the money they were worth.

DUNFERMLINE.   30/- per week, 1 ton potatoes, harvest £1.
25/- per week, 1 pint milk daily, 40 stones meal, 1 ton potatoes, ½ lb. butter weekly, insurance paid.

CUPAR.   £54 per year, 6½ bolls meal, 1 pint milk daily, 2 tons potatoes.
Single Men—£25 per six months, all found.

DUNDEE.   £56 per year, 6½ bolls meal, 1 pint milk daily, 2 tons potatoes.
28/- a week, meal, potatoes, harvest £1.
Single Men in Bothy—£35 per six months, meal, milk potatoes, coal and light.
Single Men Boarded—£30 per six months, all found.

CRIEFF.   24/- a week, 8d. milk daily, 5 stones meal per month, and potatoes.

STIRLING.   28/- per week, 2 tons potatoes, harvest £1.
30/- per week, 1 ton potatoes.

House included in each case.

Many men got less, because they asked for less.
Don't you be put off with anything less.

THESE WERE UNION MEN.

Are You in the Union, and trying to get other men into the Union?

Printed and Published for the Scottish Farm Servants' Union by JOHN BELL & CO., 82 Mitchell Street, Glasgow.

145

Handbill issued in 1893 by the Scottish Farm Servants' Union. It was only from 1912, when the later Scottish Farm Servants' Union was formed, that farm workers established a 'permanent' union. As late as then many were still working a seventy or eighty hours' week.

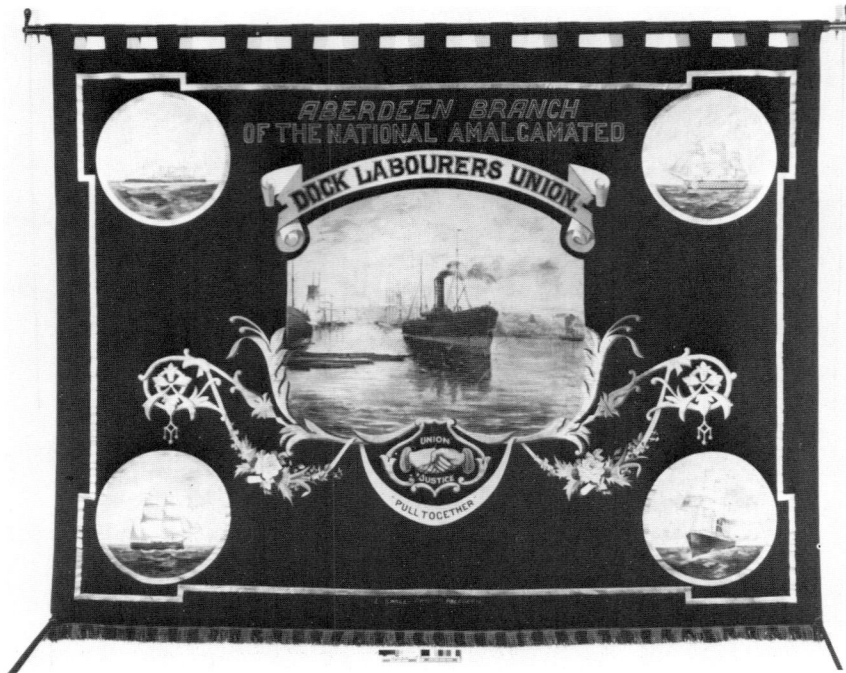

146

Aberdeen dockers' union banner, about 1900. Some Scottish dockers—at Glasgow and Leith, for example—had had unions from the middle of the nineteenth century; but the great London dock strike of 1889 gave a stimulus to wider organisation.

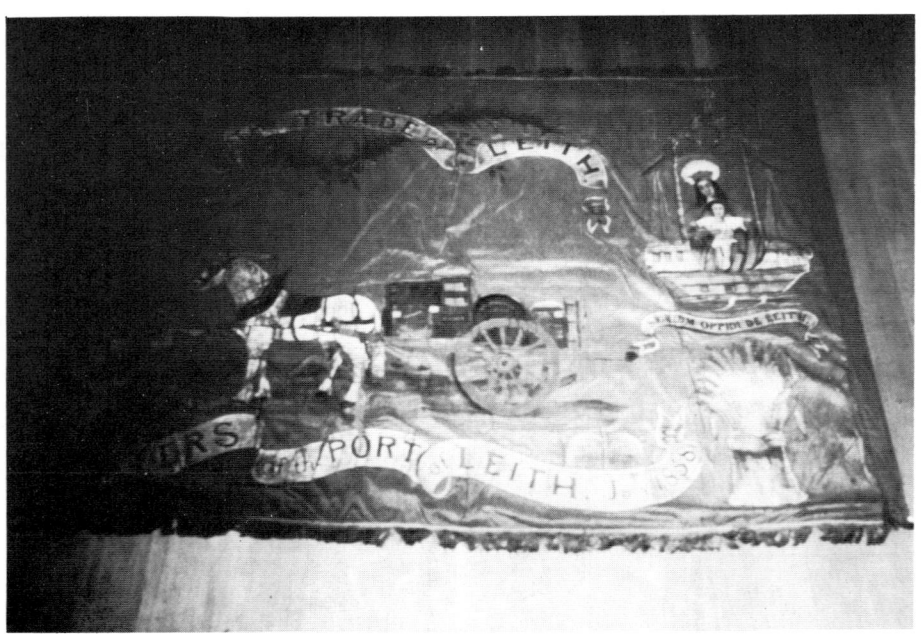

147

Road transport workers also began to organise more widely and permanently from the last years of the nineteenth century. The carters' conditions of work, like those of most unskilled workers, included extremely long hours—sometimes eighty a week—for very low wages. Like the dockers, some carters had formed unions earlier in the century: the Leith carters (whose banner here had to be photographed on the floor because of its poor state of preservation) seem to have had one from about 1858.

148

149

Shop and distributive workers, whose numbers increased substantially with the expansion of their industry in the later nineteenth century, were another group that began to unionise themselves then. These are employees of Lipton's, at Hawkhill, Dundee.

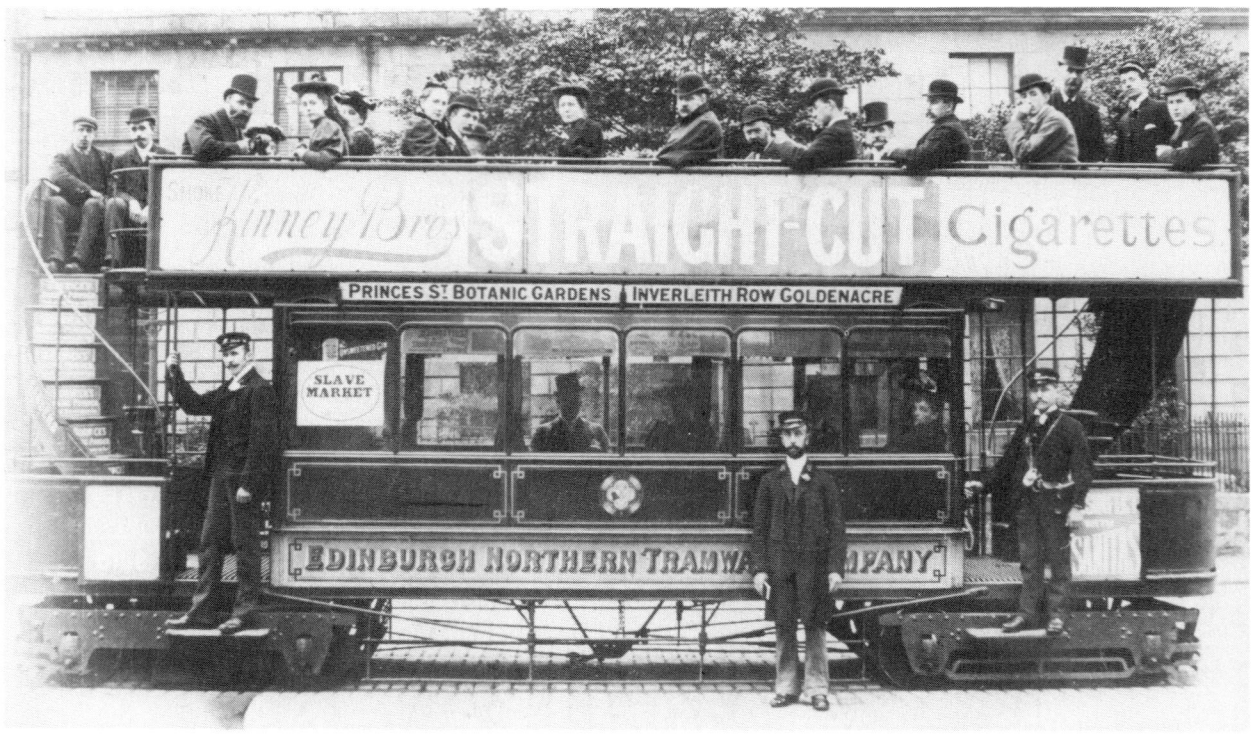

150

Public road transport was expanding in the period, and tramwaymen were among those unskilled workers attempting to form unions.

151

Textiles was one of the industries that employed many women. This photograph is of the power loom flat of Forest Mill, Selkirk, about 1895.

146

152

Many textile unions were small and local.

153

Fisher lassies gutting at Aberdeen fishmarket, 1903. Their conditions of work were extremely hard, their wages very low, the lassies living in crowded lodgings, sometimes three to a bed, when the fishing season drove them to Yarmouth and Lowestoft in search of work. The girls on the right are knitting as they walk.

THE

CONDITIONS OF WOMEN'S WORK

IN LAUNDRIES.

REPORT OF AN INQUIRY

CONDUCTED FOR

THE COUNCIL

OF THE

WOMEN'S PROTECTIVE AND PROVIDENT LEAGUE OF GLASGOW.

BY

MARGARET H. IRWIN.

154

Margaret Irwin was a full-time organiser from 1891 of the Women's Protective and Provident League and became an outstanding leader of women's trade unionism in Britain. By the beginning of the twentieth century women's trade unionism, though confronted by many difficulties, was making some headway in Scotland.

155

The 1890s were marked by several big strikes or lock-outs, one of which was the Scottish railwaymen's strike of December 1890 to the end of January 1891. The scene above is of strikers at Motherwell being batoned by police while cavalry stand by. The Amalgamated Society of Railway Servants for Scotland, its membership doubled in the enthusiasm for the New Unionism, struck on Christmas Eve for a ten-hour day: at that time many railwaymen were working between nineteen and twenty-five hours per shift or up to ninety-seven hours per week. The strike was defeated, and the A.S.R.S. for Scotland amalgamated into the English union a year later.

156

Miners at Arniston Colliery, Midlothian, about the time of the first national strike by Scottish miners from June to October 1894. The strike was against a reduction in wages but the miners had to return to work on the coalowners' terms.

149

157

Engineers at work at Mackie & Baxter's, marine engine shop, Govan, Glasgow. In 1897 a national lock-out of engineers took place, partly over a demand by the workers for an eight-hour day, but more because of the assertion by the newly formed Engineering Employers' Federation that they would 'manage their own affairs' without interference from the union. The lock-out cost the Amalgamated Society of Engineers £600,000 and the Society suffered a major defeat but the lock-out failed to destroy it.

158

Delegates to the first Scottish Trades Union Congress in March 1897. The Scottish T.U.C. was formed partly as a result of the exclusion two years earlier of trades councils from the British T.U.C. Trades councils had played a particularly important role in trade unionism in Scotland. The Scottish T.U.C. was not a rival to the British T.U.C. but was an autonomous organisation. It provided greater opportunity to its delegates to consider matters particularly affecting labour in Scotland than was normally possible at the British Congresses.

159

Among many cases taken up by the Scottish T.U.C. in its early years was a dispute between the Ballachulish slate quarrymen and their employers. Exploitation of the quarrymen by the company was severe: wages were paid only once every six weeks, excessive prices were charged for essential supplies, tools, etc. Dr Grant, a doctor paid for by the men, was dismissed for daring to criticise the insanitary company housing tenanted by the quarrymen. The company's vindictiveness against Dr Grant even extended to their securing a court interdict to prevent him practising, even privately, as a doctor in the Ballachulish district.

THE TWENTIETH CENTURY:
1900-14

Statement of steps leading up to calling of First Conference.

By George Carson, Secretary of the Conference

The Parliamentary Committee of the Scottish Trades Union Congress have remitted to them from the Trades Congress from time to time a large number of important instructions, most of them dealing with industrial legislation. In trying to have these instructions carried out the P.C. have occasion to wait upon Ministers of various Departments as well as upon many members of Parliament to impress upon them the need for these matters being looked into and at the same time to urge them to give effect to the clearly expressed wishes of the organised working-classes on these important points.

While some small concessions have been granted, no doubt due to these representations, still it may be said in this connection that the results were out of all proportion to the time, energy, & money spent by the P.C. in bringing them about, & there was the additional disadvantage that they were conceded as favours rather than recognised as rights. It therefore seemed to the P.C. that while waiting upon Ministers of State & Members of Parliament was useful in a way, & would doubtless in the meantime at least require to be continued, that some further action was wanted if the many important social & industrial reforms were to be pushed through Parliament within something like a reasonable time. After earnest consideration they came to the conclusion that the best means by which these questions would receive full attention was to

160

In January 1900, a month before the formation of the British Labour Party, the Scottish T.U.C. took up a suggestion by the Independent Labour Party and called a special conference in Edinburgh of trade unions, trades councils, the I.L.P. and Social Democratic Federation, and Co-operative societies. The conference declared in favour of independent working class representation in Parliament and formed the Scottish Workers' Parliamentary Elections Committee whose formation is described here by George Carson, its first secretary. The Committee sponsored several Labour candidates but none was elected. In 1909 the Committee merged into the Labour Party.

161

Labour parliamentary representation made little headway in Scotland before the 1914-18 War: between 1900 and 1914 only three Labour M.P.s were elected—George N. Barnes (top left) in Glasgow and Alexander Wilkie (bottom picture, seated centre of front row, with a hand on his shoulder) in Dundee, both in 1906; and in December 1910 William Adamson (top right), in West Fife. Scots Labour leaders such as Keir Hardie and Ramsay MacDonald were never elected to parliamentary seats in Scotland.

155

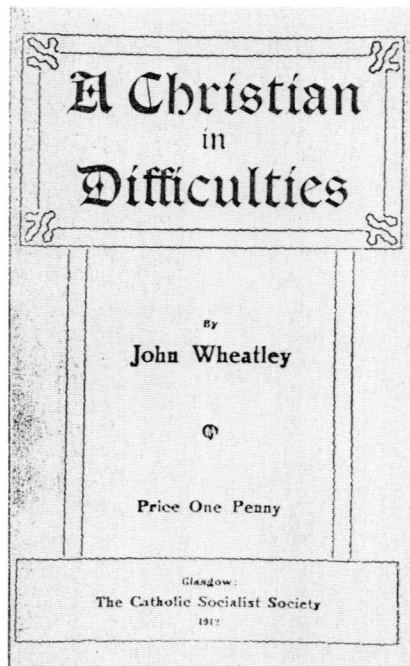

162

One of the explanations for the slow growth of electoral support for Labour in Scotland was that Catholics continued to vote Liberal to achieve Home Rule for Ireland. The Catholic Socialist Society was formed in 1906 in Glasgow by John Wheatley, a later I.L.P. leader.

163

Poster of the Labour candidate in Leith Burgh's parliamentary election, January 1910.

164

Glasgow Town Council in 1912. In local government Labour made more headway. By 1914 Glasgow had seventeen Labour councillors, Edinburgh six. There were also independent working class representatives, some of them members of the Social Democratic Federation, on parish councils and school boards.

165

Arbroath Branch of the Social Democratic Federation, 1906. By 1910 the S.D.F. had almost forty branches in Scotland.

166

John Maclean, Clydeside Marxist revolutionary schoolteacher, who joined the Social Democratic Federation in 1903. By 1914 Maclean had become one of its outstanding leaders.

THE SCOTSMAN

EDINBURGH, Tuesday, April 16, 1907.

SEIZURE OF ARMS AND AMMUNITION IN EDINBURGH.

TRAFFIC BETWEEN HAMBURG AND LEITH.

The Edinburgh police have secured what seems to be an important clue regarding the discovery of cartridges and firearms in Newcastle, Glasgow, and other centres. The discovery suggests that the authorities are on the track of an organisation whose object is the smuggling of ammunition and arms into dissatisfied districts in Russia, especially, it is thought, into Poland, as the man Keast, who is wanted at Newcastle, is understood to be of that nationality. It appears that a traffic in arms and ammunition has been going on all winter between Hamburg and Leith. The trade is said to have been conducted quite openly. No attempt was made to disguise the contents of the cases, which were stamped as containing arms and ammunition. The bills of lading were also found to be in proper order. In the circumstances, and in view of the fact that the cases were consigned to apparently responsible persons in Edinburgh, nothing was done by the authorities in regard to the matter. It has transpired that when the Newcastle police searched the house of Keast, the Pole who is "wanted" on a charge of keeping explosives in premises not licensed for the purpose, they found on some of the cases indications that they had come from Edinburgh. The Edinburgh police were communicated with, and for some days, it appears, a watch was kept upon the shop of a cycle agent in the city who was supposed to be the sender of the goods to Tyneside. This surveillance was rewarded on Saturday when information was received that a fresh consignment had been sent up from Leith to the cycle shop by the usual railway carriers. Police Inspectors Nicol and Grant, along with Inspector ... the Inspector of Explosives under the Act

167

Concern with international events had always been a feature of sections of organised labour in Scotland. This cutting from *The Scotsman* reports gun-running by socialists—members of the S.D.F.—at Leith to revolutionaries in Russia during or after the 1905 Revolution.

168

Neil Maclean, secretary of the Socialist Labour Party, formed in 1903 as a largely Scottish breakaway from the Social Democratic Federation. Maclean became Labour M.P. for Govan. Among other leaders of the Socialist Labour Party were James Connolly, the Irish socialist, and Arthur MacManus, later a leading Clyde shop steward. The Party's membership remained small but very active.

S.P.G.B. LIBRARY. No. 1.

Manifesto

OF

THE SOCIALIST PARTY

OF

GREAT BRITAIN.

With Declaration of Principles.

Fourth Edition, with Preface.

PRICE ONE PENNY.

PUBLISHED BY

THE SOCIALIST PARTY OF GREAT BRITAIN,

10, Sandland St., Bedford Row, London, W.C.

Trade Agent:

HENDERSONS, 66, Charing Cross Road, London, W.C.

169

A second breakaway from the Social Democratic Federation was the Socialist Party of Great Britain, formed in 1904, which had some members in Scotland.

JOHN PATTERSON,
HATTER AND HOSIER
(LATE WITH M'QUAKER.)

ONE PERSON HAS TOLD ANOTHER OF

PATTERSON'S HATS.

This is the reason they have forged ahead so fast.

Merit does not count for nothing after all.

102 TRONGATE, GLASGOW
(Corner of CANDLERIGGS.)

DIET CURES WHAT DIET CAUSES

THE HEALTH FOOD SUPPLY CO.'S
BREAD, BISCUITS, CAKES, & VEGETARIAN SPECIALITIES
Are the future Foods of the HEALTH REFORMER.
And those who suffer from DISORDERED STOMACHS
Write or call at one of our Stores for Booklet.
365 NEW CITY ROAD.
73 DUNDAS STREET,
434 ARGYLE STREET
GLASGOW.

TO LET

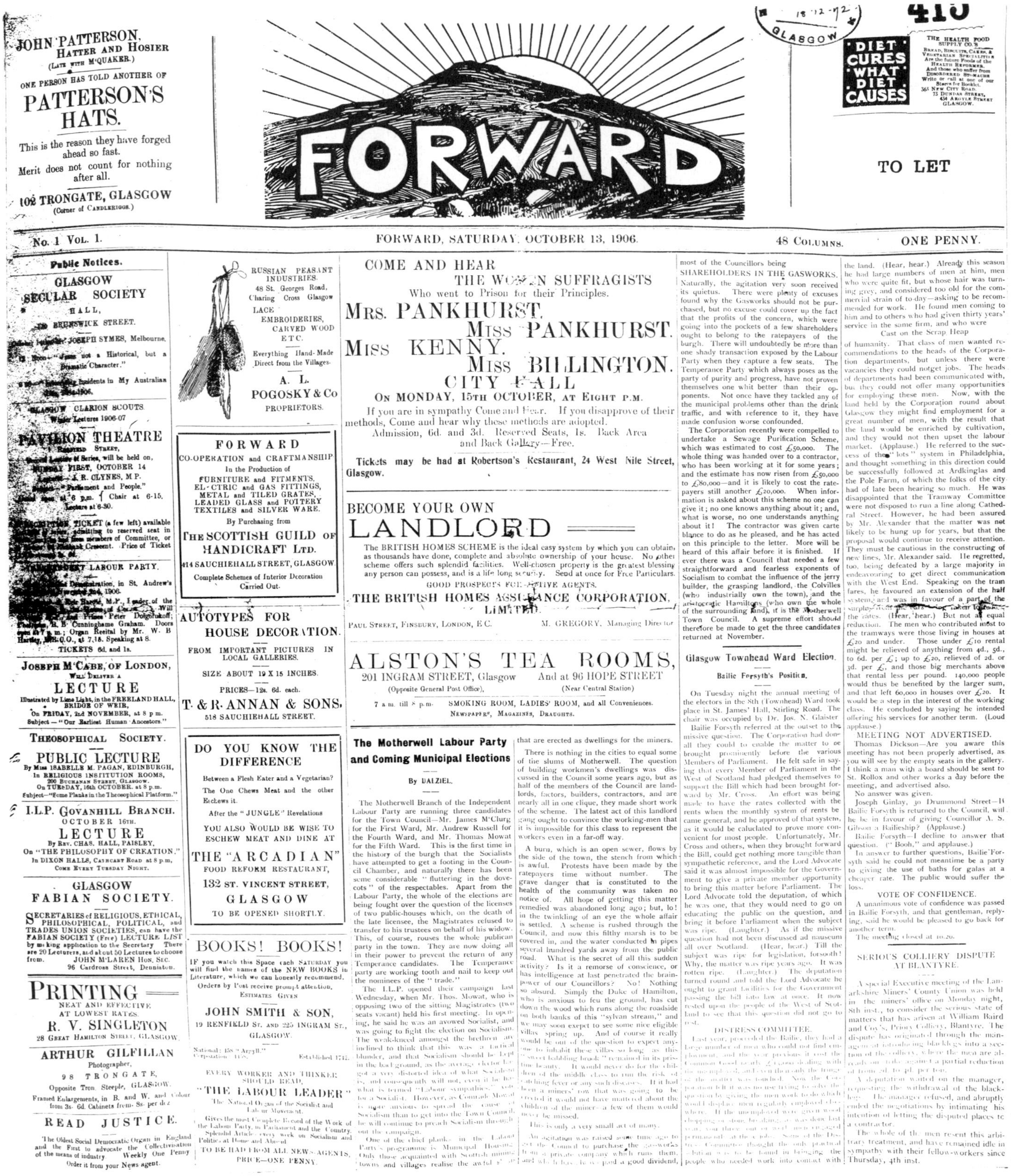

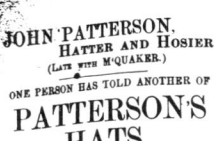

No. 1 VOL. 1. FORWARD, SATURDAY, OCTOBER 13, 1906. 48 COLUMNS. ONE PENNY.

Public Notices.

GLASGOW SECULAR SOCIETY
HALL,
[illegible] BRUNSWICK STREET.

[illegible] JOSEPH SYMES, Melbourne.

[illegible] "[illegible] not a Historical, but a Dramatic Character."

[illegible] Incidents in My Australian [illegible] 1906.

[illegible] CLARION SCOUTS.
Winter Lectures 1906-07

PAVILION THEATRE
[illegible] STREET,
[illegible] of Series, will be held on,
[illegible] FIRST, OCTOBER 14
[illegible] J. R. CLYNES, M.P.
[illegible] "Parliament and People."
[illegible] at 6 p.m. { Chair at 6-15. Lecture at 6-30.

[illegible] TICKET (a few left) available [illegible] admitting to reserved seat in [illegible] members of Committee, or [illegible] Crescent. Price of Ticket [illegible]

[illegible] LABOUR PARTY.

[illegible] Demonstration, in St. Andrew's [illegible] 2nd, 1906.

[illegible] Keir Hardie, M.P., Leader of the [illegible] Will [illegible] Prince Peter Dolgorukoff; [illegible] R. B. Cunninghame Graham. Doors open at 7 p.m.; Organ Recital by Mr. W. B. Hartley, [illegible] at 7.15. Speaking at 8.

TICKETS 6d. and 1s.

JOSEPH M'CABE, OF LONDON,
WILL DELIVER A
LECTURE
Illustrated by Lime Light, in the FREELAND HALL, BRIDGE OF WEIR,
On FRIDAY, 2nd NOVEMBER, at 8 p.m.
Subject—"Our Earliest Human Ancestors."

THEOSOPHICAL SOCIETY.
PUBLIC LECTURE
By Miss ISABELLE M. PAGAN, EDINBURGH,
In RELIGIOUS INSTITUTION ROOMS,
200 BUCHANAN STREET, GLASGOW.
On TUESDAY, 16th OCTOBER, at 8 p.m.
Subject—"Some Planks in the Theosophical Platform."

I.L.P. GOVANHILL BRANCH.
OCTOBER 16TH.
LECTURE
By REV. CHAS. HALL, PAISLEY,
On "THE PHILOSOPHY OF CREATION."
In DIXON HALLS, CATHCART ROAD at 8 p.m.
COME EVERY TUESDAY NIGHT.

GLASGOW FABIAN SOCIETY.

SECRETARIES of RELIGIOUS, ETHICAL, PHILOSOPHICAL, POLITICAL, and TRADES UNION SOCIETIES, can have the FABIAN SOCIETY (Free) LECTURE LIST by making application to the Secretary. There are 20 Lecturers, and about 50 Lectures to choose from.
JOHN M'LAREN HON. SEC.
96 Cardross Street, Dennistoun.

PRINTING
NEAT AND EFFECTIVE
AT LOWEST RATES.
R. V. SINGLETON
28 GREAT HAMILTON STREET, GLASGOW.

ARTHUR GILFILLAN
Photographer,
98 TRONGATE,
Opposite Tron Steeple, GLASGOW.
Framed Enlargements, in B. and W. and Colour from 3s. 6d. Cabinets from 8s. per doz.

READ JUSTICE.

The Oldest Social Democratic Organ in England and the First to advocate the Collectivisation of the means of industry. Weekly One Penny
Order it from your News agent.

RUSSIAN PEASANT INDUSTRIES.
48 St. Georges Road, Charing Cross Glasgow
LACE
EMBROIDERIES,
CARVED WOOD
ETC.
Everything Hand-Made Direct from the Villages.
A. L. POGOSKY & Co
PROPRIETORS.

FORWARD
CO-OPERATION and CRAFTMANSHIP
In the Production of
FURNITURE and FITMENTS.
ELECTRIC and GAS FITTINGS,
METAL and TILED GRATES,
LEADED GLASS and POTTERY
TEXTILES and SILVER WARE.
By Purchasing from
THE SCOTTISH GUILD OF HANDICRAFT LTD.
414 SAUCHIEHALL STREET, GLASGOW.
Complete Schemes of Interior Decoration Carried Out.

AUTOTYPES FOR HOUSE DECORATION.
FROM IMPORTANT PICTURES IN LOCAL GALLERIES.
SIZE ABOUT 19 X 15 INCHES.
PRICES—12s. 6d. each.
T. & R. ANNAN & SONS,
518 SAUCHIEHALL STREET.

DO YOU KNOW THE DIFFERENCE
Between a Flesh Eater and a Vegetarian?
The One Chews Meat and the other Eschews it.
After the "JUNGLE" Revelations
YOU ALSO WOULD BE WISE TO ESCHEW MEAT AND DINE AT
THE "ARCADIAN"
FOOD REFORM RESTAURANT,
132 ST. VINCENT STREET,
GLASGOW
TO BE OPENED SHORTLY.

BOOKS! BOOKS!
IF you watch this Space each SATURDAY you will find the names of the NEW BOOKS in Literature, which we can honestly recommend.
Orders by Post receive prompt attention.
ESTIMATES GIVEN
JOHN SMITH & SON,
19 RENFIELD ST. AND 225 INGRAM ST.,
GLASGOW.
National: 158 "Argyll."
Corporation: 1158. Established 1712.

EVERY WORKER AND THINKER SHOULD READ,
"THE LABOUR LEADER"
The National Organ of the Socialist and Labour Movement.
Gives the most Complete Record of the Work of the Labour Party, in Parliament and the Country. Splendid Articles every week on Socialism and Politics at Home and Abroad
TO BE HAD FROM ALL NEWS-AGENTS,
PRICE—ONE PENNY.

COME AND HEAR
THE WOMEN SUFFRAGISTS
Who went to Prison for their Principles.
MRS. PANKHURST.
MISS PANKHURST.
MISS KENNY.
MISS BILLINGTON.
CITY HALL
ON MONDAY, 15TH OCTOBER, AT EIGHT P.M.
If you are in sympathy Come and Hear. If you disapprove of their methods, Come and hear why these methods are adopted.
Admission, 6d. and 3d. Reserved Seats, 1s. Back Area and Back Gallery—Free.

Tickets may be had at Robertson's Restaurant, 24 West Nile Street, Glasgow.

BECOME YOUR OWN
LANDLORD
The BRITISH HOMES SCHEME is the ideal easy system by which you can obtain, as thousands have done, complete and absolute ownership of your house. No other scheme offers such splendid facilities. Well-chosen property is the greatest blessing any person can possess, and is a life long security. Send at once for Free Particulars.
GOOD PROSPECTS FOR ACTIVE AGENTS.
THE BRITISH HOMES ASSURANCE CORPORATION, LIMITED.
PAUL STREET, FINSBURY, LONDON, E.C. M. GREGORY, Managing Director

ALSTON'S TEA ROOMS,
201 INGRAM STREET, Glasgow (Opposite General Post Office), And at 96 HOPE STREET (Near Central Station)
7 a.m. till 8 p.m. SMOKING ROOM, LADIES' ROOM, and all Conveniences.
NEWSPAPERS, MAGAZINES, DRAUGHTS.

The Motherwell Labour Party and Coming Municipal Elections

By DALZIEL.

The Motherwell Branch of the Independent Labour Party are running three candidates for the Town Council—Mr. James M'Clurg for the First Ward, Mr. Andrew Russell for the Fourth Ward, and Mr. Thomas Mowat for the Fifth Ward. This is the first time in the history of the burgh that the Socialists have attempted to get a footing in the Council Chamber, and naturally there has been some considerable "fluttering in the dovecots" of the respectables. Apart from the Labour Party, the whole of the elections are being fought over the question of the licenses of two public-houses which, on the death of the late licensee, the Magistrates refused to transfer to his trustees on behalf of his widow. This, of course, rouses the whole publican party in the town. They are now doing all in their power to prevent the return of any Temperance candidates. The Temperance party are working tooth and nail to keep out the nominees of the "trade."

The I.L.P. opened their campaign last Wednesday, when Mr. Thos. Mowat, who is opposing two of the sitting Magistrates (two seats vacant) held his first meeting. In opening, he said he was an avowed Socialist, and was going to fight the election on Socialism. The weak-kneed amongst the brethren are inclined to think that this was a tactical blunder, and that Socialism should be kept in the background, as the average elector has got a very distorted idea of what Socialism is, and consequently will not, even if he has what is termed "Labour sympathies," vote for a Socialist. However, as Comrade Mowat is more anxious to spread the cause of Socialism than to get into the Town Council, he will continue to preach Socialism throughout the campaign.

One of the chief planks in the Labour Party's programme is Municipal Housing. Only those acquainted with Scottish mining towns and villages realise the awful s[illegible] that are erected as dwellings for the miners.

There is nothing in the cities to equal some of the slums of Motherwell. The question of building workmen's dwellings was discussed in the Council some years ago, but as half of the members of the Council are landlords, factors, builders, contractors, and are nearly all in one clique, they made short work of the scheme. The latest act of this landlord gang ought to convince the working-men that it is impossible for this class to represent the workers even in a far-off way.

A burn, which is an open sewer, flows by the side of the town, the stench from which is awful. Protests have been made by the ratepayers time without number. The grave danger that is constituted to the health of the community was taken no notice of. All hope of getting this matter remedied was abandoned long ago; but, lo! in the twinkling of an eye the whole affair is settled. A scheme is rushed through the Council, and now this filthy marsh is to be covered in, and the water conducted in pipes several hundred yards away from the public road. What is the secret of all this sudden activity? Is it a remorse of conscience, or has intelligence at last penetrated the brain-power of our Councillors? No! Nothing so absurd. Simply the Duke of Hamilton, who is anxious to feu the ground, has cut down the wood which runs along the roadside on both banks of this "sylvan stream," and we may soon exepct to see some nice eligible villas spring up. And of course it really would be out of the question to expect anyone to inhabit these villas so long as this "sweet babbling brook" remained in its pristine beauty. It would never do for the children of the middle class to run the risk of catching fever or any such diseases. If it had been a miners' row that was going to be erected it would not have mattered about the children of the miners—a few of them would never be missed.

This is only a very small act of many.

An agitation was raised some time ago to get the Council to purchase the gas-works from a private company which runs them, and which has always paid a good dividend, most of the Councillors being

SHAREHOLDERS IN THE GASWORKS.

Naturally, the agitation very soon received its quietus. There were plenty of excuses found why the Gasworks should not be purchased, but no excuse could cover up the fact that the profits of the concern, which were going into the pockets of a few shareholders ought to belong to the ratepayers of the burgh. There will undoubtedly be more than one shady transaction exposed by the Labour Party when they capture a few seats. The Temperance Party which always poses as the party of purity and progress, have not proven themselves one whit better than their opponents. Not once have they tackled any of the municipal problems other than the drink traffic, and with reference to it, they have made confusion worse confounded.

The Corporation recently were compelled to undertake a Sewage Purification Scheme, which was estimated to cost £50,000. The whole thing was handed over to a contractor, who has been working at it for some years; and the estimate has now risen from £50,000 to £80,000—and it is likely to cost the ratepayers still another £20,000. When information is asked about this scheme no one can give it; no one knows anything about it; and, what is worse, no one understands anything about it! The contractor was given carte blance to do as he pleased, and he has acted on this principle to the letter. More will be heard of this affair before it is finished. If ever there was a Council that needed a few straightforward and fearless exponents of Socialism to combat the influence of the jerry builder, the grasping landlord, the Colvilles (who industrially own the town), and the aristocratic Hamiltons (who own the whole of the surrounding land), it is the Motherwell Town Council. A supreme effort should therefore be made to get the three candidates returned at November.

Glasgow Townhead Ward Election.

Bailie Forsyth's Position.

On Tuesday night the annual meeting of the electors in the 8th (Townhead) Ward took place in St. James' Hall, Stirling Road. The chair was occupied by Dr. Jos. N. Glaister

Bailie Forsyth referred at the outset to the missive question. The Corporation had done all they could to enable the matter to be brought prominently before the various Members of Parliament. He felt safe in saying that every Member of Parliament in the West of Scotland had pledged themselves to support the Bill which had been brought forward by Mr. Cross. An effort was being made to have the rates collected with the rents when the monthly system of rents became general, and he approved of that system, as it would be caluclated to prove more convenient for most people. Unfortunately, Mr. Cross and others, when they brought forward the Bill, could get nothing more tangible than sympathetic reference, and the Lord Advocate said it was almost impossible for the Government to give a private member opportunity to bring this matter before Parliament. The Lord Advocate told the deputation, of which he was one, that they would need to go on educating the public on the question, and bring it before Parliament when the subject was ripe. (Laughter.) As if the missive question had not been discussed ad nauseum all over Scotland. (Hear, hear.) Till the subject was ripe for legislation, forsooth! Why, the matter was ripe years ago. It was rotten ripe. (Laughter.) The deputation turned round and told the Lord Advocate he ought to grant facilities for the Government passing the bill into law at once. It now rested upon the people of the West of Scotland to see that this question did not go to rest.

DISTRESS COMMITTEE.

Last year, proceeded the Bailie, they had a large number of men who could not find employment, and the year previous it cost the Common Good nearly £[illegible] dealing with the unemployed, and even then only the fringe of the matter was touched. Now the Corporation felt it was no use trying to solve the question by giving the men work to do which would displace men regularly employed elsewhere. If the unemployed were given wood chopping or stone breaking, as was done last year, you threw out of work men engaged permanently at these jobs. Some of the Distress Committee thought the only practical solution was to be found in bringing the people who needed work into contact with the land. (Hear, hear.) Already this season he had large numbers of men at him, men who were quite fit, but whose hair was turning grey, and considered too old for the commercial strain of to-day—asking to be recommended for work. He found men coming to him and to others who had given thirty years' service in the same firm, and who were

Cast on the Scrap Heap

of humanity. That class of men wanted recommendations to the heads of the Corporation departments, but unless there were vacancies they could notget jobs. The heads of departments had been communicated with, but they could not offer many opportunities for employing these men. Now, with the land held by the Corporation round about Glasgow they might find employment for a great number of men, with the result that the land would be enriched by cultivation, and they would not then upset the labour market. (Applause.) He referred to the success of the "lots" system in Philadelphia, and thought something in this direction could be successfully followed at Ardkinglas and the Pole Farm, of which the folks of the city had of late been hearing so much. He was disappointed that the Tramway Committee were not disposed to run a line along Cathedral Street. However, he had been assured by Mr. Alexander that the matter was not likely to be hung up for years, but that the proposal would continue to receive attention. They must be cautious in the constructing of new lines, Mr. Alexander said. He regretted, too, being defeated by a large majority in endeavouring to get direct communication with the West End. Speaking on the tram fares, he favoured an extension of the half system, and was in favour of a part of the surplus [illegible] the rates. (Hear, hear.) But not an equal reduction. The men who contributed most to the tramways were those living in houses at £20 and under. Those under £10 rental might be relieved of anything from 4d., 5d., to 6d. per £; up to £20, relieved of 2d. or 3d. per £, and those big merchants above that rental less per pound. 140,000 people would thus be benefited by the larger sum, and that left 60,000 in houses over £20. It would be a step in the interest of the working class. He concluded by saying he intended offering his services for another term. (Loud applause.)

MEETING NOT ADVERTISED.

Thomas Dickson—Are you aware this meeting has not been properly advertised, as you will see by the empty seats in the gallery. I think a man with a board should be sent to St. Rollox and other works a day before the meeting, and advertised also.

No answer was given.

Joseph Ginlay, 30 Drummond Street—If Bailie Forsyth is returned to the Council, will he be in favour of giving Councillor A. S. Gibson a Bailieship? (Applause.)

Bailie Forsyth—I decline to answer that question. ("Booh," and applause.)

In answer to further questions, Bailie Forsyth said he could not meantime be a party to giving the use of baths for galas at a cheaper rate. The public would suffer the loss.

VOTE OF CONFIDENCE.

A unanimous vote of confidence was passed in Bailie Forsyth, and that gentleman, replying, said he would be pleased to go back for another term.

The meeting closed at 10.20.

SERIOUS COLLIERY DISPUTE AT BLANTYRE.

A special Executive meeting of the Lanarkshire Miners' County Union was held in the miners' office on Monday night, 8th inst., to consider the serious state of matters that has arisen at William Baird and Coy's, Priory Colliery, Blantyre. The dispute has originated through the management introducing blacklegs into a section of the colliery, where the men are already on strike against a partial reduction of from 2d. to 4d. per ton.

A deputation waited on the manager, requesting the withdrawal of the blacklegs. The manager refused, and abruptly ended the negotiations by intimating his intention of letting the disputed places to a contractor.

The whole of the men resent this arbitrary treatment, and have remained idle in sympathy with their fellow-workers since Thursday, 4th inst.

170

First issue of *Forward* in 1906, a Scottish independent labour weekly paper founded and edited by Thomas Johnston.

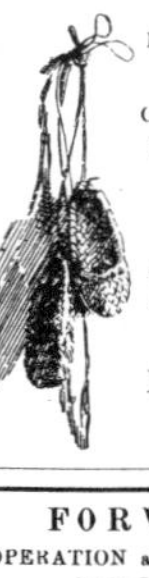

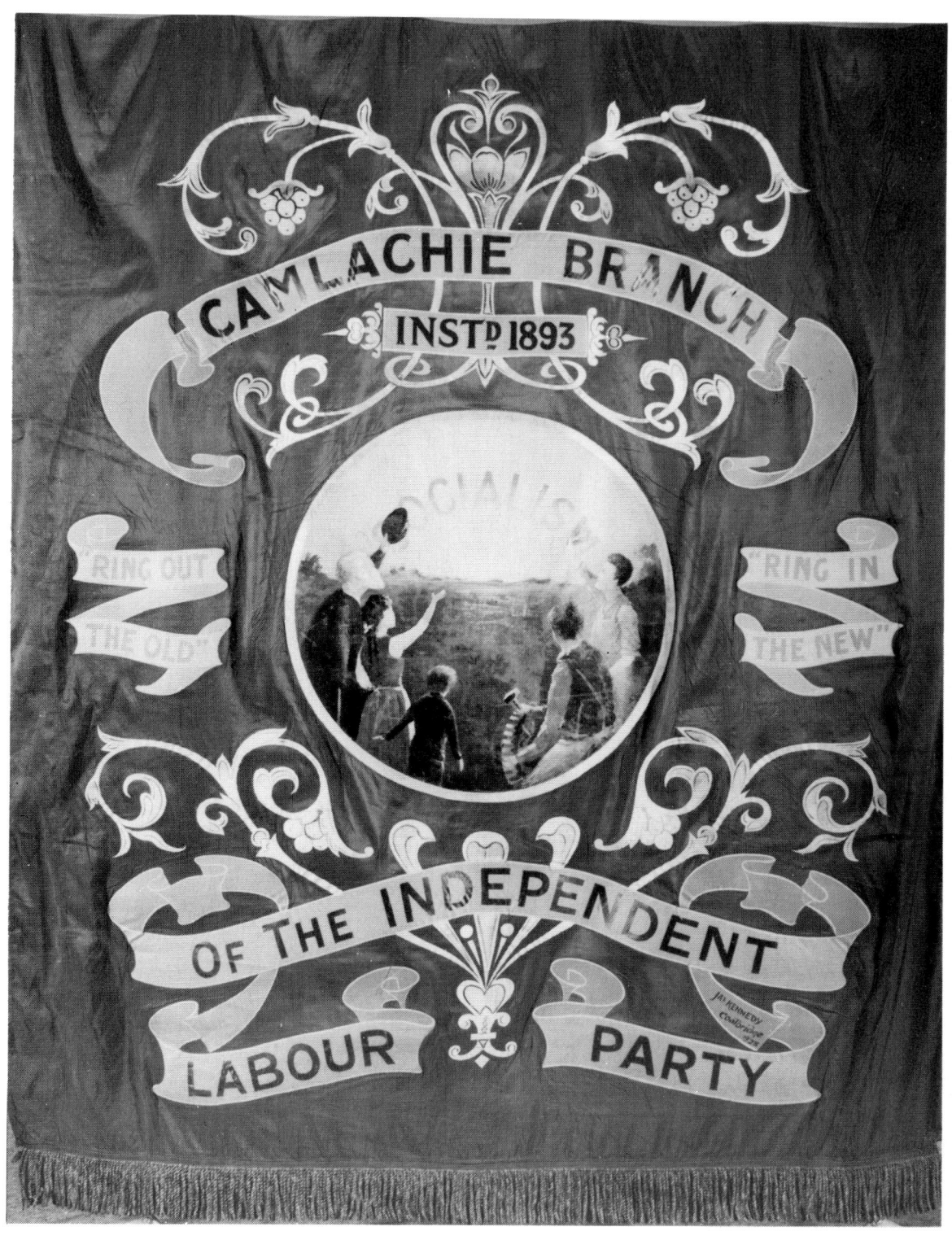

171

The Independent Labour Party was the largest socialist group in Scotland before the
1914-18 War. A Scottish Council of the Party was established in 1906.

Socialist Sunday School

Meets every Sunday at 3 P.M:

Junior Choir Practice

Every Tuesday at 7-15 P.M.

Adult Class for Reading and Discussion

Meets every Friday at 8 P.M.

Socialist Literature

On Sale at all Meetings.

D. McMillan. Printer, Dumfries.

Independent Labour Party
DUMFRIES BRANCH
Rooms: 41 English Street

Syllabus

for Winter Session, 1910-11

Chairman,	- -	F. SMITH
Vice-Chairman,	- -	R. GLOVER
Treasurer,	- -	T. MILLS
Secretary,	- -	G. PERCY

BUSINESS MEETING
Every Tuesday, at 8 p.m.

CONTRIBUTIONS 6d per month.

New Members enrolled at all Meetings.

172

173

Robert Blatchford's weekly labour paper, *The Clarion* (1891-1935), gathered around itself various supporting groups, such as Clarion Scouts, Clarion Cycling Clubs, Clarion Choirs, and Clarion Vans. This is a group of Glasgow Clarion Scouts before 1914.

University Rectorial Election, 1908.

The Socialist Torch

Contents:

The Ethics of Socialism, by the Rev. R. J. CAMPBELL.

Lord Curzon in India, by H. E. A. COTTON (Editor of *India*).

Sir Henry Campbell Bannerman's Political Career—An Indictment.

An Appeal to the Undergraduates.

Our Candidate.

(No. 1)—THURSDAY, 19th MARCH, 1908.

Published by the UNIVERSITY SOCIALIST SOCIETY,

174

Socialist student groups were developing in Scottish universities before the 1914-18 War. The *Socialist Torch* was published during the Glasgow University rectorial election of 1908, when Keir Hardie was the socialist candidate.

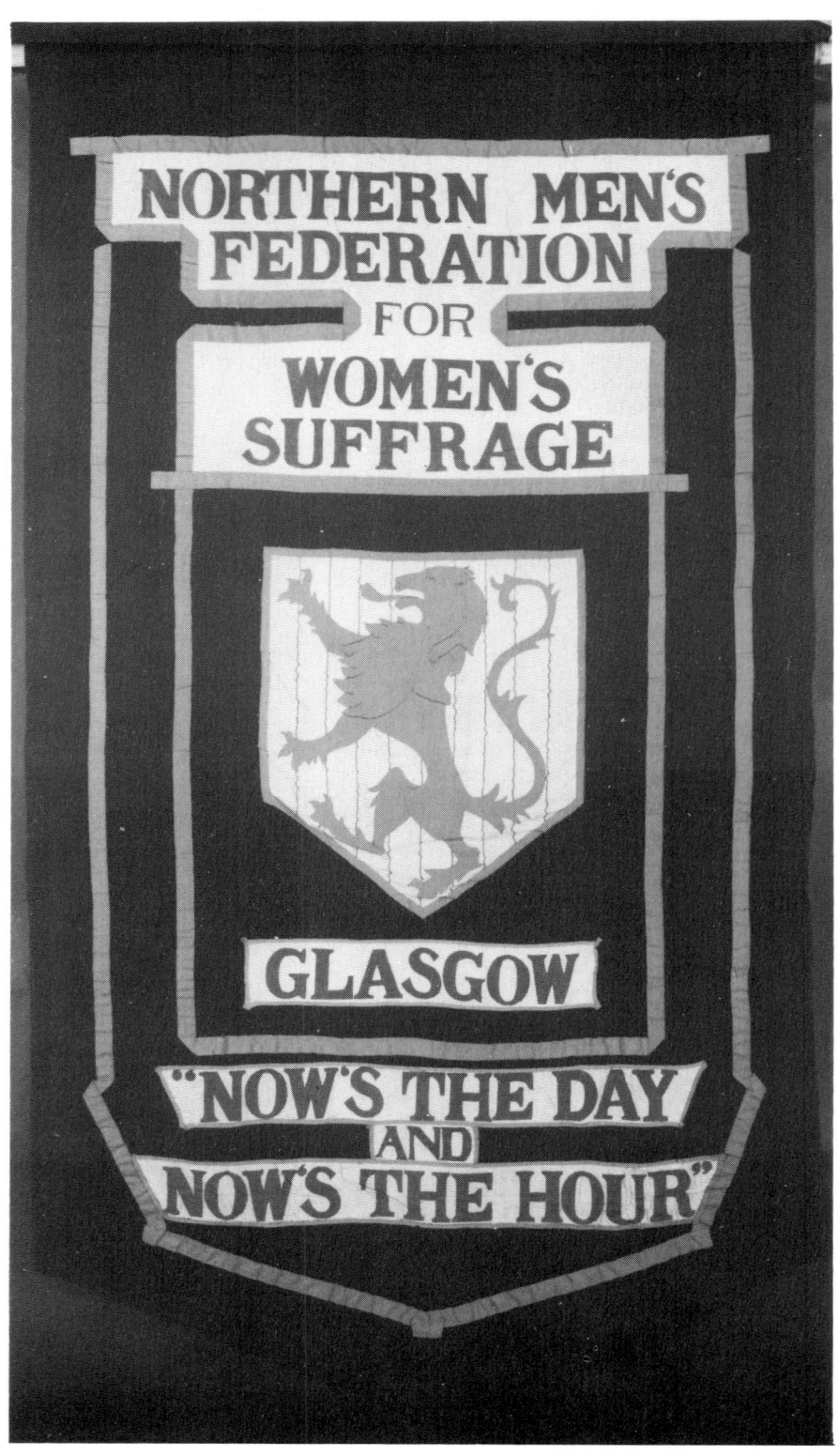

175

Many trade unionists and socialists supported the demand for the Right to Vote by women, agitation for which was carried on strongly by the Suffragettes before 1914.

FORWARD, SATURDAY, SEPTEMBER 6, 1913.

FORWARD

No. 47, Vol. 7. [REGISTERED FOR TRANSMISSION AS A NEWSPAPER] GLASGOW, SATURDAY, SEPTEMBER 6, 1913. 48 Columns. ONE PENNY.

Massacre of Working Class in Dublin.

Five Hundred Injured—Leaders in Jail—Lies about Larkin—Appeal to pay no Rent—Boss Murphy's blow—Free Speech Prohibited.

A Challenge to Scotland.

The conditions of the Tramway men in the employment of Boss Murphy, the great Dublin capitalist, are scarcely believable. *The men get 4/6 a day of twelve hours.* Murphy also owns the *Independent* newspaper, big drapery shops, has controlling railway interests, trams in Madrid and in Paisley, and is the great capitalist *par excellence*. Gradually the Labour struggles in Dublin have narrowed down to a big class contest; on the one hand we have the working class headed by Jim Larkin and on the other the federated and massed capitalist class headed by Murphy, who has also strong influence on the Government.

Murphy began operations: he first organised the employers, and then began the sacking of every known member of the Transport Workers' Union from every kind of employment that the Murphy gang controlled.

Larkin knew, of course, that Murphy would have the military and the police on his side: that the subsidised press would play the Capitalist game savagely and unscrupulously: that the press cables would be controlled: and that the Murphy group had unlimited money. Larkin also knew (and in this we are giving away no secret) that he would have to battle for Labour on an attenuated exchequer, and that at the first stroke—nay, before the first stroke for Labour—every working class leader would be arrested with or without warrants.

The sacking of the Transport Workers then began, and Larkin was given power by his organisation to call a general strike against the Murphy interests, swiftly and suddenly, at whatever moment he chose.

This he did; and was promptly arrested and charged with "inciting to class hatred" and "inciting against the Government," two crimes which can be laid at the door of every Socialist in the country. Also Jim Connolly, the Irish Correspondent of the *Forward*, Councillor Partridge and Comrades Farrelly, Meehan, Revelle, Bolger, Nolan, Brophy, and Butler were arrested. Newsboys were arrested for "intimidating" the sale of Murphy's Nationalist paper. A woman, Mrs. Rosanna Kennedy, described by the *Freeman's Journal* (also Capitalist, Nationalist and anti-Larkin) as "a respectable-looking woman, who stood in the dock holding an infant in her arms," was given 21 days without the option of a fine by Magistrate Swifte for throwing a loaf of bread at a blackleg and hissing and booing and throwing a can of porter at another.

The gauntlet had been thrown down. War had been declared.

Larkin's Manifesto.

But before Larkin was arrested, he had issued a manifesto which was widely placarded on the walls of Dublin:

"We regret," it said, "the inconvenience caused by the withdrawal of the men who worked the trams. There would have been no intention on the part of the Union or the men affected to do anything to inconvenience the public during the present Show week, but owing to the action of William Martin Murphy, the Chairman of the D.U.T.C., in dismissing some 200 men for no justifiable reason—there being no demand made on the Company for wages or conditions—the men were compelled to take action in defence of their rights. Mr. W. M. Murphy [illegible] is President of the Chamber of Commerce, which body is at present engaged in forming a Conciliation Board to allow [illegible] trade disputes. This tyrannical act of the Chamber of Commerce President will prove to every man, woman, or child with an interest in Dublin's welfare the kind of employer Dublin workers have to submit to."

The manifesto denounced in violent terms Mr. W. M. Murphy; Alderman Cotton, M.P.; Mr. Joseph Mooney, J.P.; and Colonel Vesey, of Lucan, on whom it sought to throw the responsibility for the lock-out. It concluded with an appeal to the public sympathy and support, asked the public not to patronise the cars, and accused Mr. Murphy and his friends of having made £160,000 in sixteen years out of a private monopoly, and at the expense of the ratepayers. It stated that the tramway "slaves" of Dublin work 12 hours a week longer than the Belfast tram men, and receive 20 per cent. less wages. The manifesto closed by demanding the reinstatement of the dismissed men unconditionally, improved wages, shorter hours, and the right of appeal against the secret reports of inspectors.

Cars were now held up in the streets and Murphy's blacklegs, assisted by the police, had a desperate time of it. At 7 p.m. at night, every car had to be taken off. On the Tuesday night at Liberty Hall (this was before his arrest) Larkin addressed a huge crowd and said:

They had already won the first victory in the struggle, for the trams could not run at night. They had taught Mr. Murphy a lesson, but they would teach him a greater one before he was many days older. The workers had been prevented from parading some of the streets of Dublin on Saturday night. They were now organising the greatest demonstration that had ever been seen in Dublin, and would march wherever they liked, despite the threat of the supply of police and military which was offered to Mr. Murphy by Lord Aberdeen. They would go into O'Connell Street or any other street they liked—they would, in fact, go wherever William Martin Murphy's motor cars were permitted to go. (Cheers.) They said he was already beaten, but the mighty Liberal Government and the brave and muscular Scotsman who occupied the Viceregal Lodge bowed the knee to him (Larkin) before, and they would do so again. (Cheers.) Subsequently Larkin said—Police brutality has been shown to-night. I would advise the friends and supporters of this cause to take Sir Edward Carson's advice to the men of Ulster. If he says it is right and legal for the men of Ulster to arm, why should it not be right and legal for the men of Dublin to arm themselves, so as to protect themselves? You will need it. I don't offer advice which I am not prepared to adopt myself. You know me, and you know when I say a thing I will do it. So arm, and I'll arm. You have to face hired assassins. If Sir Edward Carson is right in telling the men of Ulster to form a Provisional Government in Belfast, I think I must be right, too, in telling you to form a Provisional Government in Dublin. But whether you form a Provisional Government or not, you will require arms, for Aberdeen has promised Murphy not only the police, but the soldiers; and my advice to you is to be round the doors and corners, and whenever one of your men is shot, shoot two of theirs. (Cheers.) Now we will hold our next big meeting in O'Connell Street, come what may, and we will show them that we can use the property for which we pay. (Cheers.)

Larkin was then arrested, and was let out on bail. Then Mr. Swifte, the Chief Divisional Magistrate, proclaimed the projected Sunday demonstration as illegal. Larkin followed this announcement up with an appeal to the citizens to cease paying rent; he also publicly burned Swifte's proclamation and announced that dead or alive he would address the Sunday demonstration in O'Connell Street. He began by saying:

That the employers had decided to lock-out the members of the Irish Transport Workers' Union, and in consequence he asked those present to repeat the following pledge—"I will pay no rent until the tramwaymen have got the conditions they demand. (Cheers.) The house-owners could not evict a town."

"To-morrow," he continued, "we are going to issue our proclamation. It will not be signed by the King or by Swifte. I never knew yet that any Divisional Magistrate had the right to proclaim a meeting. We are going to ask the Lord Mayor to issue a counter proclamation giving the freedom of Dublin to the men who are going to speak on Sunday. (Cheers.) The Lord Mayor of Belfast has the right to call out troops or to proclaim a meeting, or to let it go on, but the Lord Mayor of Dublin, the capital of Ireland, is a nonentity. Well, we are patriots, and we believe that the Lord Mayor of Dublin is superior to Mr. Swifte. (Cheers.) If the Lord Mayor is too cowardly, we will issue our own proclamation. (Cheers.)

PROCLAMATION BURNED.

Mr. Larkin then, amidst cheers, set fire to the copy of the proclamation which had been served on him. "I care as much," he said, "for the King as I do for Swifte, the Magistrate. People make Kings, and people can unmake them, but what has the King of England got to do with stopping a meeting in Dublin?" (Cheers.) If they liked to stop the meeting at the dictation of Wm. Martin Murphy, Wm. Martin Murphy will take the responsibility, and as I have previously told you, for every man that falls on our side two will fall on the other. (Cheers.)

"We have a perfect right to meet in O'Connell Street," the speaker continued. "We are going to meet in O'Connell Street, and if the police or soldiers are going to stop us or try to stop us, let them take the responsibility. No one will be wanted there on Sunday but men that will stand. If Belfast Orangemen can hold a meeting, why not we? If they want revolution—well, God be with them!

"The police had said that they would take his life," Mr. Larkin said. "He knew the man who said it. He would give them a chance of doing so, but in doing so they would do what he wanted—raise a new spirit—(cheers)—and it would not be a question of paying no rent but of His Majesty losing another part of the Empire, and the sooner the better. (Cheers.) He recognised no law, but the people. (Cheers.) If William Martin Murphy was to be the lawgiver for Dublin, either he or the speaker would be broken. Keir Hardie had wired to him stating that the action taken by the Government in this fight would be dealt with by the organised workers of Great Britain. (Cheers.) From a meeting in Manchester next week the Government would get a rock that would rock it into the cradle of the deep. (Laughter and cheers.)

"Lloyd George," said the speaker, "is coming to Dublin. He had better go to Belfast. He will get a quieter meeting. (Cheers.) It will not be with Suffragettes he will have to deal with here. (Cheers.) He is coming to talk about Home Rule, and we will not be allowed to hold a meeting in our own town. We don't want Home Rule at that price! (Cheers.) Lloyd George won't buy me with an insurance stamp. (Cheers.) To-morrow we are going to raise a new standard of discontent, and a new battlecry in Ireland." (Cheers.)

Continuing, Mr. Larkin said that Mr. M'Cormick, of Tedcastle and M'Cormick, dismissed five men for refusing to deliver coal to the Deputy Lieutenant of Dublin, who had got his men on strike. The coal merchants at a meeting had declared a lock-out of the Transport Union workers.

"We want you to assemble in O'Connell St. at 12 o'clock on Sunday," he proceeded. "Board the tramcars. Go out on them as far as you can, and pay no money. (Laughter and cheers.) If they want to summon you, give them your name and address. The Tramway Company are losing more money than they will get back in 12 months. (Cheers.)

"Before to-morrow evening," Mr. Larkin declared, "there will be developments of a very far-reaching character." He announced that this evening five meetings would be held—one at Beresford Place, one at Terenure, a third at Ringsend, a fourth in Cabra, and a fifth in Inchicore. "Moral suasion" and "No rent" would win the victory for them. He advised the people to go home quietly.

THE POLICE BRUTALITY.

It was on stray sections of this crowd returning quietly home that the police zeal to execute their dastardly orders, was first made manifest. According to the *Freeman's Journal* (Saturday, 30th August), the police unprovoked rushed in gangs of 20 at peaceable civilians, knocking them down with their truncheons: even un-uniformed detectives were battered.

MURPHY'S LIES.

Even on Saturday while the police were searching high and low for Larkin, Murphy's weekly newspaper, the Irish *Weekly Independent*, came out with a dirty, lying attack upon Larkin, and Murphy himself gave one howl of exultation which unfortunately for himself, gave away his whole motive and case. Said he:

"I think I have broken the malign influence of Mr. Larkin and set him on the run. It is now up to the employers to keep him going."

(*Interview with Mr. Murphy, Irish "Weekly Independent,"* p. 7).

On the Sunday, as all the papers have reported, Larkin made a dramatic appearance on the balcony of one of Murphy's hotels, briefly addressed the crowd, and owing to the kitchen door being barred, was unable to make his exit by a back entrance before the police rushed in. The police, by the way, searched Murphy's hotel for Larkin at 11 a.m., so that they must have had some inkling of what was going to happen.

THE CARNAGE OUTSIDE.

Outside it seemed as if Hell were let loose. The police, without the slightest provocation, rushed upon unoffending spectators, clubbed, batoned and kicked them. Two were killed. Over 400 were injured. Here is part of Monday's *Freeman's Journal* description (which, by the way includes a *photograph shewing the police batoning men who are lying on the ground.*)

Some of the police charged down the street towards O'Connell Bridge, and others rushed the people into Prince's Street. Here they were met by a large body of police which were in reserve in Prince's Street, and for a few minutes a scene of terrible excitement and violence prevailed.

The people as they rushed were vigorously batoned from all sides, and in a few minutes as many as twenty people were bleeding on the ground at one time.

A youth who was in the middle of the charge was knocked down just at the corner of the Post Office. *He managed to get to his feet, and just as he did so he was surrounded by four or five constables, who plied their batons on him again, and followed him up the street past the Post Office.*

The dramatic suddenness of the whole affair was such that everyone in O'Connell Street was taken by surprise. Larkin sought to address the crowd, but the police rushed him down Sackville Place to the Police Station. Cheers and boos were raised. Immediately the police drew their batons and a terrific charge ensued [illegible] men and women were beaten indiscriminately. Soon there were scores of people scattered all over the street lying on the ground, their hands to their heads and bleeding from the wounds inflicted.

Mr. Handel Booth, Liberal M.P. for Pontefract, who is no friend of the organised working class, and who is up to the neck in Insurance, Property, etc., has made the following statement:

"I am not in a position to speak of the necessity or otherwise for the charge on the crowd, but I cannot under any circumstances understand why people when lying on the ground should be kicked. My wife saw more of the charges than I did, and she intends writing a leter to the papers about it."

Count Markievicz, another eye-witness, makes the same charge in stronger terms.

JAMES LARKIN

Stowaway—Sailor—Stevedore's Foreman—great Working Class Leader. Is over six feet in height, has the heart of a child, and would share his last shilling. Is the best hated man in Ireland by the Capitalist class, but so loved by the Poor that thousands would die for him.

James Connolly,

Our Irish Correspondent, who has got Three Months in Jail.

James Connolly, whose weekly article from Ireland has recently been such a marked feature of the *Forward*, has had a long and an honourable record of service in the Socialist movement. Over 20 years ago he was an employee in the Cleansing Department of the Edinburgh Town Council at the weekly salary of £1 per week. All his spare time was spent either in the Libraries rummaging about among the materials which were one day to give him the basis for his well-known volume, "Labour in Irish History," or spent with Bob Allan and John Leslie at the street corner, speaking for the old Social Democratic Federation. Finally he was sacked for being a Socialist, and went to Ireland, where he attempted to form a Labour Party. Then he went to the United States and edited the Socialist *Harp*. Several years ago he came back to Ireland and since then has thrown himself body and soul into the creation of an Irish Socialist opinion which shall be ready for action on the day that the Home Rule Bill is passed. He is an exceedingly able speaker and writer.

IF LARKIN GETS A LONG SENTENCE, CONNOLLY WILL HAVE SECURITIES FOUND AT ONCE, AND WILL COME OUT OF PRISON TO LEAD THE STRIKE.

Resolution.

EVERY WORKING CLASS BODY IN SCOTLAND, PLEASE NOTE.

12 Waterloo Street,
Glasgow, 2nd Sept., 1913.

Dear Comrade,

Every public meeting and every branch meeting held this week and the next under the auspices of the I.L.P. in Scotland should be made a Protest meeting against the brutal police outrages at Dublin. Get the following, or a similar resolution passed, and sent on immediately to your local Member of Parliament. Get every Trade Union with which you are connected to do the same thing, and take every possible means to get expressed the indignation of the workers.

Yours fraternally,
WILLIAM STEWART.

"That this meeting condemns in the most emphatic manner the Government and the Lord Lieutenant of Ireland for their actions in prohibiting the holding of a public meeting in Dublin, and for the brutal manner in which the citizens of that city were treated by the police, which resulted in the loss of two lives and injuries to several hundreds of people, and further calls upon the Chief Secretary of Ireland to at once re-establish the right of public meeting, and to instigate a very rigid enquiry into the conduct of the police; and, further, this meeting demands that, in view of these very serious events, a Special Session of Parliament be immediately held to enable the actions of the Government to be discussed in the proper place."

Murphy's Lie about Larkin.

Murphy the great Nationalist exploiter has said publicly in his paper that Larkin is a "convicted and mean thief." This is a low, despicable lie, and I, who was at the time Treasurer of the Larkin Defence Fund, and know all the circumstances, say so. I say

(1) That Jim Larkin was guilty of no moral offence, was not charged with personal appropriation of other people's money, and that he left the dock with his honour unbesmirched and his integrity unblemished.

(2) That, at the worst, he was guilty only of a technical misdemeanour.

The circumstances of the whole case, briefly put, are these:—Jim Larkin, organiser for the National Union of Dock Labourers, went down to Cork to organise for that Union. He was paid by that Union, and having some dispute with headquarters, he impetuously formed, or was privy to the formation of a new Union, called the Irish Transport Workers' Union. This new Union absorbed the fees and membership of the dockers in Cork who had really joined the National Union of Dock Labourers. This was the Capitalists' chance. Some five of the dockers were induced (*a la* Osborne case) to complain to the Courts that their fees, intended for the N.U.D.L., had been handed over to the Irish Transport Workers' Union. At the back of the five complainants were the sinister figures of the directors of the Shipping Federation, who had never forgiven Larkin for the trouble he gave them during the great Belfast strike. A prosecution of Larkin and the other officials of the Transport Workers' ensued. In the first trial, Sir Edward Fitzgerald, one of the judges, wanted to dismiss the whole case, but the Shipping Federation hung on. Gradually the "small fry" among the defendants were dropped out of the Shipping Federation net. Larkin was their quarry, and they finally hunted him into twelve months' imprisonment with hard labour. And this sentence was only secured after the Jury had been deliberately purged of everybody except shipowners, shippers or those connected in some way with shipping interests. Even the Judge, in giving the sentence, said that Larkin had been led to act as he did by an excess of "enthusiasm"—not a motive usually of anything mean or despicable!

Then every public body in industrial Ireland contributed its signatories to a demand for Larkin's release: great public meetings were held, and the Lord Lieutenant of Ireland was compelled to issue a free pardon.

Then, as shewing what Dublin thought of Larkin, he was elected by an enormous majority to the City Council, and after sitting there for a week and taking part in two or three divisions, the Shipping Federation touts again swept down on him and in the Law Courts it was adjudged that he had been illegally elected, inasmuch as he had been a convicted felon and that a free pardon did not wipe out the conviction. Larkin was ordered to pay heavy costs, was unseated, and was forbidden to enter a public body for five years. That was persecution number two, and it shews what the Master class and their dirty lackeys are capable of. I, for one, am proud to claim Larkin as my friend, to vouch for his spotless honour and integrity, and to make his quarrels mine. When William Martin Murphy says that Larkin is a "mean thief," he (Murphy) is a liar.

The Working Class of Scotland must keep the Dependants of the Martyrs.

Money Wanted—NOW.

This Dublin struggle is the biggest and bravest effort made by the working class in Britain for years, and the Capitalist atrocities with which it is being met are the most ruthless and brutal extremities to which the Boss spirit has been driven since the century began. On the one hand, the sheer heroism of the unarmed and semi-starving populace holding out against the baton-armed might of the Capitalist Exploiters: on the other a nervous savagery, a shameless disregard of human life, and a desperate effort to crush the incipient Labour demand for some of the decencies of civilised life, to the dust.

What, then! Where do we come in?

We, the organised workers of Scotland, must see to it that the dependents of the prisoners are fed during the incarceration of their bread-winners; we must see to it that they do not starve; our answer to Boss Murphy and his gang must be to dip our hands in our pockets: we must begin from now to shew Capitalism that every standard-bearer of ours shall have his courage tempered by the knowledge that his dear ones shall be the care of his fellow workers.

Your cash, then, friends, and at once. Whatever you can spare. It is Dublin's turn to-day. Dublin will assist you to-morrow.

I am taking it upon myself to appoint myself Treasurer. I am issuing collecting cards to the Socialist branches and the Trade Unions. We in Scotland saved Larkin before. We must save Larkin and his friends again.

If you can gather any money, write at once for a card. All subscriptions will be acknowledged through *Forward*. He gives twice who gives quickly. This is a real fight. And black shame to every sympathiser who refuses assistance.

THOMAS JOHNSTON.

176

The Dublin tramway strikers in 1913, and the general demand for Irish Home Rule, also received support from most sections of organised labour in Scotland. This is an extract from *Forward*, the Glasgow weekly independent labour paper.

177

For trade unionism there were several important developments between 1900 and 1914.
One was the gradually increasing role of women in the unions. Women were agitating
increasingly in those years for better conditions of employment, subject as many of them
were to the long hours and miserable wages of such sweated industries as tailoring and
laundries. The women shown here were delegates to the Scottish T.U.C. at Dundee in
1911.

178

A strike by Paisley mill girls, 1907.

179

Women in a Dundee jute mill. When the Dundee and District Union of Jute and Flax Workers was formed in 1906 the average wage of women jute workers was 77 pence a week—for men, it was £1.03.

180

181

Many women were involved in the strike by networkers at Kilbirnie in Ayrshire in 1913.

182

Another feature of the years before 1914 was the growth of white collar unionism. The Association of Engineering and Shipbuilding Draughtsmen was formed in Glasgow in 1913. The photograph is of draughtsmen at work in a drawing office in Greenock.

183

Strikes and lock-outs, some of them national and affecting hundreds of thousands of workers, were another salient feature of the pre-War years. Clyde shipyard workers, for instance, were locked out in 1908. Soon afterward there was a national lock-out of boilermakers arising partly from a dispute at Partick in 1910. This is a photograph of the T.T.S.S. *Munich* laid up at John Brown's yard at Clydebank during the 1908 lock-out. Three years later seamen in Scotland were involved in the great national strike of summer 1911 which won recognition for the seamen's union and also a substantial increase in wages.

184

Following the big strikes of dockers in England the previous year, Glasgow dockers struck work in January 1912. After a compromise settlement the men were locked out. The Scottish Union of Dock Labourers was formed in 1911, and this is the banner of its Glasgow Branch.

185

Leith dockers' procession during the dockers' struggles in 1912.

186

Leith dockers and their children on an outing to Stirling in July 1912.

187

A great national strike of railwaymen in 1911 was followed by the amalgamation in 1913 of several of the railway unions into the National Union of Railwaymen. This is the Edinburgh No. 1 Branch banner.

173

188

A still from a film made of the Dundee carters' strike in 1911.

189

The Executive Committee and officials of Lanarkshire Miners' County Union in 1903, with Robert Smillie, president, in centre of middle row. The publication of the pamphlet *The Miners' Next Step* by militant South Wales miners in 1912 contributed to the radicalisation of some Scots miners and to the formation of Miners' Reform Committees intent on increasing both internal Union democracy and pressure for improved wages and working conditions.

190

Miners at work underground at Camp Colliery, Motherwell, some time before the great national strike in 1912 for a minimum wage. A million miners were involved in the strike, which was the largest until then to take place in Britain.

191

The growing class consciousness of many workers, the big labour struggles of the period, and the disillusionment with or contempt for the recently formed Labour Party on the part of some of the more militant workers, helped explain the development in the years before 1914 of industrial unionism and syndicalism. The former was also to some extent a result of the impact of militant American unionism, the latter of French experience or example. Among the places in Scotland where industrial unionism found support was Singer's Sewing Machine factory at Clydebank. A big strike-cum-lock-out took place there in 1911, but the management broke the strike and the activists were dismissed from the company's employment. Many shop stewards of the 1914-18 War on Clydeside were men who had been activists at Singer's before 1911.

192

Another Clydeside establishment where industrial unionist and syndicalist influence made some headway was the Albion Motor Company. This photograph of the turners employed there in 1910-11, shows William Gallacher (second row from back, second from right), a later leading shop steward of 1914-18 and later still a leader of the Communist Party.

176

193

The years before the coming of the 1914 War were also an important period in the development of working class educational provision. This picture postcard shows members of the Amalgamated Society of Engineers in residence as full-time students at Ruskin College, Oxford, in 1906. It includes four Scots branch members: D. Tait, Pollokshaws; F. Stewart, Dennistoun; J.S. Taylor, Glasgow 3rd; and A. Rodgers, Pollokshaws. Some other Scots unions or branches, such as the Fife miners, also sent members to study at Ruskin. The dismissal of the Principal in 1908 precipitated a student strike and a secession of students and teachers. Consequently the Central Labour College was formed in London in 1909 as an independent labour college. In Scotland, John Maclean, the Clydeside revolutionary, and other Marxist agitators, held classes for workers in economics, industrial history and other subjects, and these classes were formed in 1916 into the Scottish Labour College. In 1909 the Workers' Educational Association began to organise classes in Scotland but it did not flourish before the War came.

194

Temperance was a pronounced feature of much labour organisation in Scotland until at least the 1914-18 War. This silk quilt, made in Dundee in 1904, is embroidered with the names of a hundred supporters of prohibition. A leading Dundee prohibitionist, Edwin Scrymgeour, who had been a member of the Independent Labour Party in the 1890s, was Prohibitionist and Labour M.P. for that city from 1922 to 1931.

THE TWENTIETH CENTURY:
1914-18

195

The Great War of 1914-18 had a profound impact on the labour movement in Scotland, as in other belligerent countries. Many workers rushed to join the forces, partly swept along by a wave of jingoism that is reflected in this government recruiting poster, partly driven by the urge to escape from the dull, grinding routine of factory, field, pit or workshop, with their low wages and long hours. Most people were at first convinced the War would last only a few weeks or months.

196

Front page of the British Socialist Party newspaper *Justice*, a few days after the outbreak of the War. The labour movement in Britain was divided over the War. The Labour Party and most of the official leaders of the unions were pro-War, while large sections of the Independent Labour Party, a majority of the British Socialist Party, and the Socialist Labour Party were anti-War.

197

Relatives and friends seeing off a trainload of volunteers to the War, at Newcastleton Station, Roxburghshire. The huge numbers of casualties and the unceasing demands for still more men led the Government in 1916 to impose conscription.

198

A mass meeting on Glasgow Green in 1916 against conscription. Socialists who refused to be conscripted into the army were, like conscientious objectors on religious grounds, sent to prisons such as Wormwood Scrubs and Dartmoor and some suffered severe hardship because of their opposition to the War.

199

The funeral of Keir Hardie in Glasgow in September 1915. Hardie, a pacifist, was deeply affected by the outbreak of the War and the failure of the Socialist International to oppose it. Yet some of his own statements about the War in the year before his death were, in the eyes of some socialists, equivocal.

200

One Scottish socialist who consistently and vehemently opposed the War was John Maclean, the Marxist revolutionary Clydeside schoolteacher. His anti-War speeches led to his imprisonment for five days in 1915 and to dismissal from his job as a teacher. In April 1916 he was sentenced to three years' penal servitude. In May 1918, following his early release from prison the previous summer as a result of pressure by the working class movement, Maclean was sentenced to a further five years' penal servitude for sedition.
This photograph shows Maclean (left), and some of his supporters.

201

The huge engineering and shipbuilding industries of Clydeside made Glasgow a leading centre of the War-time armaments and munitions industry. Thousands of workers came to Glasgow to work in War production. The appalling housing conditions became worse as private landlords raised rents and evicted tenants who could not pay, including wives and families of soldiers, the elderly and the unemployed. By October 1915 some 25,000 tenants were on rent strike in Glasgow. This is a photograph of one of the rent strike demonstrations that month.

184

202

Women took a leading part in the Rent Strikes. Many of the most active women rent strikers, such as Mrs Mary Barbour of Govan, were members of the Independent Labour Party.

203

Some leaders of the Rent Strike, outside Glasgow Sheriff Court in October 1915. Back row, fourth from left, is Andrew McBride, I.L.P. town councillor and secretary of the Glasgow Labour Housing Association, an outstanding organiser of the Strike. Back row, second from right, is Mrs Ferguson, secretary of the Women's Housing Association. The Rent Strike culminated in an industrial strike by shipyard workers and engineers against rent increases, and the government was forced to pass a Rent Restriction Act keeping rents at their pre-War 1914 levels and allowing an increase only if repairs were carried out.

204

The demand for labour for munitions and other War work led to 'dilution'—the employment of unskilled men and women on skilled work. These two women are at work in Stephen's Linthouse shipyard, Glasgow, about 1917.

205

Lloyd George, the Minister of Munitions—shown here seated centre—accompanied by Arthur Henderson, a Labour Party pro-War leader and member of the War-time Coalition cabinet, addressed a meeting of Clyde shop stewards at St Andrew's Hall, Glasgow, on Christmas Day 1915. The shop stewards' movement had developed earlier that year during a wages strike by engineers, and had formed the Clyde Workers' Committee, which played a leading part in the struggle over the dilution of labour. The shop stewards, many of whom were socialists opposed to the War, gave Lloyd George a hostile reception at St Andrew's Hall.

FORWARD, SATURDAY, JANUARY 1, 1916.

The Dilution of Labour—Mr. Lloyd George in Glasgow.

The best paid Munitions worker in Britain, Mr. Lloyd George (almost £100 per week), visited the Clyde last week-end in search of adventure.

He got it.

His meeting with the Clyde workers was to have taken place in the St. Andrew's Halls, on the Thursday night, but to everybody's great surprise, the newspapers on Thursday morning announced that the meeting was "off" until Saturday morning. The announcement excused it self by saying that the postponement from a night meeting, when men were not all working, to a forenoon meeting, when all the men should be working, was to suit the convenience of all concerned!

Not even Mr. Sexton Blake, the eminent detective could unravel *that!*

After all the arrangements had been made for the Thursday meeting, Messrs. Lorimer (Blacksmiths), Bunton (A.S.E.), and Sharp (Boilermakers), had been summoned by telegram to Newcastle to meet Mr. Lloyd George. Mr. Sharp did not go, but Messrs. Lorimer and Bunton went, and were informed by Mr. Lloyd George that he had changed his mind about the Thursday meeting, that he intended first to visit the workshops, and that the meeting would be postponed to the Saturday (Xmas) morning

The Committee of Trades Representatives, responsible for the Thursday meeting, met on Thursday evening, and after two hours' discussion, decided by 29 votes to 7 not to have anything to do with the Saturday meeting, owing to the shortness of time and their inability to secure a thoroughly representative gathering.

This resolution was again put to the meeting, and by 34 votes to 3 re-affirmed. It was then resolved unanimously that before any future meeting was arranged for the Ministry of Munitions that an aggregate meeting of Shop Stewards and Trade Union Officials be held, for the purpose of discussing and formulating a policy to be pursued at any future meeting with Mr. Lloyd George. Immediately after these decisions had been arrived at, someone had telephoned the result to Mr. Lloyd George's party, who viewed the decision so seriously that they desired to discuss the matter with the delegates at once. In a few minutes the Right Hon. Arthur Henderson, M.P., and three Government officials, appeared on the scene, and the whole business was re-opened. After a statement from Mr. Henderson, questions were asked and some were answered. It was then moved by Mr. Bunton (A.S.E.), and seconded by Bailie Whitehead (Brassfinishers), that the meeting rescind the previous resolutions agreed to, but by 20 votes to 13 the meeting refused to rescind their previous decisions, and, therefore, the Saturday meeting was declared off as an Official Representative Trade Union Meeting. The hour was now 11.45 p.m., and the delegates went home, but through the night letters were delivered at their homes and offices, signed by "Muray, of Elibank," asking them to meet at the Central Station Hotel, on Friday morning at 10 o'clock, and hear an appeal from Lord Murray as to reasons why they should reconsider their decision of the previous evening.

Less than half the delegates turned up at the Friday morning meeting, the absentees being chiefly men at work. It transpired that, despite the decision of *tion*, and cost the country 6/ per head in wages—this 6/ being the sum the Unions are to pay each member attending the meeting; the Unions are to be remembered by the Ministry of Munitions. In hard cash—uselessly spent hard cash—HERE GOES ONE THOUSAND POUNDS!

• ▪▪ •

THE SATURDAY MEETING.

Wild Scenes.

Mr. Lloyd George says Ramsay MacDonald "is one of my greatest personal friends."

But does not speak on Munitions Act.

Thanks Socialist for Appealing for hearing for him.

Break-up in Disorder.

On Saturday morning the St Andrew's Hall was fairly well filled. An official account of the meeting has been issued by the Censor and published in the Press. The account of Mr. Lloyd George's speech summarised very fairly the points he made, though the language has been "touched up"—at anyrate, some of his graceful periods (in the Press reports) did not reach reporters in the audience.

The comments which preface the official Press report are misleading, inasmuch as they give the impression that only a small minority of the audience was hostile to the Munitions Act. The report also is unfair, insofar as it cuts out Mr. Lloyd George's loudly-cheered expression of his friendship for Ramsay MacDonald, and his thanks to the Convener of the Parkhead Shop Stewards (Mr. Kirkwood) for rising and appealing for a hearing to him, when the interruptions threatened to overwhelm him altogether.

The Censor has passed an official report of the meeting, issued by the Press Association—probably with the idea of preventing the publication of news about munitions, guns, etc., going to the enemy as might have been the case, if the ordinary newspaper reports had been permitted. We have no desire to touch the military or "preparedness" side of the speech, but the purely political side must not go misrepresented. It is simply stupid to go about deluding people that only an insignificant minority, and not the vast overwhelming majority of the meeting was angry, and the journalist, whoever he was, who drew up the report and omitted the political references to Ramsay MacDonald and the efforts of the Socialists to secure a hearing for Mr George, is really *not* playing a patriotic part.

* * * *

We are all for free speech, and free speech not only for ourselves, but for our opponents. We, therefore, associate ourselves whole-heartedly with the Socialist effort to secure Mr. George a hearing, and regret that a mean-spirited Press report should seek to convey the impression to deal with the women workers. (Soft soap).

What is it they ask you to do? I will be done directly. (Hear, hear!) They only ask you to enable the skill of the worker to be utilised during this crisis in the best interests of the State. (Yes, in the interests of the Capitalists).

We must have the workers necessary to equip the vast army. (What about the unemployed army after the war?) The whole position will be restored to you after the war. (Question: Don't think!) It appears to me if the position is so safeguarded that you have everything restored to you after the war—(Why don't you put it in the Bill?) It is already in the Bill. I am afraid some people do not read acts of Parliament. They only read the criticisms, the false criticisms people make for their own advantage.

I want to say here in the most emphatic terms that the safeguarding of the Trade Union position is already in an Act of Parliament. And I want to tell you it was put there

BY MR. RAMSAY MACDONALD.

(Great cheering).

I hope you all believe in freedom of speech. (What about the action of the Glasgow Magistrates?) (You've made a bloomer that time, Arthur!) (Great commotion). . . . Now I am going to call upon Mr. Lloyd George, and I am quite sure, however much you may differ with him, you are prepared to give him that hearing to which his responsible position entitles him. (He has got to apologise first).

Mr. Lloyd George was sent to organise munitions, and no man has had a harder task. (Tripe: Nonsense.) If we win this war, as I believe we shall, much of the credit will be due to him. (Commotion.) After he has stated his case I am going to ask for questions, and if you do not waste too much time I think we will have sufficient time to answer all the questions that are sent up. I must ask that the questions be sent up in writing. (No, no: We're had again.) Surely in a crisis like this Mr. Lloyd George is entitled to see the questions he is going to answer. I hope you will take note, and get your questions ready, and Mr. Lloyd George will do his best to give satisfaction.

* * * *

On rising to speak Mr. Lloyd George was received with loud and continued booing and hissing. There was some cheering, certainly, and about a score of hats were waved in the area, but the meeting was violently hostile. Two verses of "The Red Flag" were sung before the Minister could utter a word. Owing to the incessant interruption and the numerous altercations going on throughout the hall, it was quite impossible to catch every word of Mr. George's speech.

My first duty, he said, is to express regret to you because I could not address the meeting on Thursday. (Leave that alone.) At this stage a delegate in the area stood upon a seat and endeavoured to speak. He only got the length of saying "Mr. Lloyd George" when apparently he was pulled down. There were loud cries of "Free Speech," and someone shouted: "This is a meeting of Trade Union officials, not police officials," evidently hinting at the surprisingly large force of police in the hall. "This is the only opportunity we have," shouted another, "they on the platform will never give us the opportunity." The Chairman appealed for quietness, and again gave the order of procedure. It was only proper, he said, that they should accept the ruling.

Mr. Lloyd George tried to resume: [illegible] to express my regret at the alteration of the arrangement—("What about the Conference at Bristol," and loud cries of "apologise.") I have addressed many meetings in Scotland and have never seen Scotsmen deny the right of free speech. The vast majority are in favour of it. Amidst the general commotion Mr. Lloyd George was understood to say that he stood with the Socialists against the South African War. He continued: I thought a small nationality was being oppressed, and I did not care whether it was being oppressed by our own people or by a foreign land. . . . Let me put this to you, friends: whilst we are comfortable at home on a Christmas day—(interruption: No sentiment; We're here for business!)—there are hundreds of thousands of our fellow-countrymen, some of them our sons, some of them our brothers, in the trenches facing death. (You're here to talk about the dilution of labour.) It's on their behalf and at their written request that I come here to put before the workmen of Glasgow their appeal for help.

We need a very large number of heavy guns and projectiles, and I am going to put to you a business proposition. (For the exploiters.) Do you think these men in the trenches are exploiters? (Don't hedge.) (The shipowners are much about the life of the worker as any man here. The responsibility of a Minister of the Crown in a great war is not an enviable one. ("The money's good," and laughter.) I can assure you it is no laughing matter.

. . . There will be unheard of changes in every country in Europe; changes that go to the root of our social system. You Socialists watch them. It is a convulsion of nature; not merely a cyclone that sweeps away the ornamental plants of modern society and wrecks the flimsy trestle-bridges of modern civilisation. It is more. It is an earthquake that upheaves the very rocks of European life.

And to go on chaffering about a regulation here and the suspension of a custom there under these conditions, why, it is just haggling with an earthquake. Workmen: may I make one appeal to you? (Interruption.) Lift up your eyes above the mist of suspicion and distrust. Rise to the height of the great opportunity now before you. If you do, you will emerge after this war is over into a future which has been the dream of many a great leader. (Cheers; loud hissing and booing).

At the close of his address, Mr. Lloyd George proceeded to answer the written questions which had been handed up from the body of the hall. He promised to reply to them all if he possibly could, but he had an engagement at 12 o'clock, and if he failed to get through them the remaining answers would be published. At 11.45, however, Mr. John Muir, of the Clyde Workers' Committee, got up on the seat and demanded an opportunity of stating the case for the workers. This, he said, had been promised, and he was not going to wait any longer. Both Mr. Lloyd George and Mr. Henderson appealed to him to resume his seat, but Mr. Muir was determined not to be put off till Mr. George had to leave. As it was impossible to hear either the Minister of Mr. Muir, the Chairman closed the proceedings, and the meeting broke up in disorder.

• ▪▪ •

Round the Yards.

Dilution of Labour.

Dramatic Discussion at Parkhead.

Socialists Agreeable but want Control of Labour in the Workshops.

Mr. George did not go to Fairfield; the men at Weir's declined to listen to him, preferring to get on with the making of munitions.

The Shop Stewards at Parkhead Forge met in the offices to greet the Minister.

A force of police, about 100 strong, guarded the entrance, and seemed surprised that common working men should be permitted to pass into the great presence. The meeting was held in the large drawing office, and the workers were gathered discussing the business before them when Mr. Lloyd George was ushered into the room in the best stage manner. His companions included the works' manager, Lord Murray, and Right Hon. Mr. Arthur Henderson, M.P. The entrance ceremony fell flat. The workers displayed little or no interest in the newcomers, but went on with their business.

After a minute or two the works' manager approached Mr. Kirkwood, the Convener of Shop Stewards, and stated that Mr. Lloyd George wished an introduction to him. Davie appeared to bear the new distinction that was thus being conferred on him with his usual modesty, for when the Minister, in the course of the usual formalities, inquired how he was, Davie replied, "No sae bad at a'." Then there were a few moments of general conversation, during which it was suggested that Kirkwood act as chairman, while Lord Murray volunteered the hint that he should introduce Mr. Lloyd George as "The Right Hon. Mr. David Lloyd George, Chief Minister of Munitions for the British Empire." Kirkwood agreed on condition that his acting as chairman did not in any way restrict him in putting questions or discussing what was said. But at the outset and before going on with the proceedings, he wished to state that the workers had been discussing a meeting that was to have

206

The independent Glasgow labour newspaper *Forward*, edited by Tom Johnston, an I.L.P. leader, was suppressed by the government in January 1916 for publishing a full and truthful account of Lloyd George's St Andrew's Hall meeting.

THE WORKER

ORGAN OF THE CLYDE WORKERS' COMMITTEE

NO. I.   JANUARY 8TH, 1916   ONE PENNY

PREPARE FOR ACTION

Now that the confusion and excitement is over, the workers are vaguely wondering what all the fuss was about, and why the Right Hon. David Lloyd George troubled the Clyde with his presence at all.

Despite the loud-mouthed professions of economy that have been made by members of the Government, public money was squandered in the most reckless manner to secure a favourable reception to the author of the Munitions Act from the men whose liberties he has persistently attacked since the very commencement of the war.

Taxi-cabs unlimited were placed at the disposal of the Trade Unions' Officials who were willing to distribute tickets among their members for the St. Andrew's Hall meeting. To their credit, be it said, out of the 24 or 25 Unions invited 20 refused to have anything to do with the wretched business. They weren't concerned about maintaining the dignity of a falling Cabinet "star," and that appeared to be the only reason for such desperate efforts to secure a meeting, regardless of what the cost might be. Special

sible." It's quite a nice arrangement. If they get all the guns they want and succeed in blowing the Germans across the Rhine, then, little Davie's the man who did it, little Davie, while little Davey takes the credit—and the cash. Little Davey goes up on a pedestal. But, if **anything** should go wrong **anywhere**, who is going to take the blame. Little Davey! Not if he knows it. That's where we come in. The politicians, press and pulpit will unite in a clamorous and lying attack on the "drunken, thriftless, shirking" workers who failed to support their brothers in the trenches, because, forsooth, they refused to sacrifice those liberties these same brothers in the trenches are presumably fighting for.

So far as little Davey is concerned, "it's heads I win and tails you lose," all the time. £100 per week for letting us know that guns are needed. What do we get for making them? Let each answer for himself.

Following the demand for guns came the demand for 80,000 skilled men. There was the "imperative necessity" for diluting labour. But what we all wanted to know was the very point the elusive Mr. George carefully avoided, to wit, whether the re-organisation of industry was to be placed in the charge of the Trade Unions, or left to the individuals whose sole concern is the

to become mere parts of the machine, ready to be used wherever or whenever the bosses may desire them. But under no consideration must these individuals be asked to relinquish their strangle-hold on industry.

"It would be a revolution," said Mr. George in reply to the C.W.C. deputation, "and it can't be done." Why not? Simply because the employers would lose the war rather than lose their power over the workers. There is no other reason can be given for his emphatic "can't be done." It is for us as workers to take that power from them. The only way to do it is by organising. Our first business, therefore, is to strengthen our Unions, or better still, amalgamate them all into one powerful industrial organisation. When that is accomplished the victory will be ours. In the meantime every effort is being made to crush what organisation we have out of existence. It was in pursuance of this object that Mr. George visited the Clyde. He came to "spy out the land," and his experience was such that he won't want to come back again. It was borne in on him beyond the slightest chance of misunderstanding that the Clyde men could not be cajoled, and that they were determined to resist any further encroachment on their hard-won liberties, so this little demagogue

207

First issue of *The Worker*, organ of the Clyde Workers' Committee. After four issues *The Worker* too was suppressed by the government on 2 February 1916, and J.W. Muir, its editor, Walter Bell, its printer, and William Gallacher, chairman of the Clyde Workers' Committee, were tried for attempting in *The Worker* 'to cause mutiny, sedition or disaffection among the civilian population'. Gallacher and Muir were sent to prison for a year, Bell for three months.

J. M. Messer.   Jas. Haggerty.   A. M'Manus.   S. Shields.   D. Kirkwood.

208

In March 1916 the government attacked the shop stewards' movement following a strike at Parkhead Forge in Glasgow. Nine shop stewards, including the five above, were deported to Edinburgh and elsewhere. Jack Smith, another shop steward, was imprisoned shortly afterward for 18 months for sedition; James Maxton of the I.L.P. and James McDougall, a lieutenant of John Maclean, were imprisoned for a year each also for sedition. John Maclean himself was sentenced to three years' penal servitude. It was these events of 1915-16 which earned the area the nickname 'Red Clydeside'.

209

Opponents of the War had criticised the alliance of Britain with reactionary Tsarist Russia. The February or March Revolution in Russia that overthrew Tsarism was therefore widely welcomed. To organised labour the Revolution held out hope that the War would soon end. The 1917 Scottish Trades Union Congress carried unanimously a resolution calling for peace negotiations. A Convention of Workers' and Soldiers' Councils, modelled on the Russian revolutionary Soviet, was held at Leeds in June, and a similar convention was held on 11 August in Glasgow. The photograph shows Ramsay MacDonald addressing the Glasgow convention.

WORKERS' AND SOLDIERS' COUNCIL

4 DUKE STREET, ADELPHI
LONDON, W.C. 2

COMRADES,   *July 12th, 1917*

In agreement with the instructions of the Leeds Convention, and as we informed you by our Circular of June 15th last, the Provisional Committee of the Workers' and Soldiers' Council has divided the area of Great Britain and Ireland into thirteen Districts and is arranging for a Conference in each District.

The Provisional Committee has decided upon holding an **All Scotland** Conference instead of two District Conferences as stated in the circular of June 15th, and this **Scottish Conference** will be held at **Glasgow, on Saturday, August 11th, at 3 p.m., in the St. Mungo Hall, South York Street.**

The following is the **Agenda for the Conference:**

1. Appointment of Chairman.

2. Chairman's Address.

3. Appointment of Tellers.

4. Resolution I.—

> This Conference, endorsing the resolutions of the Leeds Convention, hails the Russian Revolution, which has liberated the people of Russia for the great work of establishing their own political and economic freedom on a firm foundation, and undertakes to work for an agreement between the international democracies for the re-establishment of a general peace which shall not tend towards either domination by or over any nation, or the seizure of their national possessions, or the violent usurpation of their territories—a peace without annexations or indemnities and based on the right of nations to decide the own affairs. Further, and in agreement with the Leeds Convention, this Conference calls upon the Government of Great Britain to place itself in accord with the democracy of Russia by proclaiming its determination to carry into immediate effect a charter of liberties establishing complete political and social rights for all men and women.

5. Resolution II.—

> This Conference pledges itself to work for the co-ordination of working class activity in support of a peace made by the peoples of the various countries for the complete political and economic emancipation of international Labour, and for the full application of the programme outlined in the fourth resolution of the Leeds Convention. The Conference further demands from the Government for all soldiers immediately the right of association and full civil and political liberty. To that end this Conference calls upon the bodies represented at once to establish Workers' and Soldiers' Councils in their own localities. The Conference suggests that wherever possible the Trades Councils should take the initiative, but failing that or where a Trades Council does not exist, the other bodies in the district should immediately arrange to co-operate in forming a local Workers' and Soldiers' Council.

6. Election of **Two District Representatives on Provisional Committee.**

7. Chairman's closing remarks.

210

RUSSIAN PEOPLES'
EMBASSY AND
CONSULATE GENERAL
82 VICTORIA STREET, S.W.1.

Telephone: VICTORIA 9950.

5/1/18

Dear Comrade Maclean, I am writing to the Russian Consul in Glasgow (I am not sure that there exists such a person) informing him of your appointment & ordering him to hand over to you the consulate. He may refuse to do so, in which case you will open a new consulate & make it public through the press. Your position may be difficult somehow, but you will have my full support.

It is most important to keep me informed (and through me the Russian Soviets) of the labour movement in N.B.

I am writing in all haste, as I wish not to miss the occasion. It is not very safe to write by post. With best wishes

Yours sincerely
Maxim Litvinoff

211

Letter appointing John Maclean official Soviet Russian consul in Glasgow, following the Bolshevik Revolution of October–November 1917. Maclean was highly regarded by Lenin because of his opposition to the War. The Bolshevik Revolution had a profound effect on the labour movement in Scotland, as in other countries. One of its immediate effects was to contribute to the decision by the shop stewards' movement on the Clyde in January 1918 to declare officially their opposition to the War.

212

A meeting of the staff of the United Co-operative Baking Society, Glasgow, in 1917. The War greatly affected the Co-operative movement in Scotland. The U.C.B.S. itself held down the price of bread in opposition to those private bakers seeking to profiteer. Many Co-operative retail societies similarly held down the prices of other foodstuffs during the War, such as sugar. The Scottish Co-operative Wholesale Society produced tens of thousands of uniforms and pairs of boots for the army, as well as foodstuffs.

213

Crowds in George Square, Glasgow, on Armistace Day 1918. The War considerably radicalised labour in Scotland. The development of the shop stewards' movement, the anti-War struggle conducted by the more militant socialists, the Rent Strikes, and the impact of the Bolshevik Revolution, all contributed to an unusually high level of militancy at the end of the War.

214

Neil Maclean, Labour candidate for Govan, Glasgow, electioneering in the general election of December 1918. In the election Scotland increased the number of its Labour M.P.s from three to seven, including Neil Maclean.

THE TWENTIETH CENTURY:
BETWEEN THE WARS,
1919-39

To the Workers.

CALL TO ARMS!

THE JOINT COMMITTEE, representing the Official and Unofficial Section of the Industrial Movement, having carefully considered the reports of the Shop Stewards and representatives of the various industries, hereby resolve to

Demand a 40-Hours Maximum Working Week

for all workers, as an experiment with the object of absorbing the unemployed. If a 40-hour week fails to give the desired result, a more drastic reduction of hours will be demanded.

A GENERAL STRIKE

has been declared to take place on

Monday, 27th January,

and all workers are expected to respond.

By Order of Joint Committee
representing All Industries.

SUB-COMMITTEE:—

HUGH LYON.	J. CAMPBELL.	D MARSHALL.
J. THOM.	J. BURNS.	P. CAMPBELL.
J. AULD.	G. RENNIE.	J. MALONEY.
A. HOPKINS.	W. KERR.	G. KERR (Councillor)

E. SHINWELL (Councillor) Chairman.
S. NIMLIN,
D. S. MORTON, } Joint-Secretaries.
WM. SHAW,

All communications to be directed to Trades Council Office, 95 Bath Street, Glasgow. [SEE OVER

CIVIC PRESS, LTD., Printers.

215

The War over, a militant movement immediately developed on the Clyde, supported by workers in many other parts of Scotland, to establish a much shorter working week. The main object was to prevent unemployment as troops were demobilised and war production came to an end. Militants, including the shop stewards, favoured a 30-hour week, but the eventual agreed demand was for Forty Hours.

216

The Forty Hours' Strike of January-February 1919 was both official and unofficial: some unions supported it, as did the Scottish T.U.C., while other unions did not. The Lloyd George Coalition government feared the strike might be the beginning of Red Revolution in Britain. Such fears were increased by the raising of the Red Flag by strikers in front of Glasgow City Chambers.

217

The Strike was marked by a serious riot in George Square, outside Glasgow City Chambers, on 31 January. Police attacked thousands of strikers who had assembled to hear the Lord Provost's response to a request for intervention with the government to secure the Forty Hours' week. Troops occupied the centre of the city after the riot.

218

Soldiers guarding a railway bridge over the Clyde after the George Square riot.

219

Some of the Strike leaders were arrested and tried at the High Court in Edinburgh. Left to right in the front row in the dock are: Emanuel Shinwell, chairman of the Strike Committee and of Glasgow Trades Council; William Gallacher, shop stewards' leader; George Ebury, British Socialist Party; Joseph Brennan; David Kirkwood, a leading shop steward and Independent Labour Party; Harry Hopkins, District Secretary of the Engineers' union; and James Murray. Shinwell was sentenced to five months' imprisonment, Gallacher and Murray to three; the others were found not guilty. The strikers did not win a Forty Hours' week, though hours were reduced for many workers after the War.

220

A more successful strike was that by the railwaymen in 1919 when they defeated the government on a wages issue. The railwaymen's determination and solidarity, plus strong support from other sections of the trade union movement and the Co-ops, ensured their victory. This was the 1919 Strike Committee of the Kilmarnock Branch of the National Union of Railwaymen.

221

The miners, like so many other workers immediately after the War, were in a militant mood. In January 1919 the Miners' Federation demanded a thirty per cent wage increase, a six-hour day, and nationalisation of the mines, and threatened a national coal strike unless these demands were granted. The Lloyd George Coalition government persuaded the Miners to take part in the Sankey Royal Commission of enquiry into the coal industry. The Commission recommended substantial increases in wages for the miners and a reduction of hours to seven a day. But the government refused to accept the Commission's other main recommendation that the coal industry be nationalised.

222

When this aerial photograph was taken of a strike meeting at Glasgow Green in 1921, the long inter-war years of depression had already begun.

223

The beginning of the depression was marked by a three months' lock-out of the miners throughout Britain. This photograph is of the staff of a miners' soup kitchen in East Fife. The miners were forced back to work in July, their wages reduced by between a third and a half. The struggle also brought the collapse of the Triple Alliance—the alliance of miners, railwaymen and road transport workers that had aimed to give mutual support—on 'Black Friday', 15 April 1921. The defeat of the miners was followed by wage reductions forced on many other workers.

224

Shipbuilding and engineering, as well as coal, textiles, and iron and steel—Scotland's staple industries—were all badly affected by the depression, during which unemployment was never less than ten per cent and, in 1932, was almost thirty per cent. Men in the lower picture lost their jobs at John Brown's shipyard, Clydebank, when work on the giant new passenger liner *Queen Mary* (top) was stopped by the depression between 1931 and 1934.

225

Unemployed at Dundee in 1929 clearing snow from the streets in order to be able to claim benefit.

226

May Day march in Glasgow, 1920. After the 1914-18 War there was a great deal of political militancy, as well as industrial.

227

Politically, Labour's breakthrough in Scotland came in the 1922 General Election, when the number of Labour M.P.s increased from seven to thirty, of whom ten were elected in Glasgow, all Independent Labour Party. A social for the newly elected 'Clydeside Brigade' was held before their departure for Westminster, and this photograph includes James Maxton (standing, far left), David Kirkwood, Campbell Stephen and Thomas Johnston (standing, respectively fourth, third and second from right); John Wheatley and Neil Maclean (seated, respectively third and second from right).

228

Ramsay MacDonald, prime minister of the short-lived first Labour government in 1924, speaking at Kilsyth in October that year. MacDonald's election as leader of the Labour Party in 1922 was ensured by the support of the Clydeside I.L.P. M.P.s—support that many of them came later to regret.

229

William Adamson, Secretary of the Fife miners' union and Labour M.P. for West Fife from 1910 to 1931. Adamson became the first Labour Secretary of State for Scotland in 1924 and held that office again during the second Labour Government in 1929-31.

230

The 'respectability' that began to be enjoyed by some more moderate labour leaders in those years was illustrated by the appointment of James Brown, Ayrshire miners' leader and Labour M.P., as Lord High Commissioner to the General Assembly of the Church of Scotland. Brown is shown here second from left, in white plumed hat, taking the salute outside the Assembly Hall. A satirical verse published in 1924 on his appointment as Lord High Commissioner was entitled *Annus Mirabilis, or the Ascension o' Jimmie Broon.*

231

Socialists who scorned 'respectability' included John Maclean, the Clydeside revolutionary. Maclean continued after the War ceaselessly to agitate—over the Irish crisis, unemployment, and many other issues. In 1920 he formed the Tramp Trust Unlimited with four of his lieutenants shown here with him (left to right): Peter Marshall, Sandy Ross, James D. McDougall and Harry McShane. They tramped Scotland demanding a reduction in prices, a minimum wage of £1 a day, a six-hour day, rationing of work and payment of full wages to the unemployed.

232

The funeral of John Maclean in December 1923. Maclean, an indomitable agitator who spent four of the last eight years of his life in prison for his political activities, drove himself to an early grave at the age of forty-four. He refused to join the recently formed Communist Party of Great Britain and set up the Scottish Workers' Republican Party.

233

Maclean was also the founder of the Scottish Labour College, whose first full-time students are shown here with him in 1920-21: back row, left to right: R. Hunter, Ayrshire Miners, William Crawford, Lanarkshire Miners, John Bird, Fife Miners, Robert Spence, Toolmakers' Union; middle row, left to right: William Allan, Lanarkshire Miners, Andrew Fagan, Lanarkshire Miners, John Welch, Fife Miners, John McArthur, Fife Miners; front row, left to right: William McLaine, tutor, John Maclean and William Leonard, secretary of the College. Most of these men later played prominent parts in the trade union and labour movement in Scotland.

234

Though numerically small, the Communist Party of Great Britain, formed in 1920, attracted into membership in Scotland many of the most class conscious and militant workers, such as David Proudfoot, a Fife miner, seen here speaking at Methil.

235

A 1922 general election meeting in Greenock Town Hall, addressed by Alex Geddes, the Communist candidate. Geddes came close to winning the election.

236

Among left-wing fringe groups were the anarchist communists led by or associated with
Guy Aldred, an Englishman who for most of his life lived and agitated in Glasgow. In
1920, five years after this photograph of Glasgow anarchists was taken, they formed along
with others the Anti-Parliamentary Communist Federation.

237

The Independent Labour Party in the 1920s was a much larger party than the
Communists, and was particularly strong in Scotland where it had over 200 branches.
One of the I.L.P.'s outstanding leaders, and one of the few successful ministers in the first
Labour Government, was John Wheatley, M.P. for Glasgow Shettleston. Wheatley is
seen here addressing a May Day demonstration on Glasgow Green.

238

Delegates to the I.L.P. Scottish conference at Edinburgh in 1924.

239

James Maxton, with hand on chest, addressing a large crowd in 1934. Maxton was one of the most popular leaders of the Independent Labour Party, though many commentators considered him a less able leader than John Wheatley, who died in 1930.

240

Some of the staff of the Gorebridge Co-operative Society store, Midlothian, in the early inter-War years. Mass unemployment reduced purchasing power and affected the Co-ops. Many Co-ops, especially in mining areas, played a supporting role in some of the big labour struggles of the period, such as the miners' lock-out in 1921 and 1926.

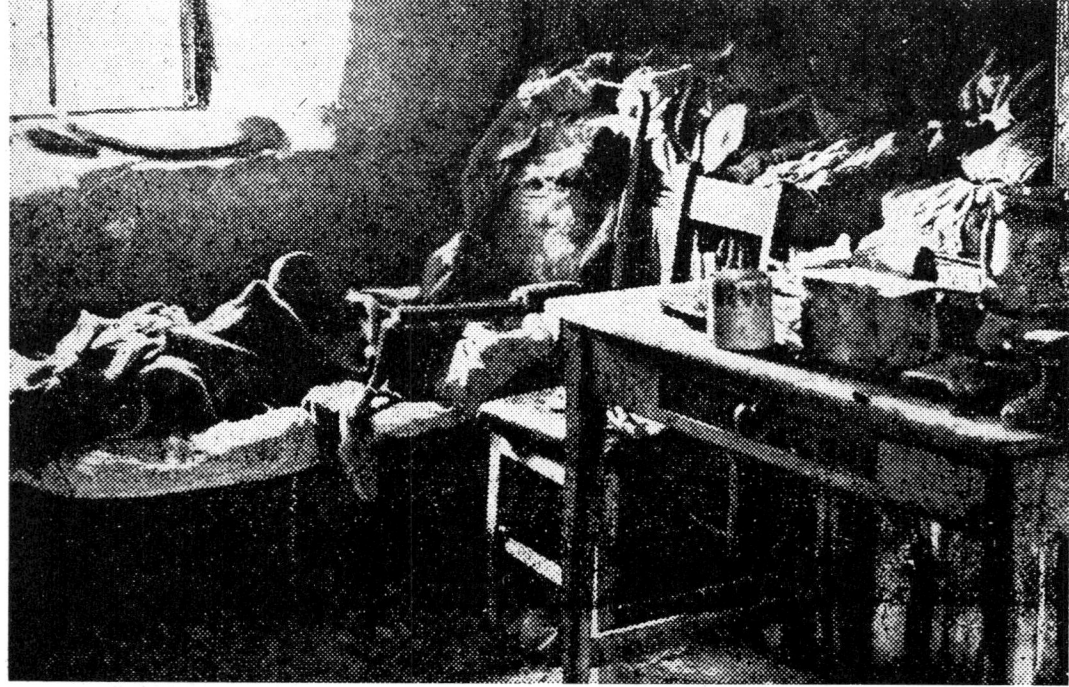

241

Working class housing in Scotland remained notoriously inadequate in the inter-War period, although local authority building schemes enabled some of the worst slum housing to be replaced. The Royal Commission on Housing at the end of the 1914-18 War had estimated the shortage of houses in Scotland at one million. Overcrowding had been defined as more than three people per room, whereas in England and Wales it was defined as more than two per room. At the end of the 1920s over a third of the population of Scotland were living more than two per room; in England and Wales only about seven per cent of the population were as overcrowded as that. In 1939 it was estimated that Scotland still needed 250,000 new houses, mainly to end overcrowding and replace slums. These photographs are of miners' housing in Lanarkshire, as revealed by the Sankey Commission in 1919.

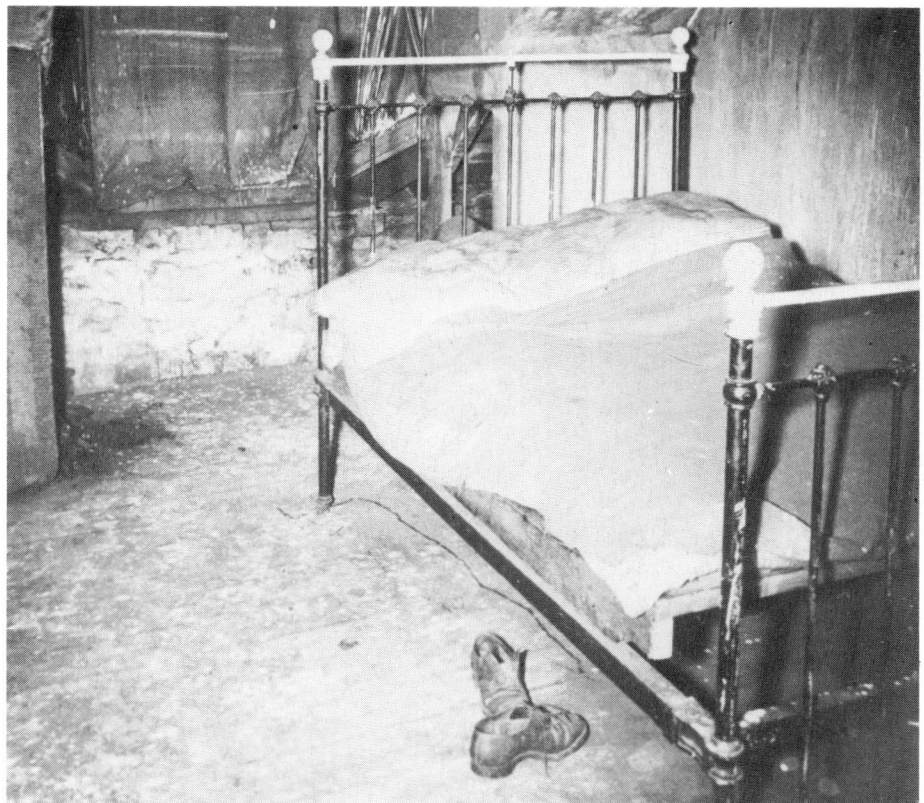

242

Slum housing in Dundee. The precise date of these two photographs is uncertain but they were taken some time before 1953.

The Bulletin, Tuesday, August 24, 1920.

WINTER FOOD PRICES TO BE DEARER IF MINERS STRIKE

The Bulletin

No. 1631. [REGISTERED AT G.P.O. AS A NEWSPAPER] Tuesday, August 24, 1920. One Penny.

THE STRIKE: JAMAICA BRIDGE WITHOUT A TRAMCAR ON IT!

Undoubtedly the most noticeable effect in Glasgow of yesterday's rent strike was the absence of tramcars from the streets. Indeed, one could cross from Jamaica Street to Union Street at a leisurely saunter! Our photo on the left shows strikers, at Jamaica Bridge, making their way home, on foot, from Glasgow Green. Right—The women's exhortation.

With no tramcars running, members of office staffs, shopkeepers, etc., had to travel to and from business by railway or subway. Both had a very busy day, long queues having generally to form up. Our photo on the right shows subway travellers lining up at St Enoch. Strikers of course formed a fair proportion of the numbers. The other photo shows Edinburgh demonstrators in St Andrew's Square.

243

Scenes from the national rent strike in Scotland in August 1920 against a new Rent Act. The strike was centred on Glasgow (top, and bottom right), where at least two-thirds of the workers came out on strike and the crowd that gathered to hear the strike leaders at Glasgow Green was estimated to be 60,000. The picture at bottom left is of demonstators in St Andrew Square, Edinburgh. In this rent strike women took a prominent part, as they had done in the 1915 rent strikes.

244

A feature of trade unionism in Scotland between the Wars was the continuing amalgamation of purely Scottish unions, such as the Farm Servants, into English or United Kingdom unions.

245

Tailors at work, at Strathaven in Lanarkshire. The Scottish tailors' and tailoresses' union also amalgamated into a British tailors' union after the 1914-18 War.

246

Nonetheless numbers of purely Scottish unions survived, especially in the textile industry. This photograph shows weft pirn winders and handloom weavers in a textile mill at Selkirk about 1930.

247

General Council of the Scottish T.U.C., 1926. The S.T.U.C. had followed the example of the British Congress in forming a General Council in the early 1920s to replace its earlier Parliamentary Committee. About the same time the secretaryship of the S.T.U.C. became a full-time appointment and was held efficiently for almost a quarter of a century by William Elger, shown here fourth from left in front row, with arms folded. Elger contributed to the growing importance of the S.T.U.C. as a central organisation of trade unionism in Scotland.

Minority Movement Conference in Battersea

248

Some of the more militant trade unionists in Scotland supported the Red International of Trade Unions—founded in Moscow in 1921 as a rival to the Amsterdam-based International Federation of Trade Unions—and also the National Minority Movement, formed in Britain in 1924 under Communist auspices. The photograph is of the Minority Movement conference in London in 1925.

249

Poster pinned up in April 1926 by militant miners at Wellesley Colliery, Methil, Fife, denouncing new reduced wage scales proposed by the private coalowners. The renewed conflict in the coal industry led to another national lock-out of miners and to the great sympathetic General Strike of 4-12 May by millions of other workers.

250

A bus overturned by strikers in Glasgow during the General Strike. There were many
conflicts between strikers and police, especially in connection with running blackleg
trains, buses or tramcars, during the Strike. Hundreds of arrests were made in Glasgow
and there were also many in other Scottish cities and towns and mining areas.

251

Peter Kerrigan, an active leader of the General Strike in Glasgow. Kerrigan, an engineer,
was convener of the Industrial Committee of Glasgow Trades Council. The Trades
Union Congress did not call out engineers and shipyard workers until two days before
the Strike was abruptly called off. So the 'Red Clyde' played a less active part than might
otherwise have been the case. Some commentators believed that was a deliberate policy
by the T.U.C., to prevent the strike becoming too militant.

252

The *Scottish Worker* was published by the Scottish T.U.C., but only after the General Strike had already been under way for almost a week. The British T.U.C. was very reluctant to permit any strike papers to be printed other than its own *British Worker*. The Scottish T.U.C. saw itself as operating during the Strike very much as the agent of the British T.U.C.

OFFICIAL STRIKE BULLETIN OF THE PARTICK AREA STRIKE
COMMITTEE --- 8th MAY, 1926.

ISSUED IN CONJUNCTION WITH THE SCOTTISH TRADE UNION CONGRESS.

Price ½d.

Fellow Workers,

The following Official Bulletin is being issued by
the above Strike Committee daily for the purpose of diseminating
information as to the true position in regard to the present General
Strike. The news contained in the Emergency Press contains only a
modicum of truth, and that spread by the Wireless is mainly "stunt"
Government news. The purpose of these two methods is to break the
morale of the strikers. We call upon you to stand firm and accept
only the news given through official Trade Union sources. The
news you will receive through these bulletins is brought direct from
the British and Scottish T. U. C. and is, therefore, absolutely
reliable.

The situation is as follows, generally.-

RAILWAYS.- From all over the country the reports are the same.
Everything at a standstill, and while it is true to say that one or

---

NO. I.   OFFICIAL STRIKE BULLETIN   4/5/26.

(EDINBURGH & DISTRICT STRIKE COMMITTEE.)

The response to the General Council's appeal has been
magnificent. The Scottish Horse & Motormen, although not
affiliated to the British Trades Union Congress have decided to
throw in their lot with the Trade Union Movement as a whole. The
Railwaymen have come out solidly. The response from the Tramwaymen
and Busmen is excellent, the few buses and cars running being in
many cases manned by University students. As a result of the
Corporation refusing the request of the Strike Committee that the
cars run by blacklegs be stopped, labour (E.T.U., A.E.U., and
Corporation Workers) has been withdrawn from Power Stations. The
"News" has ceased publication as a result of the magnificent
solidarity of the Printing Trades. The Building Trades are solid
in their support and many other groups of workers have taken
strike action. The Miners, of course, are standing by to a man.

No attention should be paid to rumours. The Official
Bulletin, which will be issued at least daily, will keep you
advised. The Bulletin will be circulated to all Branch and Strike
Committee rooms.

STAND TOGETHER! DISCIPLINE AND SOLIDARITY WILL
BRING SUCCESS.

Issued from 5, Hillside Crescent, Edinburgh.

253

Some local strike bulletins published in Scotland during the General Strike. They helped
keep up the morale of the strikers and satisfy the thirst for news when so many
newspapers were either prevented from appearing by the printers' strike or were
boycotted because of their anti-Strike bias.

254

John Bird, a militant Fife miner and 'stunt merchant', disguised as a special constable
during the General Strike. This photograph, made into a picture postcard, circulated
widely in aid of miners' funds.

255

After nine days the General Council of the T.U.C. suddenly called off the General Strike. The miners remained locked out: they had refused to accept the Samuel Memorandum as a basis for a settlement—a fact the General Council concealed from trade unionists for a couple of days after the General Strike ended. The General Council in fact was in such a hurry to end the Strike that it did not even ensure that those it had called out in support of the miners would return to work on pre-Strike conditions. Consequently victimisation occurred or was attempted by many employers. In Glasgow, for example, of the Corporation tramwaymen who had been on strike over 300—one of them a wartime hero with the Victoria Cross—were refused re-employment for eight months.

GEORGE OUTRAM & CO., Ltd.
JAMES HEDDERWICK & SONS, Ltd.

PROPRIETORS OF

THE GLASGOW HERALD   THE EVENING TIMES
THE BULLETIN   THE CITIZEN

Owing to the action of certain Trade Unions in breaking agreements with us, to which they were parties, we can have no confidence that any contracts which might be entered into in future would be observed.   As continuity of publication is essential in the interests of newspaper readers and advertisers, we are compelled to protect them and ourselves against any repetition of what has taken place on this occasion.   We quite recognise the difficult position in which so many of our former employees found themselves, and desire to say that we have no unfriendly feelings towards them individually.

We therefore give notice that, in future, Non-Union Labour only will be employed in the production of our publications.

The terms of employment will be as follow :—

1. Employment will be secure except in cases of incompetence or misdemeanour.

2. Retiring allowances will be paid to those who retire through age or infirmity.

3. Funeral and sickness allowances will be paid.

4. The rates of pay will be :—

DEPARTMENTS	NIGHT RATES PER WEEK. 45 Hours Week	DAY RATES PER WEEK 48 Hours Week.
TYPOGRAPHICAL— Case Hands, Readers, Linotype Operators ...	£7 . 10 . 0	£6 . 15 . 0
MACHINE ROOM— Minders......................	£5 . 15 . 0	£5 . 5 . 0
Labourers — i.e., Fly, Reel, and Floor Hands.	£4 . 7 . 6	£4 . 5 . 0
DESPATCH ROOM.........	£4 . 10 . 0	£4 . 5 . 0
STEREOTYPERS............	£5 . 10 . 0	£5 . 5 . 0
PROCESS WORKERS.....	£5 . 5 . 0	£5 . 5 . 0
Two Weeks Holiday each year with pay.		

Applications in writing can now be forwarded by post and addressed to "THE SECRETARY" from those desiring employment on the above terms when normal publication and conditions are resumed.

Applications in person will not be considered.

GEORGE OUTRAM and COMPANY, Limited.
JAMES HEDDERWICK and SONS, Limited.

256

The failure of the General Strike encouraged newspaper proprietors in Scotland to enforce non-unionism on printers and journalists. The announcement above was published the day after the Strike ended. Similar conditions were forced on newspaper staffs in Edinburgh, Aberdeen and Dundee and some smaller towns. The Scottish Typographical Association, the compositors' union, lost about one-tenth of its total membership; Glasgow Branch of the National Union of Journalists lost almost half its members. The sacrifices of the strikers in all industries seemed to have been in vain since the miners remained locked out.

257

The miners' lock-out lasted a further six months after the end of the General Strike. A.J. Cook, militant General Secretary of the Miners' Federation of Great Britain, addressed this huge crowd of locked-out miners at Buckhaven, Fife, on 6 August 1926.

258

The acute hardship suffered by the miners and their families during the prolonged lock-out was eased to some extent by their own intensive fund-raising activities, and by the support given by other trade unionists. Here the left-wing Workers' International Relief organisation distributes parcels to miners and their families at Lochore in Fife.

259

Fund-raising was carried on all over Scotland by miners' bands and concert groups such as this one—Kydd's Jazz Band from East Fife.

260

Miners' soup kitchen staff at Leven, Fife, 1926. In November 1926, six-and-a-half months after the lock-out began, the miners throughout Britain were forced back to work on severe wage reductions. There was widespread victimisation of union activists by the private coal companies.

261

The failure of the miners' long struggle in 1926, and growing criticism—especially in Lanarkshire and Fife—of their leaders in Scotland, led to divisions within the National Union of Scottish Mine Workers. In Fife, the two rival miners' unions—the Reform Union and the county union—reunited in 1927 but there was a further split the following year. This photograph shows the 'moderate' miners' leaders of the period: Robert Smillie (second from left), William Adamson (extreme left), James Brown and James Hood of Ayrshire, and Andrew Clarke of the Mid and East Lothian miners.

262

The United Mineworkers of Scotland was formed in 1929 as a militant, largely Communist, rival to the National Union of Scottish Mine Workers. Here some of the leaders of the U.M.S., along with veteran miners and the outstanding agitator Tom Mann, stand in front of the U.M.S. banner which was gifted by Soviet miners. Back row, third and fourth from the left, the brothers Alex and Abe Moffat of the Fife miners; immediately to their left, William Gallacher, Communist M.P. for West Fife from 1935 to 1950, and John McArthur and, standing to right in front row, with light raincoat, Bob Eadie, both Fife miners. Tom Mann is seated in middle of front row, with hat in hand.

263

Ramsay MacDonald, prime minister in the second Labour Government in 1929-31, was denounced as a traitor by organised labour for his action in forming a Coalition Government with Conservatives and Liberals in 1931 amid the worsening economic situation arising from the Wall Street Crash two years earlier. The Labour Party suffered a catastrophic defeat at the subsequent 1931 general election, losing in Scotland all but seven of its thirty-seven seats. Here MacDonald, is shown with his new 'National' cabinet: back row, left to right: Cunliffe-Lister, J.H. Thomas, Lord Reading, Neville Chamberlain, Sir Samuel Hoare; front row, left to right: Philip Snowden, Stanley Baldwin, MacDonald, Sir Herbert Samuel and Lord Sankey.

264

The decision in 1932 by the Independent Labour Party to disaffiliate from the Labour Party following years of increasing friction between the two parties over policy and other issues, was followed by the rapid decline of the I.L.P. Some leading Scottish I.L.P.ers, such as David Kirkwood, resigned in order to remain in the Labour Party; some others, led by Patrick Dollan, broke away from the I.L.P. and formed the Scottish Socialist Party, which affiliated to the Labour Party. This photograph shows Scots I.L.P. leaders at a social occasion in Glasgow in 1935: James Maxton, seated centre, George Buchanan, behind him, Campbell Stephen, standing, third from left, all M.P.s; Councillors James Carmichael (front, extreme right) and Myer Galpern standing, second from left; and William Stewart, the veteran secretary of the I.L.P. in Scotland seated, extreme left.

265

A meeting of Glasgow Town Council in December 1937. In local government Labour made considerable headway in Scotland between the Wars. A majority, dependent on I.L.P. support, was captured on Glasgow Town Council from 1933, and there were also majorities won on the councils at Motherwell, Clydebank, Dundee, Falkirk and some others. In some areas, such as Fife, Communists won seats on local councils.

266

The 1930s brought the rise of Fascism, following the Wall Street Crash of 1929 and the arrival of Hitler and the Nazis in power in Germany in 1933. Fascism had already had Italy in its grip, under Mussolini, since 1922. In Scotland, the Fascists, led nationally by Sir Oswald Mosley, did not make much headway, but among their leaders was Dr Robert Forgan, formerly Labour M.P. for West Renfrew. Forgan is seen here (second left) at Mosley's Buckinghamshire country house in June 1931, a year before the formation of the British Union of Fascists. Others in the group are Mosley second from left, his wife Lady Cynthia, W.E.D. Allen (extreme left) and John Strachey.

267

About 200 Scots, many of them members of the Communist Party or the I.L.P., went to fight Fascism in Spain during the Civil War there between 1936 and 1939. The Spanish Civil War was seen by many in the working class movement as the beginning of a European or world war against Fascist aggression. This photograph of the Anti-Tank Unit of the XV Battalion of the International Brigade includes Hugh Sloane of Methil (front row, second from left).

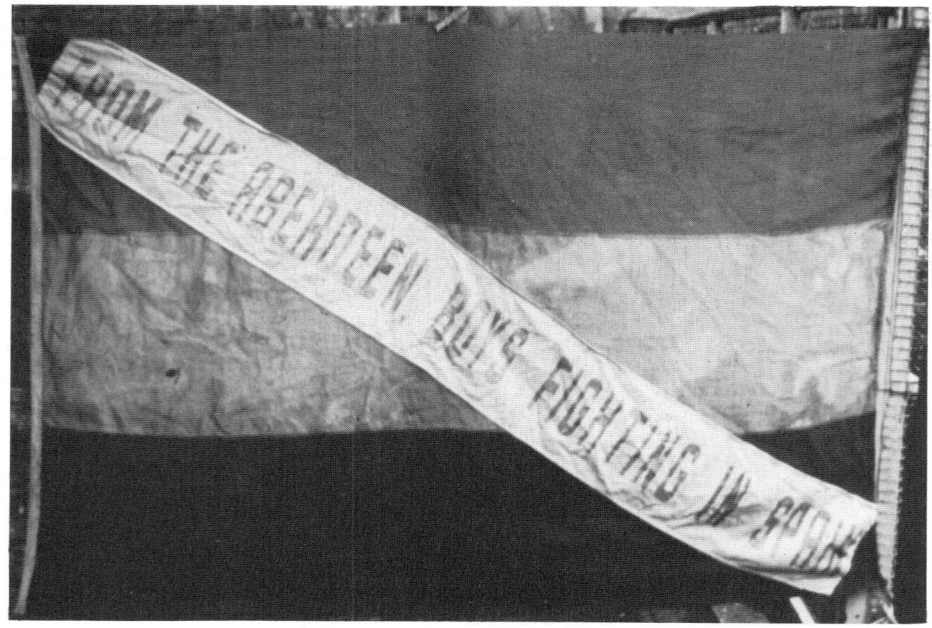

268

Banner of the Aberdeen men who fought Fascism in Spain in the Civil War.

269

Banner of the British Battalion of the International Brigade in the Spanish Civil War,
carried at the Scottish Miners' Gala in 1972.

270

Unemployment, at its worst in the early 1930s, was a prolonged and depressing feature of
the inter-War period. The National Unemployed Workers' Movement was formed in
1921 and was under the leadership of militant workers such as Wal Hannington and, in
Scotland, Harry McShane, both of whom were engineers and Communists. This
photograph is of a march, headed by a flute band, by Vale of Leven unemployed to
Alexandria in the early 1930s to demand increased relief. Two local activists leading the
march are George Halkett (extreme left) and Dan O'Hare (extreme right).

271

Fife unemployed march to Dundee in the 1930s to demonstrate against the Means Test
(introduced by the 'National' government in 1931 and hated by the working class as a
disruption of family solidarity) and 'slave camps' (Government training or instructional
residential centres where the unemployed were re-trained for new jobs, and where the
conditions were—in Harry McShane's words—'terrible').

272

National Unemployed Workers' Movement Hunger marchers washing at the street
water fountain in Princes Street, Edinburgh's main thoroughfare, in June 1933.

273

Women's contingent of the Scottish Hunger March to London in February 1934, near Barnet in Hertfordshire.

274

The Scottish contingent of the Hunger March by the unemployed to London in
February 1934 entering Hyde Park.

275

Chalking the streets was a cheap and effective way for labour movement activists to put
their message. Here two Vale of Leven militants, George Halkett and Brian McGougan,
are chalking their message in Bank Street, Alexandria, c. 1934.

276

Scottish Labour College, Edinburgh District Committee, 1920-21. The Scottish College became from 1921 part of the National Council of Labour Colleges whose secretary was J.P.M. Millar, seen here in second row, third from left. Another leading figure in the N.C.L.C. was Arthur Woodburn, second row, fourth from left. The head office of the N.C.L.C. moved from London to Tillicoultry during the 1939-45 War and remained there until the N.C.L.C.'s dissolution in the 1960s. By the outbreak of the War the N.C.L.C. had almsot 40,000 students in day and week-end schools, evening classes and postal courses. Its recently published history claims that the N.C.L.C. 'made a bigger quantitative contribution to working class education than did the trade unions themselves and the Workers' Educational Association put together'.

277

Between the National Council of Labour Colleges and the Workers' Educational Association there was considerable rivalry. Joseph F. Duncan, leader of the Scottish farm workers' union, was chairman of the W.E.A. for many years. It failed, however, to make much headway in the labour movement in Scotland before the 1939-45 War.

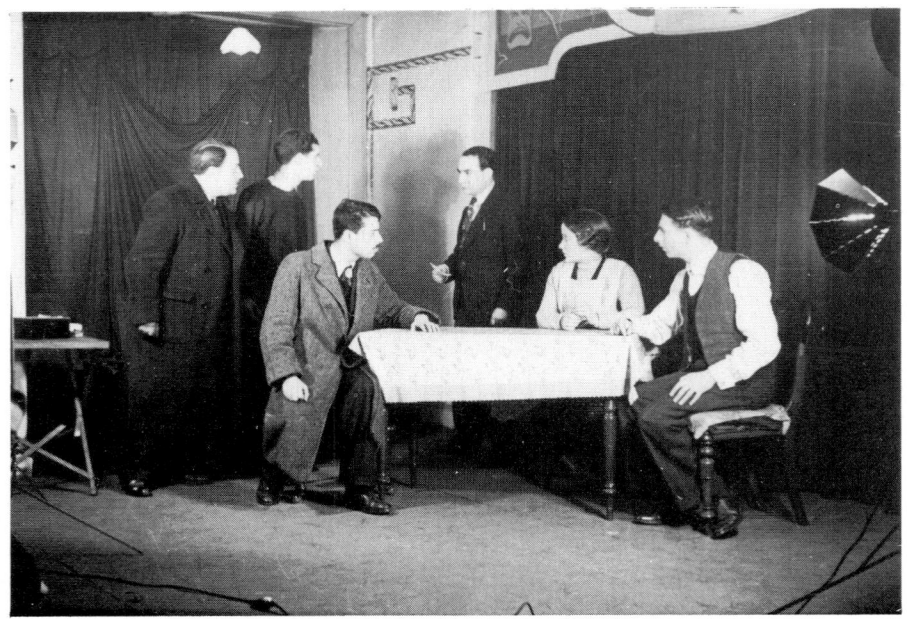

278

Several workers' libraries, bookstalls, film and theatre and other cultural groups were established between the Wars. One of the most active was the Glasgow Workers' Theatre group, shown here.

279

Another feature of the inter-War period was the formation and growth of youth sections in the labour movement. The Scottish T.U.C. Youth Advisory Council, for example, was formed in 1938, the Labour Party League of Youth in 1926. Here Arthur Woodburn, later Secretary of State for Scotland, lectures to members of the Labour League of Youth at Newbattle Abbey College, Dalkeith, in 1939.

280

Delegates to an Independent Labour Party Guild of Youth conference in Glasgow, c. 1933.

281

The Communist Party had its Young Pioneers, Young Comrades, and Young Communist League. This is a Young Comrades' social in Cowdenbeath Public Hall in 1928.

282

Socialist Sunday Schools, founded many years earlier, also continued to flourish between the Wars.

THE TWENTIETH CENTURY:
SECOND WORLD WAR,
1939-45

283

The Second World War, like the first, greatly affected labour in Scotland.
Unemployment virtually disappeared; trade union membership increased; support for
both the Labour Party and the Communist Party increased. But the early years of the
War also brought the blitz. This was Dalmuir West tramway terminus after the
Luftwaffe bombed Clydebank in March 1941. Some 1,200 lives were lost on Clydeside in
these raids.

244

284

Staff of the Blackburn Aircraft Factory at Vale of Leven in Dunbartonshire, 1942.
Membership of women in trade unions increased during the War—when the
Engineering Union opened its ranks to women in 1943 some 139,000 were recruited in the
first year, including many thousands in Scotland.

285

Tom Johnston, Labour M.P. for West Stirlingshire, was appointed Secretary of State for Scotland during the War by the Churchill Coalition government, and proved an efficient administrator and innovator. He could claim much of the credit for the establishment of the publicly owned North of Scotland Hydro-Electric Board, the Scottish Council on Industry, and over 700 new or enlarged industrial undertakings. For the first time since the Union of 1707 a meeting of Scottish M.P.s was called by Johnston in Edinburgh in 1941 but the experiment was unsuccessful.

286

The Independent Labour Party, led by James Maxton, was opposed to the Second World War and refused to accept the electoral truce accepted by the Labour, Conservative and Liberal Parties. The Communist Party, after first opposing the War reversed its view and became a whole-hearted supporter of the War effort from June 1941 when Nazi Germany invaded the Soviet Union. The call for a second front to help relieve the intense pressure on Russia was kept up until the Normandy landings of 1944. Here a soldier in a Scottish regiment speaks at a Second Front Now demonstration in 1943.

287

Among changes in labour organisation during the War was the reorganisation of the
miners' union. The Miners' Federation of Great Britain was reconstructed from January
1945 as the National Union of Mineworkers. In Scotland the old county miners' unions
merged in 1944 into a single National Union of Scottish Mine Workers which a year later
became the National Union of Mineworkers (Scottish Area).

288

The Co-operative movement, like other sections of the broad labour movement, was deeply affected by the War. Here Field Marshal Montgomery visits a Scottish Co-operative Wholesale Society sheet metal factory producing Flying Dustbin landmines.

289

A particularly important part in War production was played by the Clyde shipyards
which between 1939 and 1945 produced on average 400,000 tons of shipping each year.
This is the yard of Alexander Stephen and Son at Linthouse.

290

Scotland elected 37 labour M.P.s in the General Election of 1945. In addition, three I.L.P.
and one Communist were elected. These are some of the Scottish Group of Labour M.P.s
on the terrace of the House of Commons after the election.

THE TWENTIETH CENTURY:
SINCE 1945

291

Since 1945 Labour Party parliamentary representation has remained strong in Scotland, despite pressure in the 1960s and '70s from the Scottish National Party and, more recently, from the formation of the Social Democratic Party. This photograph is of the May Day procession in Glasgow in 1951 led by Aneurin Bevan, whose resignation then from the Labour Government in protest against the imposition of National Health Service charges reflected some of the tensions within the Party that, in varying forms and over varying issues, have continued to the present.

292

William Gallacher lost his seat as Communist M.P. for West Fife in 1950 and no Communist has been elected to Parliament since then. Though the Party's strength declined because of the Cold War, the Hungarian crisis of 1956, and other factors, Communists have remained among the most active and articulate members of the working class movement in Scotland, playing a notably active role in industrial struggles. The two men seated are Abe Moffat (right) and John McArthur (centre), leaders of the Scottish miners and both Communists.

293

James Maxton, leader of the Independent Labour Party, in his last years, with a
pensioners' petition at the House of Commons in 1943. His death three years later tolled
virtually the end of the Independent Labour Party as a noticeable force.

294

The opening in 1968 of Centenary House, Glasgow, magnificent new headquarters of the Scottish Co-operative Wholesale Society, by the queen. Within five years, however, the S.C.W.S. found itself in serious financial difficulties and merged into the Co-operative Wholesale Society. The merger created a United Kingdom Co-operative organisation with huge actual and potential buying power. Since the War retail Co-operative societies in Scotland have faced increasingly powerful competition from multiple private stores. Many local societies have merged into regional societies and some of these have been very successful. But some earlier working class loyalty to 'the store' seems to have weakened.

295

Since 1945 the number of purely Scottish trade unions has continued to decline. The Scottish Bakers, whose Edinburgh Branch banner this is, amalgamated into the Union of Shop, Distributive and Allied Workers. Only half-a-dozen Scottish unions remain, the largest being the Educational Institute of Scotland, the main teachers' union.

296

The Scottish Trades Union Congress developed both its affiliated membership and its influence considerably after the Second World War. Its General Secretary between 1949 and 1963 was George Middleton.

297

This photograph illustrates one of many issues, agitations, marches, strikes, sit-ins, successes and defeats that have marked the history of labour in Scotland in recent years as in earlier periods. Mrs Kay Carmichael, wife of Neil Carmichael, Glasgow Labour M.P., is second from right and Rita Baxter, Joint-Secretary, Glasgow and West of Scotland Council for Peace in Vietnam, third from left.

298

299

Pickets at the newspaper and periodical publishers, D.C. Thomson, at Dundee in April 1952. The firm had gone non-union at the time of the 1926 General Strike and remains so.

300

Tenants at Forfar protest about high rents and rates, April 1957.

301

March against pit closures by miners at Lochgelly in Fife, December 1958.

302

The Scottish miners' annual gala at Holyrood Park, Edinburgh, has been a notable occasion for organised labour since the Second World War. This procession down Canongate on the way to the Park in 1976 was led by Michael McGahey, fourth from left, President of the Scottish miners, Eric Heffer, M.P., fifth from left, and Arthur Scargill, Yorkshire miners, second from right. The late William McLean, General Secretary of the Scottish Miners, is on the extreme left.

303

One of the great struggles of the post-war period was at Upper Clyde Shipbuilders, threatened with closure in the summer of 1971. This is the head of the huge march of protest on 18 August from George Square, to Glasgow Green, when an estimated 80,000 took part and 200,000 Scottish workers stopped work in sympathy. Left to right are Roddy McKenzie, U.C.S. treasurer; Alex Murray, Scottish Secretary, Communist Party; Bob Cook, Govan Division, U.C.S.; Willie McInnes, Linthouse; Victor Feather, General Secretary, Trades Union Congress; Daniel McGarvey, President, Boilermakers' Union; Hugh Scanlon, President, Engineering Union; James Airlie, U.C.S. shop steward; Anthony Wedgwood Benn, M.P.; James Reid, U.C.S. shop steward; William Ross, M.P.; Sam Barr, Scotstoun U.C.S.; Bobby Dickie, Clydebank; and James Jack, General Secretary, Scottish T.U.C.

304

An Equal Pay for Women lobby at the Scottish T.U.C. in the 1960s.

305

The Industrial Relations Bill passed by the Conservative government in 1971, like the Criminal Law Amendment Act passed a century earlier by a Liberal government, was the subject of massive demonstrations of protest by trade unionists.

306

Plessey shop stewards, supported by John Henry, Deputy General Secretary, Scottish
T.U.C. (extreme right), march through Bathgate to celebrate a successful stage in their
struggle with the company in March 1982.

307

Many Labour activists have taken an energetic part in the campaign against nuclear weapons. Here thousands simulate in George Square, Glasgow, the mass casualties that would result from nuclear war.

308

The struggle against mass unemployment has been a dominant feature of the past few years. The Hunger Marchers of the inter-war period have had latter-day equivalents. Here the People's March for Jobs crosses a bridge at Uplawmoor on the way from Scotland to London in April 1983.

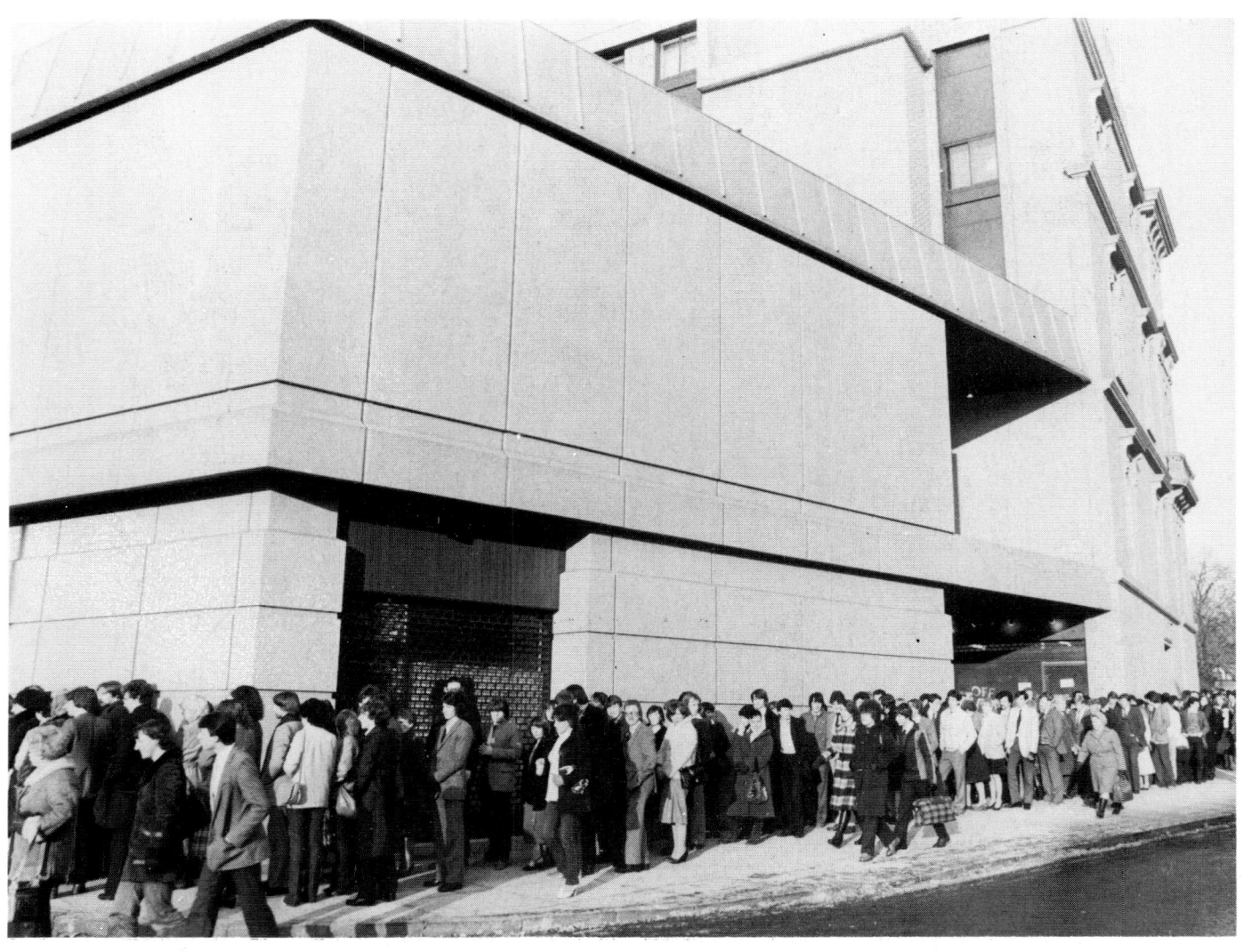

309

Part of a queue of 2,500 applicants who waited for hours in the hope of getting a job at the
Grosvenor Hotel, Glasgow, in January 1982.

310

Joseph Vickery, a campaigner against unemployment, 'on his bike' (in the phrase of a Conservative Minister for Employment) at the Hillhead by-election, Glasgow, in March 1982, with the former deputy leader of the Labour Party, Roy Jenkins, standing as Social Democratic Party candidate, canvassing electors in the background.

311

In the General Election of June 1983 Labour held its position relatively well in Scotland
while suffering a serious defeat in Britain as a whole. Robin Cook M.P., (centre, with
thumbs up) proclaims his victory at Livingston.

312

Pickets at Henry Robb's shipyard, Leith, try to prevent the yard's closure by British
Shipbuilders, in January 1984.

313

The prolonged strike by the miners in 1984, which reminded many of the lengthy miners' struggles in the 1920s, was marked by violent clashes between police and pickets. Here mounted police gallop past an unconscious picket lying on the ground, at Hunterston in Ayrshire, on 8 May.

Some Further Reading

R. Page Arnot, *A History of the Scottish Miners*. (London. 1955).

P.S. Bagwell, *The Railwaymen: the History of the National Union of Railwaymen. 2 vols.* (London. 1963 and 1982).

Kenneth D. Buckley, *Trade Unionism in Aberdeen, 1878 to 1900*. (Edinburgh. 1955).

Bulletin of the Society for the Study of Labour History.

Alan B. Campbell, *The Lanarkshire Miners: A Social History of their Trade Unions, 1775-1874.* (Edinburgh. 1979).

G.D.H. Cole, *A Short History of the British Working Class Movement*. (London. 1948).

G.D.H. Cole, *A Century of Co-operation*. (Manchester. 1945).

R.E. Dowse, *Left in the Centre*. (London. 1966).

Robert Duncan, *James Leatham, 1865-1945*. (Aberdeen. 1978).

W. Hamish Fraser, *Trade Unions and Society. The Struggle for Acceptance, 1850-1880.* (London. 1974).

William Gallacher, *Revolt on the Clyde*. (London. 1936).

C. Desmond Greaves, *The Life and Times of James Connolly*. (London. 1961).

James Hinton, *The First Shop Stewards' Movement*. (London. 1973).

James Hunter, *The Making of the Crofting Community*. (Edinburgh. 1976).

Thomas Johnston, *History of the Working Classes in Scotland*. (Glasgow. 1946).

Walter Kendall, *The Revolutionary Movement in Britain, 1900-21*. (London. 1969).

James Kinloch and John Butt, *History of the Scottish Co-operative Wholesale Society Ltd.* (Manchester. 1981).

W. Knox (ed.), *Scottish Labour Leaders, 1918-1939: A Biographical Dictionary*. (Edinburgh. 1984).

Sheila Lewenhak, *Women and Trade Unions*. (London. 1977).

Kenneth Logue, *Popular Disturbances in Scotland, 1780-1815*. (Edinburgh. 1979).

Ian MacDougall (ed.), *Essays in Scottish Labour History*. (Edinburgh. 1978).

Ian MacDougall, *Militant Miners*. (Edinburgh. 1981).

Ian MacDougall (ed.), *Minutes of Edinburgh Trades Council, 1859-73*. (Edinburgh. 1968).

Stuart McIntyre, *Little Moscows*. (London. 1980).

Iain McLean, *The Legend of Red Clydeside*. (Edinburgh. 1983).

Harry McShane, *No Mean Fighter*. (London. 1978).

W.H. Marwick, *A Short History of Labour in Scotland*. (Edinburgh. 1967).

Joseph Melling, *Rent Strikes. Peoples' Struggle for Housing in West Scotland, 1890-1916.* (Edinburgh. 1983)

R.K. Middlemas, *The Clydesiders*. (London. 1965)

Nan Milton, *John Maclean*. (London. 1973).

Kenneth O. Morgan, *Keir Hardie, Radical and Socialist*. (London. 1975).

Norman Murray, *The Scottish Hand Loom Weavers, 1790-1850: a Social History*. (Edinburgh. 1978).

Henry Pelling, *A History of British Trade Unionism*. (London. 1972).

Fred Reid, *James Keir Hardie, the Making of a Socialist, 1856-95*. (London. 1978).

Scottish Labour History Journal.

J.H. Smith, *Joseph Duncan, Scottish Farm Servants and British Agriculture*. (Edinburgh. 1973).

E.P. Thompson, *William Morris, Romantic to Revolutionary*. (London. 1956).

E.P. Thompson, *The making of the English working class*. (London. 1963).

William M. Walker, *Juteopolis: Dundee and its textile workers, 1885-1923*. (Edinburgh. 1979).

Alexander Wilson, *The Chartist Movement in Scotland*. (Manchester. 1970).

Gordon M. Wilson, *Alexander McDonald, Leader of the Miners*. (Aberdeen. 1982).

James D. Young, *The Rousing of the Scottish Working Class*. (London. 1979).